TRYING TRUMP

TRYING TRUMP

A Guide to His First Election Interference Criminal Trial

Edited by Norman Eisen

SDDF Books
Washington, DC

A publication of SDDF Books

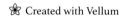 Created with Vellum

Dedicated to my Hollywood High School Class of 1980 pals,
the dearest of friends still:
Eric Berg, Kevin Crowell, Burt Hara, Evan Hochstein, Mark
Hope, Krista Jacobsen, Russell Levan, John Sovec, and Michael
Tannourji

TABLE OF CONTENTS

FOREWORD: MORE THAN A HUSH MONEY CASE

By Barbara McQuade

This essential volume offers a comprehensive overview of the first criminal prosecution of a former president in American history. It is Manhattan District Attorney Alvin Bragg's campaign corruption and cover up case against Donald Trump. Far from only a "hush money" case, the DA has charged 34 felonies related to serious alleged 2016 election misconduct. As this book details, that alleged 2016 misconduct—and the fact that Trump previously faced no accountability for it—was a precursor to Trump's 2020 election wrongdoing. Conviction carries serious penalties. That includes, as this book explains, the possibility and even the likelihood of a sentence of incarceration.

The editor of this volume, Ambassador Norman Eisen, is an ideal guide to the 2016 election interference trial. He is a seasoned criminal lawyer who has actually had the experience of prosecuting Donald Trump for high crimes and misdemeanors as counsel in the first impeachment of the former president. That included investigating the identical allegations that are at issue in the Bragg prosecution. Eisen and his expert co-authors of the essays in the book were among the first and most vigorous champions of the case. Their views have been borne out by a series of legal successes DA Bragg has secured that are described in this volume.

Eisen and his co-authors assess that the DA will likely secure a conviction of Trump, and this volume offers the most detailed public explanation of why. The core of the book is its detailed analysis of what to expect at the trial. It covers every aspect of trial proceedings from jury selection to sentencing; from opening statements to jury instructions; from the prosecution case and witnesses to those of the defense; and from pretrial motions to what appeals might look like. Eisen's and his co-authors' views on what will happen at every stage of the proceedings are an important contribution to the public understanding of one of the most important election and democracy trials in the history of our nation.

This volume is in a sense something that is familiar to every trial lawyer, whether prosecution or defense: a trial notebook. We litigators can typically be seen toting a thick binder under one arm as we ascend the courthouse steps to attend trial. It contains the most essential material that we need to have at our fingertips throughout the case. We never know when we'll need to flip to a tab to deal with a particular development.

This volume puts that trial notebook for DA Bragg's case in the hands of every member of the public and the press. It includes annotated versions of the indictment and other key filings; a detailed list of every potential trial witness and their role; a comprehensive chronology of the events and evidence in the case; and much, much more. This book is the ultimate insider's guide to what has happened and will happen in the 2016 election interference case.

However the trial turns out, the prosecution illustrates the resilience of the rule of law in the American legal and political systems. A fair trial, in which Trump will be judged guilty or not under the facts and the law by a jury of his peers, is a concrete demonstration of perhaps the foundational American principle. No one—not even a former president—is above the law. This magnificent book is above all a testament to that idea and provides an exceptional resource to the public.

Barbara McQuade served as the United States Attorney for the Eastern District of Michigan from 2010 to 2017. She is a professor of law at the University of Michigan Law School, the author of "Attack from Within" and a legal analyst for NBC News and MSNBC.

INTRODUCTION: WHAT TO EXPECT AT TRIAL AND IN THIS BOOK

In this volume, we provide a complete guide to the prosecution of former President Donald Trump in a New York state court. In April 2023, Manhattan District Attorney Alvin Bragg announced that his office had charged Trump with 34 felony counts of falsifying business records in the first degree. The case is historic. It is the first ever prosecution of an American president (current or former), and one of the most important trials of alleged election wrongdoing in American history. This book is a complete guide to understanding what will happen and why it matters.

What's the Trial About?

As DA Bragg has explained, the Manhattan case charges Trump with "conspiring to corrupt a presidential election and then lying in New York business records to cover it up." The trial will center on Trump's alleged efforts to conceal a hush money payment made to Stephanie Clifford, an adult film star also known as Stormy Daniels, for the exclusive rights to her story of a sexual encounter with Trump. As part of an alleged "catch and kill" scheme orchestrated by Trump with his fixer Michael Cohen and David Pecker, the former CEO of American Media, Inc. (AMI), which published supermarket tabloids including the *National Enquirer*, Cohen paid Daniels $130,000. Trump reimbursed Cohen, and Trump and Cohen allegedly falsified their business records to conceal the true nature of those payments, which the District Attorney's Office alleges should have been claimed as a campaign-related expense. The 34 counts consist of one count for each of the 11 checks to reimburse Cohen, also for 11 fake corresponding invoices and 12 corresponding false ledger entries.

Make no mistake: The Manhattan case is not just about hush money. According to the presiding judge, Justice Juan Merchan, "the charges arise from allegations that Defendant attempted to conceal an illegal scheme to influence the 2016 presidential election." As Bragg described it, the "core" of the case "is not money for sex... It's about conspiring to corrupt a presidential election and then... lying in New York business records to cover it up... That's the heart of the case." Bragg and his team built the case as a "clear-cut instance of election interference, in which a candidate defrauded the American people to win the White House in 2016."

The timing of the scheme establishes its connection to the election. The hush money arrangement with Daniels occurred just after the "Access Hollywood" scandal, when Trump boasted about committing sexual assaults, and was consummated on October 27, 2016, 12 days before the election. As described in the charging documents, Trump initially directed Cohen to delay the payments to Daniels until after the election, "because at that point it would not matter if the story became public." However, "with pressure mounting and the election approaching," Trump ultimately agreed to the payoff.

The "catch and kill" scheme was squarely aimed at influencing voters' perceptions. When Cohen pleaded guilty to eight charges in 2018, the Department of Justice (DOJ) explained that the hush money payments made to Clifford and another woman were "intend[ed] to influence the 2016 presidential election." Similarly, in its non-prosecution agreement with the DOJ, AMI admitted that the hush money paid to another woman (former *Playboy* model Karen McDougal) was intended to prevent her from "publiciz[ing] damaging allegations about" Trump "before the 2016 presidential election and thereby influence that election." And as I explained for *The New York Times*, it is "entirely possible that the alleged election interference might have altered the outcome of the 2016 contest, which was decided by just under 80,000 votes in three states. Coming on the heels of the 'Access Hollywood' disgrace, the effort to keep the scandal from voters may have saved Trump's political prospects."

Trump and his defense team dismiss the case as simply a revenge prosecution by a partisan Democratic district attorney. As with his two impeachments, three other criminal prosecutions, and multiple civil suits, Trump has denounced this case as a "witch hunt" In addition to Trump's denunciations, the charging decision was met with early and ongoing skepticism. Some observers have criticized the case as unlikely to succeed because it is too political or legally convoluted.

But those criticisms are misplaced. As explained throughout this volume, DA Bragg has built a robust case along a narrowly tailored theory of prosecution: falsifying business records to conceal criminal conduct that hid damaging information during the 2016 presidential campaign. Despite the historical significance of being the first indictment of a former president, the core allegations of falsifying business records are routine.

What's in This Book?

As the case proceeds to trial, we offer this book as a complete guide to the case. We cover what the landmark prosecution is all about, what has happened so far, the remaining pretrial proceedings, and most important, the trial and possible sentencing.

In **Part I, Chapter 1**, we provide annotated versions of the documents that represent the foundation of the case—including the indictment, the statement of facts, and the response to request for a bill of particulars. **Chapter 2** goes beyond those filings to survey the voluminous public record and offer a complete chronology of events. It provides a preview of the narrative that the approximately two months of trial will unfold. **Chapter 3** covers the cast of characters, including both well-known and obscure ones, to assist observers. Like the chronology, this also offers a trial preview, but of the universe of possible witnesses. Part I concludes with **Chapter 4**, which lays out the relevant statutes that Trump is alleged to have violated or that otherwise come into play.

Part II provides an authoritative guide to the trial itself, including key pre- and post-trial proceedings. We forecast what to expect, including the key evidentiary issues, witnesses, and relevant jury instructions. As we explain, all inexorably lead to the fact that Trump will likely face conviction and with it, a sentence of incarceration. **Chapter 5** explains the pretrial proceedings—the key rulings by the court to prepare to present the case to a jury, as well as the jury selection process and the likely composition of the jury. It also includes logistical information such as on the courthouse and how to access the courtroom. **Chapter 6** covers trial proceedings from opening statements to the prosecution and defense cases; from Trump's presence to whether or not he will testify; and from the "other crimes" proof the DA must establish to Trump's main defenses. When all of that concludes, the jury will be instructed on the law and on how to apply it, and **Chapter 7** presents the likely jury instructions.

Chapter 8 addresses sentencing. We summarize New York sentencing law, and digest past cases in New York and in Bragg's office, which underscore that the DA has not singled Trump out for disparate treatment. Chapter 8 also explains why if Trump is convicted, as is likely, a sentence of incarceration is also probable. In a **conclusion to the book**, we review the considerable terrain we have surveyed and explain why the case is stronger than some think. We also provide a series of appendices exploring in more depth key legal issues.

The overarching theme of the coming trial will be DA Bragg's argument to the judge, the jury, and the court of public opinion that this case is about our democracy. In

America, we value our freedoms—including our freedom to elect leaders who govern in our name. The legitimacy of American governance rests upon the honesty of our elections, and when information is withheld from voters, as Bragg alleges happened here, that undermines democracy. Indeed, the alleged 2016 campaign corruption and cover up may be viewed as setting the pattern for Trump's presidency and its culmination: his alleged 2020 election interference. For these reasons, we believe the trial is deeply important to our democracy, and so worth understanding in depth. This book is our effort to help readers do just that.

PART I

THE BASICS

In Chapter 1, we analyze the three legal documents that are the foundation of District Attorney Alvin Bragg's case: the indictment, the statement of facts, and the response to the request for a bill of particulars. Our annotations to each document are intended to serve as a guide to key facts and legal issues.

Chapter 2 goes beyond these three filings to survey the voluminous public record and offer a complete chronology of events. The chronology provides additional context for the charges against Trump and highlights some key legal developments in the case.

Chapter 3 provides a cast of characters, including well-known and obscure ones. Like the chronology, this chapter offers a preview of the trial, as we identify and offer brief biographies of all who are likely to appear in court.

Chapter 4 lays out the relevant statutes that Trump is alleged to have violated or that otherwise come into play, including both New York state and federal laws.

1

THE ESSENTIAL COURT FILINGS
EXPLAINED

I n this chapter, we analyze the three legal documents that
are the foundation of District Attorney Alvin Bragg's case:
the indictment, the statement of facts, and the response to
the request for a bill of particulars. Our annotations in each document are intended to highlight key legal and factual claims that
may not be immediately obvious to the reader. The indictment
establishes the crimes Donald Trump allegedly committed—
namely, 34 counts of falsifying business records to cover up a
hush money payment to Stephanie Clifford (also known as
Stormy Daniels) during the 2016 presidential election.

As THE DA's office has explained, the charges in the indictment
"are merely allegations" and Trump "is presumed innocent unless
and until proven guilty." He denies any wrongdoing. The annotated statement of facts supplements the indictment, explaining
how Trump's allegedly criminal acts were committed as part of a
broader "catch and kill" scheme to keep negative stories about
Trump out of the press prior to Election Day in November 2016.
The third key document is an annotated bill of particulars, which

Trump's defense team requested from the DA's Office. In the New York court system, a bill of particulars is merely intended to clarify the indictment. Though DA Bragg argued that such clarification was unnecessary in this matter, his office did provide insight into the prosecution's legal theory of the case in its response to the request.

OUR ANNOTATIONS in this chapter are not in the original documents but are intended to provide the reader with additional context on the charges.

The Indictment: Annotated

SUPREME COURT OF THE STATE OF NEW YORK
COUNTY OF NEW YORK

THE PEOPLE OF THE STATE OF NEW YORK
-against-
DONALD J. TRUMP,
Defendant.

THE GRAND JURY OF THE COUNTY OF NEW YORK, by this indictment, accuses the defendant of the crime of **FALSIFYING BUSINESS RECORDS IN THE FIRST DEGREE**, in violation of Penal Law §175.10, committed as follows:

Annotation 1: The Manhattan District Attorney's indictment is a historically significant document. Trump is the first U.S. president—current or former—to be indicted. Others including Bill Clinton and Richard Nixon have been investigated. Ulysses Grant was arrested for speeding, put up $20 in collateral, and ultimately forfeited that sum when he did not appear in court to contest the citation.

Annotation 2: Trump is charged with 34 felony counts of Falsifying Business Records in the First Degree. In New York, violating Penal Law §175.10 is a felony if the defendant(s) falsifies business records with the intent to defraud, including the intent to commit, aid, or conceal another crime. The Manhattan

DA's office alleges in each of the 34 counts that the former president had the "intent to defraud and intent to commit another crime and aid and conceal the commission thereof." Specifically, as explained in Chapter 7, Trump allegedly falsified business records with the intent to cover up other violations of New York and federal election laws, as well as state tax laws.

The defendant, in the County of New York and elsewhere, on or about February 14, 2017, with intent to defraud and intent to commit another crime and aid and conceal the commission thereof, made and caused a false entry in the business records of an enterprise, to wit, an invoice from Michael Cohen dated February 14, 2017, marked as a record of the Donald J. Trump Revocable Trust, and kept and maintained by the Trump Organization.

Annotation 3: Eleven of the 34 charges against Trump cite invoices submitted by Michael Cohen, Trump's longtime personal attorney, to the Trump Organization. Cohen's invoices were ostensibly submitted for legal services he provided through 2017. The first invoice, cited in this charge and dated Feb. 14, 2017, stated: "Pursuant to the retainer agreement, kindly remit payment for services rendered for the months of January and February, 2017." However, the DA's office alleges that these invoices were fraudulent, as there was no retainer agreement in place and Cohen did not provide the claimed legal services. According to the DA's office, the invoices were intended to cover up Trump's repayment of the $130,000 in hush money Cohen paid to Stephanie Clifford (also known as Stormy Daniels) in October 2016.

Annotation 4: Other than Trump himself, Cohen is the only other figure named in the indictment. However, according to the

DA's statement of facts, Cohen facilitated Trump's "catch and kill" scheme in 2015 and 2016. Trump, Cohen, and David Pecker, then CEO of American Media Inc. (AMI published the *National Enquirer* and other tabloids at the time), allegedly agreed to the scheme in August 2015—just two months after Trump declared his candidacy for president. The three men allegedly agreed to prevent women from coming forward with sordid stories from Trump's past during the 2016 presidential election. Trump did not want such negative stories to hurt his odds of winning. In late October 2016, as part of this "catch and kill" scheme, Cohen set up a shell company to pay Clifford hush money. He allegedly transferred $131,000 from a home equity loan to a bank account for the shell company and then paid Clifford's lawyer $130,000. In 2018, Cohen pleaded guilty to eight charges, admitting that the hush money payments made to Clifford and another woman were "intend[ed] to influence the 2016 presidential election." Cohen will likely be a key witness during the Manhattan trial.

Annotation 5: The Trump Organization is mentioned throughout the indictment. In the related statement of facts, the DA's office alleges that several Trump Organization officials— either knowingly or unknowingly—helped Trump conceal the purpose of his payments to Cohen throughout 2017. Separately, in September 2022, New York Attorney General Letitia James brought a civil fraud case against Donald Trump, Trump Organization entities, and several officials in the organization alleging that they engaged in financial fraud and other illegal conduct. In September 2023, New York State Supreme Court Justice Arthur Engoron granted James' motion for partial summary judgment, ruling that Trump and the other defendants had committed fraud by artificially inflating the value of Trump's assets. In February 2024, Justice Engoron ordered the *defendants to pay more than $450 million in disgorgement and prejudgment interest. That civil matter is separate from the criminal case brought by the Manhattan DA's case but involves many of the same individuals.*

SECOND COUNT:

AND THE GRAND JURY AFORESAID, by this indictment, further accuses the defendant of the crime of **FALSIFYING BUSINESS RECORDS IN THE FIRST DEGREE**, in violation of Penal Law §175.10, committed as follows:

The defendant, in the County of New York and elsewhere, on or about February 14, 2017, with intent to defraud and intent to commit another crime and aid and conceal the commission thereof, made and caused a false entry in the business records of an enterprise, to wit, an entry in the Detail General Ledger for the Donald J. Trump Revocable Trust, bearing voucher number 842457, and kept and maintained by the Trump Organization.

Annotation 6: Twelve of the 34 counts in the indictment cite allegedly fraudulent entries that were made in the general ledgers maintained by the Trump Organization. Two of the 12 allegedly fraudulent entries were made in the general ledger for the Donald J. Trump Revocable Trust, which holds some of Trump's assets. The remaining 10 allegedly fraudulent entries cited in the indictment reference a general ledger for Trump's personal account(s). The DA alleges that these 12 entries falsely referred to payments made to Cohen as "legal expenses," when in fact they were really made to repay the hush money transferred to Clifford in October 2016.

[Beginning of Page 2 in original]

THIRD COUNT:

AND THE GRAND JURY AFORESAID, by this indictment, further accuses the defendant of the crime of **FALSI-
FYING BUSINESS RECORDS IN THE FIRST DEGREE**, in
violation of Penal Law §175.10, committed as follows:

The defendant, in the County of New York and elsewhere, on or about February 14, 2017, with intent to defraud
and intent to commit another crime and aid and conceal the
commission thereof, made and caused a false entry in the
business records of an enterprise, to wit, an entry in the
Detail General Ledger for the Donald J. Trump Revocable
Trust, bearing voucher number 842460, and kept and maintained by the Trump Organization.

FOURTH COUNT

AND THE GRAND JURY AFORESAID, by this indictment, further accuses the defendant of the crime of **FALSI-
FYING BUSINESS RECORDS IN THE FIRST DEGREE**, in
violation of Penal Law §175.10, committed as follows:

The defendant, in the County of New York and elsewhere, on or about February 14, 2017, with intent to defraud
and intent to commit another crime and aid and conceal the
commission thereof, made and caused a false entry in the
business records of an enterprise, to wit, a Donald J. Trump
Revocable Trust Account check and check stub dated
February 14, 2017, bearing check number 000138, and kept
and maintained by the Trump Organization.[1]

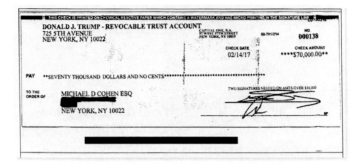

This is an image of the first allegedly fraudulent check written by
the Donald J. Trump Revocable Trust Account, dated Feb. 14, 2017,
and sent to Cohen. It is the subject of the fourth count. This image
was not originally found in the indictment.

*Annotation 7: Eleven of the 34 counts in the indictment cite
allegedly fraudulent checks and check stubs that Trump and
his trust used to repay Cohen for the $130,000 in hush money
provided to Clifford in October 2016. All 11 checks were issued
to Cohen between February and December 2017—that is,
during Trump's first year in office. According to the statement
of facts, the first check, cited here, was issued by Trump's trust
and signed by two trustees: Allen Weisselberg (then the
Trump Organization's CFO) and Donald Trump, Jr. Weisselberg also allegedly negotiated the fraudulent repayment
scheme, which was intended to mask the true purpose of the
payments. Weisselberg allegedly agreed to pay Cohen
$420,000 total. This figure includes a $130,000 repayment
for the hush money paid to Clifford and an additional
$50,000 in expenses owed Cohen, for a total of $180,000.
According to the DA, Weisselberg then agreed to double this
figure to $360,000 so Cohen could "characterize the payment
as income on his tax returns" and would be left with
$180,000 "after paying approximately 50% in income taxes."
Weisselberg also allegedly agreed to tack on an "additional*

$60,000 as a supplemental year-end bonus," bringing the
total figure to $420,000.

FIFTH COUNT:

AND THE GRAND JURY AFORESAID, by this indictment, further accuses the defendant of the crime of **FALSI-
FYING BUSINESS RECORDS IN THE FIRST DEGREE**, in
violation of Penal Law §175.10, committed as follows:

[Beginning of Page 3 in original]

The defendant, in the County of New York and elsewhere, on or about March 16, 2017 through March 17, 2017,
with intent to defraud and intent to commit another crime
and aid and conceal the commission thereof, made and
caused a false entry in the business records of an enterprise,
to wit, an invoice from Michael Cohen dated February 16,
2017 and transmitted on or about March 16, 2017, marked as
a record of the Donald J. Trump Revocable Trust, and kept
and maintained by the Trump Organization.

SIXTH COUNT:

AND THE GRAND JURY AFORESAID, by this indictment, further accuses the defendant of the crime of **FALSI-
FYING BUSINESS RECORDS IN THE FIRST DEGREE**, in
violation of Penal Law §175.10, committed as follows:

The defendant, in the County of New York and elsewhere, on or about March 17, 2017, with intent to defraud
and intent to commit another crime and aid and conceal the
commission thereof, made and caused a false entry in the
business records of an enterprise, to wit, an entry in the

Detail General Ledger for the Donald J. Trump Revocable Trust, bearing voucher number 846907, and kept and maintained by the Trump Organization.

SEVENTH COUNT:

AND THE GRAND JURY AFORESAID, by this indictment, further accuses the defendant of the crime of **FALSIFYING BUSINESS RECORDS IN THE FIRST DEGREE**, in violation of Penal Law §175.10, committed as follows:

[Beginning of Page 4 in original]

The defendant, in the County of New York and elsewhere, on or about March 17, 2017, with intent to defraud and intent to commit another crime and aid and conceal the commission thereof, made and caused a false entry in the business records of an enterprise, to wit, a Donald J. Trump Revocable Trust Account check and check stub dated March 17, 2017, bearing check number 000147, and kept and maintained by the Trump Organization.

This is an image of an allegedly fraudulent check dated March 17, 2017 and issued by the Donald J. Trump Revocable Trust Account. It was sent to Cohen and is the subject of the seventh count. This image was not originally found in the indictment.

Annotation 8: According to the Manhattan DA's office, the second check from Trump's trust to Cohen was "signed by two trustees," but they are not otherwise identified in the charging documents.

EIGHTH COUNT:

AND THE GRAND JURY AFORESAID, by this indictment, further accuses the defendant of the crime of **FALSIFYING BUSINESS RECORDS IN THE FIRST DEGREE**, in violation of Penal Law §175.10, committed as follows:

The defendant, in the County of New York and elsewhere, on or about April 13, 2017 through June 19, 2017, with intent to defraud and intent to commit another crime and aid and conceal the commission thereof, made and caused a false entry in the business records of an enterprise, to wit, an invoice from Michael Cohen dated April 13, 2017, marked as a record of Donald J. Trump, and kept and maintained by the Trump Organization.

NINTH COUNT:

AND THE GRAND JURY AFORESAID, by this indictment, further accuses the defendant of the crime of **FALSIFYING BUSINESS RECORDS IN THE FIRST DEGREE**, in violation of Penal Law §175.10, committed as follows:

The defendant, in the County of New York and elsewhere, on or about June 19, 2017, with intent to defraud and intent to commit another crime and aid and conceal the commission thereof, made and caused a false entry in the business records of an enterprise, to wit, an entry in the Detail General Ledger for Donald J. Trump, bearing

voucher number 858770, and kept and maintained by the
Trump Organization.

[Beginning of Page 5 in original]

TENTH COUNT:

AND THE GRAND JURY AFORESAID, by this indictment, further accuses the defendant of the crime of **FALSI-
FYING BUSINESS RECORDS IN THE FIRST DEGREE**, in
violation of Penal Law §175.10, committed as follows:

The defendant, in the County of New York and elsewhere, on or about June 19, 2017, with intent to defraud and
intent to commit another crime and aid and conceal the
commission thereof, made and caused a false entry in the
business records of an enterprise, to wit, a Donald J. Trump
account check and check stub dated June 19, 2017, bearing
check number 002740, and kept and maintained by the
Trump Organization.

> *Annotation 9: The indictment cites nine checks that were
> "personally" signed by Trump and made payable to Cohen.
> Each of the checks was allegedly stapled to an allegedly
> fraudulent invoice from Cohen, and then sent to the Trump
> Organization. Trump's last check to Cohen was issued in
> December 2017. Images of five of these checks allegedly
> bearing Trump's signature can be found in the following
> pages.*

ELEVENTH COUNT:

AND THE GRAND JURY AFORESAID, by this indict-
ment, further accuses the defendant of the crime of **FALSI-**

FYING BUSINESS RECORDS IN THE FIRST DEGREE, in violation of Penal Law §175.10, committed as follows:

The defendant, in the County of New York and elsewhere, on or about May 22, 2017, with intent to defraud and intent to commit another crime and aid and conceal the commission thereof, made and caused a false entry in the business records of an enterprise, to wit, an invoice from Michael Cohen dated May 22, 2017, marked as a record of Donald J. Trump, and kept and maintained by the Trump Organization.

TWELFTH COUNT:

AND THE GRAND JURY AFORESAID, by this indictment, further accuses the defendant of the crime of FALSIFYING BUSINESS RECORDS IN THE FIRST DEGREE, in violation of Penal Law §175.10, committed as follows:

[Beginning of Page 6 in original]

The defendant, in the County of New York and elsewhere, on or about May 22, 2017, with intent to defraud and intent to commit another crime and aid and conceal the commission thereof, made and caused a false entry in the business records of an enterprise, to wit, an entry in the Detail General Ledger for Donald J. Trump, bearing voucher number 855331, and kept and maintained by the Trump Organization.

THIRTEENTH COUNT:

AND THE GRAND JURY AFORESAID, by this indictment, further accuses the defendant of the crime of FALSI-

FYING BUSINESS RECORDS IN THE FIRST DEGREE, in violation of Penal Law §175.10, committed as follows:

The defendant, in the County of New York and elsewhere, on or about May 23, 2017, with intent to defraud and intent to commit another crime and aid and conceal the commission thereof, made and caused a false entry in the business records of an enterprise, to wit, a Donald J. Trump account check and check stub dated May 23, 2017, bearing check number 002700, and kept and maintained by the Trump Organization.

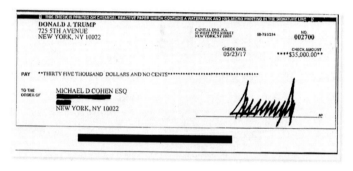

This is an image of an allegedly fraudulent check sent to Cohen. Trump allegedly signed nine checks personally, including this one, dated May 23, 2017. This check is the subject of the 13th count. This image was not originally found in the indictment.

FOURTEENTH COUNT:

AND THE GRAND JURY AFORESAID, by this indictment, further accuses the defendant of the crime of **FALSIFYING BUSINESS RECORDS IN THE FIRST DEGREE**, in violation of Penal Law §175.10, committed as follows:

The defendant, in the County of New York and elsewhere, on or about June 16, 2017 through June 19, 2017, with intent to defraud and intent to commit another crime and aid and conceal the commission thereof, made and caused a false entry in the business records of an enterprise, to wit, an invoice from Michael Cohen dated June 16, 2017, marked as a record of Donald J. Trump, and kept and maintained by the Trump Organization.

[Beginning of Page 7 in original]

FIFTEENTH COUNT:

AND THE GRAND JURY AFORESAID, by this indictment, further accuses the defendant of the crime of **FALSIFYING BUSINESS RECORDS IN THE FIRST DEGREE**, in violation of Penal Law §175.10, committed as follows:

The defendant, in the County of New York and elsewhere, on or about June 19, 2017, with intent to defraud and intent to commit another crime and aid and conceal the commission thereof, made and caused a false entry in the business records of an enterprise, to wit, an entry in the Detail General Ledger for Donald J. Trump, bearing voucher number 858772, and kept and maintained by the Trump Organization.

SIXTEENTH COUNT:

AND THE GRAND JURY AFORESAID, by this indictment, further accuses the defendant of the crime of **FALSIFYING BUSINESS RECORDS IN THE FIRST DEGREE**, in violation of Penal Law §175.10, committed as follows:

The defendant, in the County of New York and elsewhere, on or about June 19, 2017, with intent to defraud and intent to commit another crime and aid and conceal the commission thereof, made and caused a false entry in the business records of an enterprise, to wit, a Donald J. Trump account check and check stub dated June 19, 2017, bearing check number 002741, and kept and maintained by the Trump Organization.

SEVENTEENTH COUNT:

AND THE GRAND JURY AFORESAID, by this indictment, further accuses the defendant of the crime of **FALSIFYING BUSINESS RECORDS IN THE FIRST DEGREE**, in violation of Penal Law §175.10, committed as follows:

[Beginning of Page 8 in original]

The defendant, in the County of New York and elsewhere, on or about July 11, 2017, with intent to defraud and intent to commit another crime and aid and conceal the commission thereof, made and caused a false entry in the business records of an enterprise, to wit, an invoice from Michael Cohen dated July 11, 2017, marked as a record of Donald J. Trump, and kept and maintained by the Trump Organization.

EIGHTEENTH COUNT:

AND THE GRAND JURY AFORESAID, by this indictment, further accuses the defendant of the crime of **FALSIFYING BUSINESS RECORDS IN THE FIRST DEGREE**, in violation of Penal Law §175.10, committed as follows:

The defendant, in the County of New York and elsewhere, on or about July 11, 2017, with intent to defraud and intent to commit another crime and aid and conceal the commission thereof, made and caused a false entry in the business records of an enterprise, to wit, an entry in the Detail General Ledger for Donald J. Trump, bearing voucher number 861096, and kept and maintained by the Trump Organization.

NINETEENTH COUNT:

AND THE GRAND JURY AFORESAID, by this indictment, further accuses the defendant of the crime of **FALSIFYING BUSINESS RECORDS IN THE FIRST DEGREE**, in violation of Penal Law §175.10, committed as follows:

The defendant, in the County of New York and elsewhere, on or about July 11, 2017, with intent to defraud and intent to commit another crime and aid and conceal the commission thereof, made and caused a false entry in the business records of an enterprise, to wit, a Donald J. Trump account check and check stub dated July 11, 2017, bearing check number 002781, and kept and maintained by the Trump Organization.

[Beginning of Page 9 in original]

TWENTIETH COUNT:

AND THE GRAND JURY AFORESAID, by this indictment, further accuses the defendant of the crime of **FALSIFYING BUSINESS RECORDS IN THE FIRST DEGREE**, in violation of Penal Law §175.10, committed as follows:

The defendant, in the County of New York and elsewhere, on or about August 1, 2017, with intent to defraud and intent to commit another crime and aid and conceal the commission thereof, made and caused a false entry in the business records of an enterprise, to wit, an invoice from Michael Cohen dated August 1, 2017, marked as a record of Donald J. Trump, and kept and maintained by the Trump Organization.

TWENTY-FIRST COUNT:

AND THE GRAND JURY AFORESAID, by this indictment, further accuses the defendant of the crime of **FALSIFYING BUSINESS RECORDS IN THE FIRST DEGREE**, in violation of Penal Law §175.10, committed as follows:

The defendant, in the County of New York and elsewhere, on or about August 1, 2017, with intent to defraud and intent to commit another crime and aid and conceal the commission thereof, made and caused a false entry in the business records of an enterprise, to wit, an entry in the Detail General Ledger for Donald J. Trump, bearing voucher number 863641, and kept and maintained by the Trump Organization.

TWENTY-SECOND COUNT:

AND THE GRAND JURY AFORESAID, by this indictment, further accuses the defendant of the crime of **FALSIFYING BUSINESS RECORDS IN THE FIRST DEGREE**, in violation of Penal Law §175.10, committed as follows:

[Beginning of Page 10 in original]

The defendant, in the County of New York and elsewhere, on or about August 1, 2017, with intent to defraud and intent to commit another crime and aid and conceal the commission thereof, made and caused a false entry in the business records of an enterprise, to wit, a Donald J. Trump account check and check stub dated August 1, 2017, bearing check number 002821, and kept and maintained by the Trump Organization.

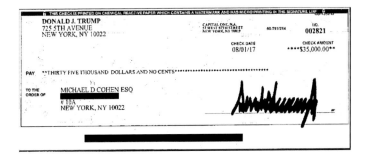

This check, which is allegedly fraudulent and signed by Trump, is dated August 1, 2017. It is the subject of the indictment's 22nd count. This image was not originally found in the indictment.

TWENTY-THIRD COUNT:

AND THE GRAND JURY AFORESAID, by this indictment, further accuses the defendant of the crime of **FALSIFYING BUSINESS RECORDS IN THE FIRST DEGREE**, in violation of Penal Law §175.10, committed as follows:

The defendant, in the County of New York and elsewhere, on or about September 11, 2017, with intent to defraud and intent to commit another crime and aid and conceal the commission thereof, made and caused a false entry in the business records of an enterprise, to wit, an invoice from Michael Cohen dated September 11, 2017, marked as a record of Donald J. Trump, and kept and maintained by the Trump Organization.

TWENTY-FOURTH COUNT:

AND THE GRAND JURY AFORESAID, by this indictment, further accuses the defendant of the crime of **FALSIFYING BUSINESS RECORDS IN THE FIRST DEGREE**, in violation of Penal Law §175.10, committed as follows:

The defendant, in the County of New York and elsewhere, on or about September 11, 2017, with intent to defraud and intent to commit another crime and aid and conceal the commission thereof, made and caused a false entry in the business records of an enterprise, to wit, an entry in the Detail General Ledger for Donald J. Trump, bearing voucher number 868174, and kept and maintained by the Trump Organization.

[Beginning of Page 11 in original]

TWENTY-FIFTH COUNT:

AND THE GRAND JURY AFORESAID, by this indictment, further accuses the defendant of the crime of **FALSIFYING BUSINESS RECORDS IN THE FIRST DEGREE**, in violation of Penal Law §175.10, committed as follows:

The defendant, in the County of New York and elsewhere, on or about September 12, 2017, with intent to defraud and intent to commit another crime and aid and conceal the commission thereof, made and caused a false entry in the business records of an enterprise, to wit, a

Donald J. Trump account check and check stub dated September 12, 2017, bearing check number 002908, and kept and maintained by the Trump Organization.

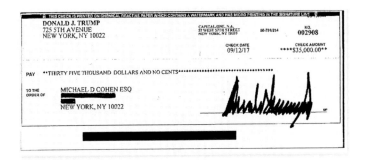

This check, which is allegedly fraudulent and signed by Trump, is dated September 12, 2017. It is the subject of the indictment's 25th count. This image was not originally found in the indictment.

TWENTY-SIXTH COUNT:

AND THE GRAND JURY AFORESAID, by this indictment, further accuses the defendant of the crime of **FALSIFYING BUSINESS RECORDS IN THE FIRST DEGREE**, in violation of Penal Law §175.10, committed as follows:

The defendant, in the County of New York and elsewhere, on or about October 18, 2017, with intent to defraud and intent to commit another crime and aid and conceal the commission thereof, made and caused a false entry in the business records of an enterprise, to wit, an invoice from Michael Cohen dated October 18, 2017, marked as a record of Donald J. Trump, and kept and maintained by the Trump Organization.

TWENTY-SEVENTH COUNT:

AND THE GRAND JURY AFORESAID, by this indictment, further accuses the defendant of the crime of **FALSIFYING BUSINESS RECORDS IN THE FIRST DEGREE**, in violation of Penal Law §175.10, committed as follows:

[Beginning of Page 12 in original]

The defendant, in the County of New York and elsewhere, on or about October 18, 2017, with intent to defraud and intent to commit another crime and aid and conceal the commission thereof, made and caused a false entry in the business records of an enterprise, to wit, an entry in the Detail General Ledger for Donald J. Trump, bearing voucher number 872654, and kept and maintained by the Trump Organization.

TWENTY-EIGHTH COUNT:

AND THE GRAND JURY AFORESAID, by this indictment, further accuses the defendant of the crime of **FALSIFYING BUSINESS RECORDS IN THE FIRST DEGREE**, in violation of Penal Law §175.10, committed as follows:

The defendant, in the County of New York and elsewhere, on or about October 18, 2017, with intent to defraud and intent to commit another crime and aid and conceal the commission thereof, made and caused a false entry in the business records of an enterprise, to wit, a Donald J. Trump account check and check stub dated October 18, 2017, bearing check number 002944, and kept and maintained by the Trump Organization.

TWENTY-NINTH COUNT:

AND THE GRAND JURY AFORESAID, by this indictment, further accuses the defendant of the crime of **FALSI-FYING BUSINESS RECORDS IN THE FIRST DEGREE**, in violation of Penal Law §175.10, committed as follows:

The defendant, in the County of New York and else-where, on or about November 20, 2017, with intent to defraud and intent to commit another crime and aid and conceal the commission thereof, made and caused a false entry in the business records of an enterprise, to wit, an invoice from Michael Cohen dated November 20, 2017, marked as a record of Donald J. Trump, and kept and main-tained by the Trump Organization.

[Beginning of Page 13 in original]

THIRTIETH COUNT:

AND THE GRAND JURY AFORESAID, by this indict-ment, further accuses the defendant of the crime of **FALSI-FYING BUSINESS RECORDS IN THE FIRST DEGREE**, in violation of Penal Law §175.10, committed as follows:

The defendant, in the County of New York and else-where, on or about November 20, 2017, with intent to defraud and intent to commit another crime and aid and conceal the commission thereof, made and caused a false entry in the business records of an enterprise, to wit, an entry in the Detail General Ledger for Donald J. Trump, bearing voucher number 876511, and kept and maintained by the Trump Organization.

THIRTY-FIRST COUNT:

AND THE GRAND JURY AFORESAID, by this indict-ment, further accuses the defendant of the crime of **FALSI-**

FYING BUSINESS RECORDS IN THE FIRST DEGREE, in violation of Penal Law §175.10, committed as follows:

The defendant, in the County of New York and elsewhere, on or about November 21, 2017, with intent to defraud and intent to commit another crime and aid and conceal the commission thereof, made and caused a false entry in the business records of an enterprise, to wit, a Donald J. Trump account check and check stub dated November 21, 2017, bearing check number 002980, and kept and maintained by the Trump Organization.

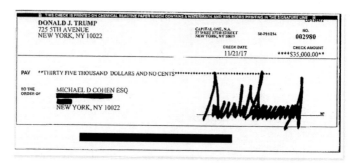

This check, which is allegedly fraudulent and signed by Trump, is dated November 21, 2017. It is the subject of the indictment's 31st count. This image was not originally found in the indictment.

THIRTY-SECOND COUNT:

AND THE GRAND JURY AFORESAID, by this indictment, further accuses the defendant of the crime of **FALSIFYING BUSINESS RECORDS IN THE FIRST DEGREE**, in violation of Penal Law §175.10, committed as follows:

[Beginning of Page 14 in original]

The defendant, in the County of New York and elsewhere, on or about December 1, 2017, with intent to defraud and intent to commit another crime and aid and conceal the commission thereof, made and caused a false entry in the business records of an enterprise, to wit, an invoice from Michael Cohen dated December 1, 2017, marked as a record of Donald J. Trump, and kept and maintained by the Trump Organization.

THIRTY-THIRD COUNT:

AND THE GRAND JURY AFORESAID, by this indictment, further accuses the defendant of the crime of **FALSIFYING BUSINESS RECORDS IN THE FIRST DEGREE**, in violation of Penal Law §175.10, committed as follows:

The defendant, in the County of New York and elsewhere, on or about December 1, 2017, with intent to defraud and intent to commit another crime and aid and conceal the commission thereof, made and caused a false entry in the business records of an enterprise, to wit, an entry in the Detail General Ledger for Donald J. Trump, bearing voucher number 877785, and kept and maintained by the Trump Organization.

THIRTY-FOURTH COUNT:

AND THE GRAND JURY AFORESAID, by this indictment, further accuses the defendant of the crime of **FALSIFYING BUSINESS RECORDS IN THE FIRST DEGREE**, in violation of Penal Law §175.10, committed as follows:

The defendant, in the County of New York and elsewhere, on or about December 5, 2017, with intent to defraud and intent to commit another crime and aid and conceal the commission thereof, made and caused a false entry in the business records of an enterprise, to wit, a Donald J. Trump account check and check stub dated December 5, 2017, bearing check number 003006, and kept and maintained by the Trump Organization.

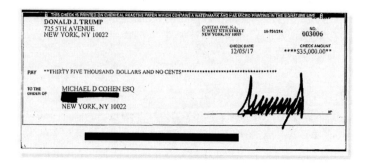

This check, dated December 5, 2017, is the last of 11 allegedly fraudulent checks sent by Trump or an affiliate to Cohen. Like each monthly check between April and December, Trump allegedly signed this check personally. This is the subject of the indictment's 34th and final count. This image was not originally found in the indictment.

ALVIN L. BRAGG, JR.
District Attorney

The Statement of Facts: Annotated

SUPREME COURT OF THE STATE OF NEW YORK
COUNTY OF NEW YORK

THE PEOPLE OF THE STATE OF NEW YORK
-against-
DONALD J. TRUMP,
Defendant.

STATEMENT OF FACTS

INTRODUCTION

1. The defendant DONALD J. TRUMP repeatedly and fraudulently falsified New York business records to conceal criminal conduct that hid damaging information from the voting public during the 2016 presidential election.

> *Annotation 1:* The DA's office's statement of facts supplements the indictment, placing the charged criminal conduct in the broader context of Donald Trump's scheme to prevent voters from learning salacious allegations about his past.

> *Annotation 2:* At the outset, the Manhattan DA's office makes clear that Trump's alleged falsification of business records was part of his effort to prevent Stephanie Clifford (also known as Stormy Daniels) and other sources from sharing their stories with the public just prior to the 2016 presidential election. This

*is why the Manhattan prosecution is not a hush money case
but rather an election fraud case.*

2. From August 2015 to December 2017, the Defendant orchestrated a scheme with others to influence the 2016 presidential election by identifying and purchasing negative information about him to suppress its publication and benefit the Defendant's electoral prospects. In order to execute the unlawful scheme, the participants violated election laws and made and caused false entries in the business records of various entities in New York. The participants also took steps that mischaracterized, for tax purposes, the true nature of the payments made in furtherance of the scheme.

Annotation 3: The dates of the alleged scheme are important for understanding Trump's alleged criminal conduct. Trump declared his presidential candidacy in June 2015. Just two months later, in August 2015, he allegedly "orchestrated" what is known as a "catch and kill" scheme to suppress negative stories from reaching the public. Trump repaid Cohen the hush money he paid to Clifford throughout 2017—that is, throughout Trump's first year in office as president.

3. One component of this scheme was that, at the Defendant's request, a lawyer who then worked for the Trump Organization as Special Counsel to Defendant ("Lawyer A"), covertly paid $130,000 to an adult film actress shortly before the election to prevent her from publicizing a sexual encounter with the Defendant. Lawyer A made the $130,000 payment through a shell corporation he set up and funded at a bank in Manhattan. This payment was illegal, and Lawyer A has since pleaded guilty to making

an illegal campaign contribution and served time in prison.

Annotation 4: "*Lawyer A*" *is Michael Cohen—Trump's long-time personal lawyer.*

[Beginning of Page 2 in original]

Further, false entries were made in New York business records to effectuate this payment, separate and apart from the New York business records used to conceal the payment.

4. After the election, the Defendant reimbursed Lawyer A for the illegal payment through a series of monthly checks, first from the Donald J. Trump Revocable Trust (the "Defendant's Trust")—a Trust created under the laws of New York which held the Trump Organization entity assets after the Defendant was elected President—and then from the Defendant's bank account. Each check was processed by the Trump Organization, and each check was disguised as a payment for legal services rendered in a given month of 2017 pursuant to a retainer agreement. The payment records, kept and maintained by the Trump Organization, were false New York business records. In truth, there was no retainer agreement, and Lawyer A was not being paid for legal services rendered in 2017. The Defendant caused his entities' business records to be falsified to disguise his and others' criminal conduct.

BACKGROUND

5. The Defendant is the beneficial owner of a collection of business entities known by the trade name the Trump Organization. The Trump Organization comprises approxi-

mately 500 separate entities that, among other business activities, own and manage hotels, golf courses, commercial real estate, condominium developments, and other properties. The Trump Organization is headquartered at 725 Fifth Avenue in New York County.

6. From approximately June 2015 to November 2016, the Defendant was a candidate for the office of President of the United States. On January 20, 2017, he became President of the United States.

[Beginning of Page 3 in original]

THE SCHEME

I. The Catch and Kill Scheme to Suppress Negative Information

7. During and in furtherance of his candidacy for President, the Defendant and others agreed to identify and suppress negative stories about him. Two parties to this agreement have admitted to committing illegal conduct in connection with the scheme. In August 2018, Lawyer A pleaded guilty to two federal crimes involving illegal campaign contributions, and subsequently served time in prison. In addition, in August 2018, American Media, Inc. ("AMI"), a media company that owned and published magazines and supermarket tabloids including the *National Enquirer*, admitted in a non-prosecution agreement that it made a payment to a source of a story to ensure that the source "did not publicize damaging allegations" about the Defendant "before the 2016 presidential election and thereby influence that election."

Annotation 5: On Sept. 21, 2018, the Department of Justice and AMI entered a non-prosecution agreement in connection with AMI's role in the catch and kill scheme.

A. The 2015 Trump Tower Meeting

8. In June 2015, the Defendant announced his candidacy for President of the United States.

9. Soon after, in August 2015, the Defendant met with Lawyer A and AMI's Chairman and Chief Executive Officer (the "AMI CEO") at Trump Tower in New York County. At the meeting, the AMI CEO agreed to help with the Defendant's campaign, saying that he would act as the "eyes and ears" for the campaign by looking out for negative stories about the Defendant and alerting Lawyer A before the stories were published. The AMI CEO also agreed to publish negative stories about the Defendant's competitors for the election.

Annotation 6: David Pecker was AMI's chairman and chief executive officer at the time.

B. Suppressing the Doorman's Story

10. A few months later, in or about October or November 2015, the AMI CEO learned that a former Trump Tower doorman (the "Doorman") was trying to sell information regarding a child that the Defendant had allegedly fathered out of wedlock. At the AMI CEO's direction, AMI negotiated and signed an agreement to pay the Doorman $30,000 to acquire exclusive rights to the story.

Annotation 7: The "Doorman" is Dino Sajudin.

[Beginning of Page 4 in original]

AMI falsely characterized this payment in AMI's books and records, including in its general ledger. AMI purchased the information from the Doorman without fully investigating his claims, but the AMI CEO directed that the deal take place because of his agreement with the Defendant and Lawyer A.

11. When AMI later concluded that the story was not true, the AMI CEO wanted to release the Doorman from the agreement. However, Lawyer A instructed the AMI CEO not to release the Doorman until after the presidential election, and the AMI CEO complied with that instruction because of his agreement with the Defendant and Lawyer A.

> ***Annotation 8:*** *The Manhattan DA's office alleges Trump's lawyer at the time, Michael Cohen, "instructed" AMI CEO David Pecker not to release Sajudin from a non-disclosure agreement until after the 2016 presidential election. And Pecker complied "because of his agreement" with Trump and Cohen. This further supports the DA's argument that the alleged criminal acts charged in the indictment are fundamentally part of an election interference case—as Trump and Cohen were only concerned with keeping Sajudin's story out of the press until after all the votes had been cast. Indeed, AMI did eventually release Sajudin from the non-disclosure agreement, which was obtained by CNN and published online.*

C. Suppressing Woman 1's Account

12. About five months before the presidential election, in or about June 2016, the editor-in-chief of the *National Enquirer* and AMI's Chief Content Officer (the "AMI Editor-

in-Chief") contacted Lawyer A about a woman ("Woman 1") who alleged she had a sexual relationship with the Defendant while he was married. The AMI Editor-in-Chief updated Lawyer A regularly about the matter over text message and by telephone. The Defendant did not want this information to become public because he was concerned about the effect it could have on his candidacy. Thereafter, the Defendant, the AMI CEO, and Lawyer A had a series of discussions about who should pay off Woman 1 to secure her silence.

Annotation 9: Dylan Howard was AMI's chief content officer ("Editor-in-Chief") at the time and The New York Times has identified him as the AMI editor in contact with Cohen.

Annotation 10: The press has identified "Woman 1" as Karen McDougal, a former Playboy model.

Annotation 11: Although the Manhattan DA's office does not identify the source for this claim, it is (again) noteworthy that Trump was allegedly concerned that McDougal's story could have an "effect" on the 2016 presidential election.

13. AMI ultimately paid $150,000 to Woman 1 in exchange for her agreement not to speak out about the alleged sexual relationship, as well as for two magazine cover features of Woman 1 and a series of articles that would be published under her byline. AMI falsely characterized this payment in AMI's books and records, including in its general ledger. The AMI CEO agreed to the deal after discussing it with both the Defendant and Lawyer A, and on the understanding from Lawyer A that the Defendant or the Trump Organization would reimburse AMI.

Annotation 12: While none of the criminal charges against Trump directly involve the hush money payment to McDougal, the Manhattan DA's office alleges AMI falsely characterized the payment in its general ledger—just as Trump and the Trump Organization are alleged to have done with respect to Trump's repayment of Cohen.

[Beginning of Page 5 in original]

14. In a conversation captured in an audio recording in approximately September 2016 concerning Woman 1's account, the Defendant and Lawyer A discussed how to obtain the rights to Woman 1's account from AMI and how to reimburse AMI for its payment. Lawyer A told the Defendant he would open up a company for the transfer of Woman 1's account and other information, and stated that he had spoken to the Chief Financial Officer for the Trump Organization (the "TO CFO") about "how to set the whole thing up." The Defendant asked, "So what do we got to pay for this? One fifty?" and suggested paying by cash. When Lawyer A disagreed, the Defendant then mentioned payment by check. After the conversation, Lawyer A created a shell company called Resolution Consultants, LLC on or about September 30, 2016.

Annotation 13: The New York Times and CNN reported that Michael Cohen recorded some of his conversations with Trump, including their discussion of a hush money payment to Karen McDougal. It appears that the "audio recording" cited here is from one of Cohen's tapes.

Annotation 14: The Trump Organization's CFO was Allen Weisselberg. In August 2022, Weisselberg pleaded guilty to 15 *charges in another case, admitting that he had devised and operated "a 15-year scheme to defraud federal, New York State, and New York City tax authorities, evading payment of taxes due on $1.76 million in unreported income." As part of his plea deal, Weisselberg served five months in prison. In March 2024, Weisselberg pleaded guilty to two additional counts of perjury.*

15. Less than two months before the election, on or about September 30, 2016, the AMI CEO signed an agreement in which AMI agreed to transfer its rights to Woman 1's account to Lawyer A's shell company for $125,000. However, after the assignment agreement was signed but before the reimbursement took place, the AMI CEO consulted with AMI's general counsel and then told Lawyer A that the deal to transfer the rights to Lawyer A's shell company was off.

D. Suppressing Woman 2's Account

16. About one month before the election, on or about October 7, 2016, news broke that the Defendant had been caught on tape saying to the host of *Access Hollywood*: "I just start kissing them [women]. It's like a magnet. Just kiss. I don't even wait. And when you're a star, they let you do it. You can do anything. Grab 'em by the [genitals]. You can do anything." The evidence shows that both the Defendant and his campaign staff were concerned that the tape would harm his viability as a candidate and reduce his standing with female voters in particular the understanding from Lawyer A that the Defendant or the Trump Organization would reimburse AMI.

Annotation 15: The "Access Hollywood" tape was a so-called October surprise. Released just weeks prior to the 2016 election, it had the potential to sway voters. Additional allegations and unfavorable stories could have negatively impacted voters' perceptions of Trump even further.

[Beginning of Page 6 in original]

17. Shortly after the *Access Hollywood* tape became public, the AMI Editor-in-Chief contacted the AMI CEO about another woman ("Woman 2") who alleged she had a sexual encounter with the Defendant while he was married. The AMI CEO told the AMI Editor-in- Chief to notify Lawyer A.

Annotation 16: "Woman 2" is Stephanie Clifford, the adult film actress also known as Stormy Daniels.

18. On or about October 10, 2016, the AMI Editor-in-Chief connected Lawyer A with Woman 2's lawyer ("Lawyer B"). Lawyer A then negotiated a deal with Lawyer B to secure Woman 2's silence and prevent disclosure of the damaging information in the final weeks before the presidential election. Under the deal that Lawyer B negotiated, Woman 2 would be paid $130,000 for the rights to her account.

Annotation 17: "Lawyer B" is Clifford's former attorney, Keith Davidson.

19. The Defendant directed Lawyer A to delay making a payment to Woman 2 as long as possible. He instructed Lawyer A that if they could delay the payment until after the election, they could avoid paying altogether, because at that point it would not matter if the story became public. As reflected in emails and text messages between and among

Lawyer A, Lawyer B, and the AMI Editor-in-Chief, Lawyer A attempted to delay making payment as long as possible.

> *Annotation 18:* Trump's suggestion that Cohen "could delay the payment until after the election" because they could then avoid payment entirely is another piece of evidence indicating that the hush money paid to Clifford was intended solely to prevent her from sharing her story with voters prior to Election Day 2016.

20. Ultimately, with pressure mounting and the election approaching, the Defendant agreed to the payoff and directed Lawyer A to proceed. Lawyer A discussed the deal with the Defendant and the TO CFO. The Defendant did not want to make the $130,000 payment himself, and asked Lawyer A and the TO CFO to find a way to make the payment. After discussing various payment options with the TO CFO, Lawyer A agreed he would make the payment. Before making the payment, Lawyer A confirmed with the Defendant that Defendant would pay him back.

[Beginning of Page 7 in original]

21. On or about October 26, shortly after speaking with the Defendant on the phone, Lawyer A opened a bank account in Manhattan in the name of Essential Consultants LLC, a new shell company he had created to effectuate the payment. He then transferred $131,000 from his personal home equity line of credit ("HELOC") into that account. On or about October 27, Lawyer A wired $130,000 from his Essential Consultants LLC account in New York to Lawyer B to suppress Woman 2's account.

E. Post-Election Communications with AMI CEO

22. On November 8, 2016, the Defendant won the presidential election and became the President-Elect. Thereafter, AMI released both the doorman and Woman 1 from their non- disclosure agreements.

23. The Defendant was inaugurated as President on January 20, 2017. Between Election Day and Inauguration Day, during the period of the Defendant's transition to his role as President, the Defendant met with the AMI CEO privately in Trump Tower in Manhattan. The Defendant thanked the AMI CEO for handling the stories of the Doorman and Woman 1, and invited the AMI CEO to the Inauguration. In the summer of 2017, the Defendant invited the AMI CEO to the White House for a dinner to thank him for his help during the campaign.

II. The Defendant Falsified Business Records

24. Shortly after being elected President, the Defendant arranged to reimburse Lawyer A for the payoff he made on the Defendant's behalf. In or around January 2017, the TO CFO and Lawyer A met to discuss how Lawyer A would be reimbursed for the money he paid to ensure Woman 2's silence. The TO CFO asked Lawyer A to bring a copy of a bank statement for the Essential Consultants account showing the $130,000 payment.

25. The TO CFO and Lawyer A agreed to a total repayment amount of $420,000. They reached that figure by adding the $130,000 payment to a $50,000 payment for another expense for which Lawyer A also claimed reimbursement, for a total of $180,000.

[Beginning of Page 8 in original]

The TO CFO then doubled that amount to $360,000 so that Lawyer A could characterize the payment as income on his tax returns, instead of a reimbursement, and Lawyer A would be left with $180,000 after paying approximately 50% in income taxes. Finally, the TO CFO added an additional $60,000 as a supplemental year-end bonus. Together, these amounts totaled $420,000. The TO CFO memorialized these calculations in handwritten notes on the copy of the bank statement that Lawyer A had provided.

26. The Defendant, the TO CFO, and Lawyer A then agreed that Lawyer A would be paid the $420,000 through twelve monthly payments of $35,000 over the course of 2017. Each month, Lawyer A was to send an invoice to the Defendant through Trump Organization employees, falsely requesting payment of $35,000 for legal services rendered in a given month of 2017 pursuant to a retainer agreement. At no point did Lawyer A have a retainer agreement with the Defendant or the Trump Organization.

27. In early February 2017, the Defendant and Lawyer A met in the Oval Office at the White House and confirmed this repayment arrangement.

28. On or about February 14, 2017, Lawyer A emailed the Controller of the Trump Organization (the "TO Controller") the first monthly invoice, which stated: "Pursuant to the retainer agreement, kindly remit payment for services rendered for the months of January and February, 2017." The invoice requested payment in the amount of $35,000 for each of those two months. The TO CFO approved the payment, and, in turn, the TO Controller sent the invoice to the Trump Organization Accounts Payable Supervisor (the "TO Accounts Payable Supervisor") with the following

instructions: "Post to legal expenses. Put 'retainer for the months of January and February 2017' in the description."

Annotation 19: The "TO [Trump Organization] Controller" at the time was Jeffrey McConney.

[Beginning of Page 9 in original]

29. Lawyer A submitted ten similar monthly invoices by email to the Trump Organization for the remaining months in 2017. Each invoice falsely stated that it was being submitted "[p]ursuant to the retainer agreement," and falsely requested "payment for services rendered" for a month of 2017. In fact, there was no such retainer agreement and Lawyer A was not being paid for services rendered in any month of 2017.

30. The TO Controller forwarded each invoice to the TO Accounts Payable Supervisor. Consistent with the TO Controller's initial instructions, the TO Accounts Payable Supervisor printed out each invoice and marked it with an accounts payable stamp and the general ledger code "51505" for legal expenses. The Trump Organization maintained the invoices as records of expenses paid.

31. As instructed, the TO Accounts Payable Supervisor recorded each payment in the Trump Organization's electronic accounting system, falsely describing it as a "legal expense" pursuant to a retainer agreement for a month of 2017. The Trump Organization maintained a digital entry for each expense, called a "voucher," and these vouchers, like vouchers for other expenses, became part of the Trump Organization's general ledgers.

32. The TO Accounts Payable Supervisor then prepared checks with attached check stubs for approval and signa-

ture. The first check was paid from the Defendant's Trust and signed by the TO CFO and the Defendant's son, as trustees. The check stub falsely recorded the payment as "Retainer for 1/1-1/31/17" and "Retainer for 2/1-2/28/17." The second check, for March 2017, was also paid from the Trust and signed by two trustees. The check stub falsely recorded the payment as "Retainer for 3/1-3/31/17."

33. The remaining nine checks, corresponding to the months of April through December of 2017, were paid by the Defendant personally. Each of the checks was cut from the Defendant's bank account and sent, along with the corresponding invoices from Lawyer A, from the Trump Organization in New York County to the Defendant in Washington, D.C.

[Beginning of Page 10 in original]

The checks and stubs bearing the false statements were stapled to the invoices also bearing false statements. The Defendant signed each of the checks personally and had them sent back to the Trump Organization in New York County. There, the checks, the stubs, and the invoices were scanned and maintained in the Trump Organization's data system before the checks themselves were detached and mailed to Lawyer A for payment.

34. The $35,000 payments stopped after the December 2017 payment.

III. The Investigation into Lawyer A and the Defendant's Pressure Campaign

35. On or about April 9, 2018, the FBI executed a search warrant on Lawyer A's residences and office. In the months

that followed, the Defendant and others engaged in a public and private pressure campaign to ensure that Lawyer A did not cooperate with law enforcement in the federal investigation.

36. On the day of the FBI searches, Lawyer A called to speak with the Defendant to let him know what had occurred. In a return call, the Defendant told Lawyer A to "stay strong."

37. On or about April 21, 2018, the Defendant publicly commented on Twitter encouraging Lawyer A not to "flip," stating, "Most people will flip if the Government lets them out of trouble, even if . . . it means lying or making up stories. Sorry, I don't see [Lawyer A] doing that...."

38. In mid-April 2018, Lawyer A was also approached by an attorney ("Lawyer C"), who offered to represent him in the interest of maintaining a "back channel of communication" to the Defendant. On or about April 21, 2018, Lawyer C emailed Lawyer A, highlighting that he had a close relationship with the Defendant's personal attorney ("Lawyer D") and stating, "[T]his could not be a better situation for the President or you." Later that day, Lawyer C

[Beginning of Page 11 in original]

emailed Lawyer A again, writing, "I spoke with [Lawyer D]. Very Very Positive. You are 'loved.' . . . [Lawyer D] said this communication channel must be maintained. . . . Sleep well tonight, you have friends in high places."

Annotation 20: "Lawyer C" is attorney Robert Costello.

Annotation 21: "Lawyer D" is former New York City Mayor Rudy Giuliani.

39. On or about June 14, 2018, Lawyer C emailed Lawyer A a news clip discussing the possibility of Lawyer A cooperating, and continued to urge him not to cooperate with law enforcement, writing, "The whole objective of this exercise by the [federal prosecutors] is to drain you, emotionally and financially, until you reach a point that you see them as your only means to salvation." In the same email, Lawyer C, wrote, "You are making a very big mistake if you believe the stories these 'journalists' are writing about you. They want you to cave. They want you to fail. They do not want you to persevere and succeed."

40. On August 21, 2018, Lawyer A pleaded guilty in the federal investigation. The next day, on or about August 22, 2018, the Defendant commented on Twitter, "If anyone is looking for a good lawyer, I would strongly suggest that you don't retain the services of [Lawyer A]!" Later that day, the Defendant posted to Twitter again, stating, "I feel very badly for" one of his former campaign managers who had been criminally charged, saying, "[U]nlike [Lawyer A], he refused to 'break' – make up stories in order to get a 'deal.'"

IV. Lawyer A and AMI Admit Guilt in Connection with Payoffs of Woman 1 and Woman 2

41. Ultimately, other participants in the scheme admitted that the payoffs were unlawful.

42. In or about September 2018, AMI entered into a non-prosecution agreement with the United States Attorney's Office for the Southern District of New York in connection with AMI's payoff of Woman 1, admitting that "[a]t no time during the negotiation or acquisition of [Woman 1's] story did AMI intend to publish the story or disseminate information about it publicly."

[Beginning of Page 12 in original]

Rather, AMI admitted that it made the payment to ensure that Woman 1 "did not publicize damaging allegations" about the Defendant "before the 2016 presidential election and thereby influence that election."

43. On Aug. 21 2018, Lawyer A pleaded guilty to a felony in connection with his role in AMI's payoff to Woman 1, admitting in his guilty plea that he had done so at the Defendant's direction:

[O]n or about the summer of 2016, **in coordination with, and at the direction of, a candidate for federal office**, I and the CEO of a media company at the request of the candidate worked together to keep an individual with information that would be harmful to the candidate and to the campaign from publicly disclosing this information. After a number of discussions, we eventually accomplished the goal by the media company entering into a contract with the individual under which she received compensation of $150,000. I participated in this conduct, which on my part took place in Manhattan, for the principal purpose of influencing the election (emphasis added).

44. Lawyer A also pleaded guilty to a felony in connection with his payoff of Woman 2 to secure her silence, again at the Defendant's direction. Lawyer A admitted as part of his guilty plea:

[O]n or about October of 2016, **in coordination with, and at the direction of, the same candidate,** I arranged to make a payment to a second individual with information that would be harmful to the candidate and to the campaign to keep the individual from disclosing the information. To accomplish this, I used a company that was under my control to make a payment in the sum of $130,000. The monies I advanced through my company were later repaid to me by the candidate. I participated in this conduct, which on my part took place in Manhattan, for the principal purpose of influencing the election (emphasis added).

This Statement of Facts contains certain of the information that is relevant to the events described herein, and does not contain all facts relevant to the charged conduct.

[Beginning of Page 13 in original]

DATED: New York, New York
    April 4, 2023

                ALVIN L. BRAGG, JR.
            District Attorney New York County

The Response to Request for Bill of Particulars: Annotated

In April 2023, former President Donald J. Trump's defense team requested a "bill of particulars" from the Manhattan District Attorney's Office. The DA's office responded with this response to request for a bill of particulars, noting that the "sole function" of a "bill of particulars" is to "clarify... the indictment." Bragg and his team argued that such a clarification was unnecessary in this case because there was more than enough information in the indictment and statement of facts (both of which are annotated above) to "provide all the particulars to which defendant is entitled." In addition, the Manhattan DA's team pointed out that they informed defendant of their intent "to provide millions of pages of discovery."

The DA's team was wary that the defense was conducting a fishing expedition, writing that "to the extent that defendant asks the People to identify specific pieces of evidence or preview the People's legal strategy," he has "failed to meet his burden." Even though the DA's office said it would not "preview" its "legal strategy," the prosecutors did offer an important insight into the case. As explained above, "falsification of business records" can be charged as a misdemeanor in New York. But that same crime can be charged as a felony if prosecutors have concluded that the defendant(s) falsified business records with the intent to commit or conceal another crime.

In "People's Response to Request No. 2," the DA's office identified the additional crimes Trump "may" have intended to cover up by allegedly falsifying business records, including: New York Election Law § 17-152; New York Tax Law §§ 1801(a)(3) and 1802; New York Penal Law §§ 175.05 and 175.10; or violations of the Federal Election Campaign Act, 52 U.S.C. § 30101. Each of these relevant statutes is excerpted in Chapter 4 of this book.

SUPREME COURT OF THE STATE OF NEW YORK
COUNTY OF NEW YORK: PART 59

THE PEOPLE OF THE STATE OF NEW YORK
-against-
DONALD J. TRUMP,
Defendant.

PEOPLE'S RESPONSE TO DEFENDANT DONALD J. TRUMP'S APRIL 27 REQUEST FOR A BILL OF PARTICULARS

PURSUANT TO CPL 200.95(2) and 200.95(4), the People provide the following response to defendant Donald J. Trump's April 27, 2023 request for a bill of particulars, attached hereto as Exhibit 1.

I. Legal standard.

A bill of particulars specifies "items of factual information which are not recited in the indictment and which pertain to the offense charged... including the substance of each defendant's conduct encompassed by the charge which the people intend to prove at trial on their direct case." CPL 200.95(1)(a). "The sole function of a bill of particulars is to clarify... the indictment." *People v. Elliott,* 299 A.D.2d 731, 732 (3d Dep't 2002). A bill of particulars is not a statement of the prosecution's legal theory or a discovery device. *See* CPL 200.95(1)(a) (limiting a bill of particulars to "items of factual information"); *People v. Davis,* 41 N.Y.2d 678, 680 (1977) ("A bill of particulars serves to clarify the pleading; it is not a discovery device.").

To be entitled to a bill of particulars, a defendant must demonstrate that the requested information is "authorized to be included in a bill of particulars" and "necessary to enable the defendant adequately to prepare or conduct his defense." CPL 200.95(4); *see* CPL 200.95(1)(b), 200.95(5).

The People "are not required to list every action undertaken by the defendant in the course of the crime." *People v. Kessler,* No. 11307/95, 1996 WL 903952, at *3 (Sup. Ct. N.Y. Cty. Dec. 2, 1996); *see also People v. Iannone,* 45 N.Y.2d 589, 599 (1978) ("To require a listing of every action undertaken by the defendant in the course of this crime would serve no useful purpose, and would instead mark a step back towards the needless complexities of the common-law indictment."); *People v. Rondon,* 67 Misc.3d 1228(A), at *5 (Cty. Ct. Orange Cty. 2020) (denying the defendant's "overly broad" request for "all factual information which is not recited in the indictment that pertains to each offense charged"). In addition, the People are not required to include "matters of evidence relating to how the people intend to prove the elements of the offense charged or how the people intend to prove any item of factual information included in the bill of particulars." CPL 200.95(1)(a).

II. The People are already providing defendant with more information than a bill of particulars would require.

Defendant has already received and will receive far more factual information than the People are required to provide in a bill of particulars, and has more than sufficient information to prepare his defense.

First, the facts set forth in the indictment and the accompanying Statement of Facts provide all the particulars to which defendant is entitled because they provide "the substance of... defendant's conduct encompassed by the charge[s] which the people intend to prove at trial on their direct case." CPL 200.95(1)(a). The 15-page, 34-count indictment and 13- page Statement of Facts fully inform defendant of the nature of the charges against him, including by specifying the business records defendant allegedly falsified and by describing the details of his allegedly unlawful scheme. *See, e.g., People v. Morris,* 28 Misc.3d 1215(A), at *48-49 (Sup. Ct. N.Y. Cty. July 29, 2010) (denying the defendant's motion for a bill of particulars where, among other things, the indictment included a 17-page narrative of the allegedly unlawful scheme).

Second, as the People advised the Court and defendant at arraignment, the People are prepared to provide millions of pages of discovery to defendant pursuant to CPL Article 245 once defendant has been advised on the record of the terms and content of, and conduct prohibited by, the protective order entered by this Court on May 8, 2023. *See* Tr. of Apr. 4, 2023 Arraignment at 16-17 (describing the People's intent to make rolling productions of discovery in several stages once a protective order is in place). That discovery will include grand jury minutes, grand jury exhibits, prior witness statements, financial documents, subpoena compliance, and extensive additional materials. The production of these voluminous discovery materials further ensures that defendant is fully informed of the charges against him so he may prepare a defense. *See, e.g., People v. Kyoung Ja Choi* 259 A.D.2d 423, 424 (1st Dep't 1999) ("The indictment together with the People's response to defendant's omnibus motion and discovery material provided to defendant gave adequate notice of the charges against her and the prosecution was not required to include evidentiary material in a bill of particulars."); *Morris,* 28 Misc.3d 1215(A), at *48-49 (denying motion for a bill of particulars and noting that where the People "turned over two million documents it had in its possession from its investigation into the defendants and their co-conspirators' activities, ... [the defendant) cannot in good faith complain that he needs a bill of particulars in order to prepare for trial"); *see generally Iannone,* 45 N.Y.2d at 598 ("[T]he development of modern discovery rules in criminal cases has diminished the significance of the indictment's function as a provider of information." (citing CPL Article 240, which was replaced in 2020 by the more expansive CPL Article 245)).

Third, to the extent that defendant asks the People to identify specific pieces of evidence or preview the People's legal strategy, defendant has failed to meet his burden of demonstrating that the requested information is "authorized to be included in a bill of particulars." CPL 200.95(4); *see also* CPL 200.95(1)(b), 200.95(5); *Davis,* 41 N.Y.2d at 680.

III. Responses to defendant's specific requests.

The People's further responses to each of defendant's specific requests follow.

<u>REQUEST NO. 1</u>: "Describe the substance of Donald J. Trump's conduct and specify as to each offense charged:"

<u>PEOPLE'S RESPONSE to Request No. 1</u>: To the extent that Request No. 1 seeks factual information describing the

substance of defendant's conduct as to each offense charged, that factual information is contained in the Indictment and Statement of Facts, and will be contained in the discovery that the People will provide pursuant to CPL Article 245. Defendant is not entitled to any further information in response to this request. *See* CPL 200.95(I)(a).

To the extent that Request No. I is an attempt to incorporate Request Nos. 2, 3, and 4 into the request for information describing the substance of defendant's conduct as to each offense charged, the People refer to the responses below.

REQUEST No. 2: "Specify the criminal statute (i.e., 'other crime') which Donald J. Trump is alleged to have committed or intended to commit or to aid or conceal the commission thereof by means of the allegedly false business record; a. If the 'other crime' you are relying on is N.Y. Elec. Law § 17-152, please identify (i) what are the 'unlawful means,' and (ii) who are the other members of the alleged conspiracy. b. If the 'other crime' is a tax crime, identify the tax returns which were intended to be incorrect or false and specify the manner in which they were intended to be false or incorrect."

PEOPLE'S RESPONSE to Request No. 2: Defendant is not entitled to the information requested in Request No. 2. Where an intent to commit or conceal another crime is an element of an offense, the People need not prove intent to commit or conceal a particular crime; thus, the indictment need not identify any particular crime that the defendant intended to commit or conceal, and defendant is not entitled to such information in a bill of particulars. *See People v.*

Mackey, 49 N.Y.2d 274, 277-79 (1980). Notwithstanding that defendant is not entitled to the requested information, and expressly without limiting the People's theory at trial, *see People v. Barnes,* 50 N.Y.2d 375, 379 n.3 (1980); the People respond that the crimes defendant intended to commit or to aid or conceal may include violations of New York Election Law § 17-152; New York Tax Law §§ 1801(a)(3) and 1802; New York Penal Law§§ 175.05 and 175.10; or violations of the Federal Election Campaign Act, 52 U.S.C. § 30101 *et seq.;* and the People further refer defendant to certain facts, among others, set forth in the Statement of Facts relating to:

- an agreement to unlawfully suppress negative stories about defendant before an election in order to influence the outcome of the election (Statement of Facts ¶¶ 1-2, 7, 9-14, 17-21, 23);
- multiple false statements in the business records of different entities to advance that agreement, including but not limited to a series of false statements that both furthered the conspiracy and concealed earlier unlawful conduct and payments (Statement of Facts ¶¶ 2-4, 13, 26, 28-33);
- disguising reimbursement payments by doubling them and falsely characterizing them as income for tax reasons (Statement of Facts ¶¶ 2, 25); and
- multiple admissions of specific crimes by participants, including by guilty pleas to felonies (Statement of Facts ¶¶ 2-3, 7, 40, 42-44).

The factual information requested in Request Nos. 2(a)(i), 2(a)(ii), and 2(b) is contained in the Indictment and Statement of Facts, and will be contained in the discovery that the People will provide pursuant to CPL Article 245.

REQUEST NO. 3: "Identify the person or entity who Donald J. Trump is alleged to have intended to defraud by means of the allegedly false business record."

PEOPLE'S RESPONSE to Request No. 3: Defendant is not entitled to the information requested in Request No. 3. Under Penal Law § 175.10, the People are not required to establish that a defendant "acted with intent to defraud a particular person or business entity." *Morgenthau v. Khalil,* 73 A.D.3d 509, 510 (1st Dep't 2010); *see also People v. Coe,* 131 Misc. 2d 807,813 (Sup. Ct. N.Y. Cty. 1986) ("Intent to defraud anyone is sufficient.").

REQUEST NO. 4: "Identify what Donald J. Trump intend to defraud from the person or entity identified in response to item 1(b)."

PEOPLE'S RESPONSE to Request No. 4: The People note that there is no item "1(b)" in defendant's requests and it is unclear what is requested by "[i]dentify what Donald J. Trump intend to defraud." To the extent that Request No. 4 seeks factual information, that factual information is contained in the Indictment and Statement of Facts, and will be contained in the discovery that the People will provide pursuant to CPL Article 245. To the extent that Request No. 4 seeks "matters of evidence relating to how the people intend to prove the elements of the offense charged," CPL 200.95(1)(a), that information is outside the scope of a bill of particulars.

RESPECTFULLY SUBMITTED,
　/s/ *Becky Mangold*

_____

　Becky Mangold
　Assistant District Attorney

DATED: New York, New York
　May 12, 2023

2

CHRONOLOGY OF EVENTS

I n this section, we build on the court documents included in Chapter 1. We survey the voluminous public record to offer a complete chronology of events. It offers a preview of the narrative that will unfold during the approximately two months of trial. We rely upon court filings, contemporaneous media reports, and extracts from a Pulitzer Prize-winning team's account of the events, The Fixers, *and much more. We begin in* 2004, with the origins of Donald Trump's relationship with American Media Inc., the parent company of the National Enquirer. We conclude with the most recent March 2024 filings and opinions of the court as this book went to press.

This chronology was originally published by Gretchen Knaut, Norm Eisen, McKenzie Carrier, Vicka Heidt, Greg Phea, and Madison Gee as "Detailed Chronology in Trump-Cohen Hush Money Investigation," in Just Security *on March 29, 2023. It has been updated to reflect subsequent events.*

2004 - 2015

<u>Beginning around 2004</u>: Former American Media Inc. ("AMI") employees claim that the company and its publications routinely turned away stories and tips that could paint Donald Trump in a bad light. AMI CEO David Pecker had a strong friendship with Trump throughout this period, attending Trump's wedding to Melania in 2005 (AP News; *The Wall Street Journal*; *The New Yorker*; see also Michael Cohen congressional testimony, "these catch and kill scenarios existed between David Pecker and Mr. Trump long before I started working for him in 2007").

<u>2005</u>: While in conversation with Billy Bush, an anchor at the time for "Access Hollywood," Trump identified a "young woman through a bus window" and began making lewd, sexually aggressive remarks. Bush recorded Trump's comments on a hot mic: "I'm automatically attracted to beautiful women—I just start kissing them, it's like a magnet. Just kiss. I don't even wait. And when you're a star, they let you do it. You can do anything... Grab 'em by the pussy" (*NBC News*).

<u>June 2006</u>: Karen McDougal met Trump while "The Celebrity Apprentice" was being filmed at the Playboy Mansion. McDougal had been hired to work as an extra at a pool party scene. At the end of the night, Trump reportedly asked McDougal for her phone number. They talked "right away on the phone... for about a week before [Trump's] next visit to [Los Angeles]" (*CNN*; *The New Yorker*).

<u>June 12, 2006</u>: According to McDougal, she and Trump went on their first "date" at the Beverly Hilton hotel. McDougal claims that Trump's bodyguard brought her to a bungalow in the back of the hotel, where she and Trump were "intimate." Trump reportedly tried to pay McDougal afterward. By McDougal's account, she and Trump then began an extended affair, meeting up in Los Angeles, Lake Tahoe, and even his New York apartment in Trump Tower (*NPR*; *POLITICO*).

<u>July 2006</u>: Stephanie Clifford (also known as "Stormy Daniels") met Trump at a celebrity golf tournament in Lake Tahoe. Clifford claims that the two had sex in Trump's hotel room. At dinner, Trump reportedly told Clifford that he could "make [her appearing on *The Apprentice*] happen" (*CBS News*; *The Fixers*, p. 72). McDougal claims that she also attended the Lake Tahoe golf tournament and had sex with Trump (*The New Yorker*).

<u>2007</u>: Michael Cohen entered into employment as "an attorney and employee of a Manhattan-based real estate company," the Trump Organization, under the titles "Executive Vice President" and "Special Counsel" to Trump (Cohen criminal information, p. 1).

<u>Jan. 2007</u>: According to McDougal, she attended a launch party for Trump Vodka in Los Angeles and sat at a table with "Kim Kardashian, Trump, Donald Trump, Jr., and Trump, Jr.'s wife, Vanessa, who was pregnant." At another point (no date specified in source), McDougal claims she worked as a

costumed Playboy bunny at a party hosted by Trump and took pictures together with him and his family (*The New Yorker*).

APR. 2007: After nine months, McDougal reportedly ended her relationship with Trump. A friend of McDougal's later claimed that "the breakup was prompted in part by McDougal's feelings of guilt" (*The New Yorker*).

THROUGHOUT 2007: According to a lawsuit Clifford filed against Trump in March 2018, their "intimate relationship" lasted "well into the year 2007" and "'included, among other things, at least one 'meeting' with Mr. Trump' at the Beverly Hills Hotel" (*The Washington Post*).

JULY 2007: Trump asked Clifford to meet with him "privately at the Beverly Hills Hotel in Los Angeles." Clifford later claimed that "they did not have sex, but he wanted to" (*PBS*).

AUG. 2007: Trump reportedly called Clifford to tell her that he "[was not] able to get her a spot" on *The Apprentice*. According to Clifford, they did not meet again (*PBS*).

2009 OR 2010: Clifford and Trump had their last conversation, by Clifford's account. According to Clifford, Trump called her after she appeared on television "and was like, 'Hey, I just saw you on CNN' or Fox or something...

'You looked great. I love how you give it to 'em'" (*The Washington Post*).

<u>MAY 2011</u>: Clifford "agreed to tell her story to a sister publication of *In Touch* magazine [*Life & Style*] for $15,000." At the magazine's request, she and other witnesses reportedly took and passed polygraph exams about her alleged affair with Trump. Two employees of the magazine at the time later claimed that "the story never ran because after the magazine called Mr. Trump seeking comment, his attorney Michael Cohen threatened to sue." Clifford has also claimed that she was never paid (CBS News; *The Fixers*, p. 121).

<u>MAY 2011</u>: Weeks after the *In Touch* story was squashed, Clifford alleges she "was threatened by a man who approached her in Las Vegas." Clifford claims that the man came up to her and said, "Leave Trump alone. Forget the story," before looking at her daughter and saying, "That's a beautiful little girl. It'd be a shame if something happened to her mom" (CBS News).

<u>OCT. 2011</u>: *TheDirty.com*, a gossip site, published rumors about an extramarital affair between Clifford and Trump in July 2006 (Cohen warrant, p. 39).

<u>OCT. 11, 2011</u>: Clifford's attorney, Keith Davidson, "sent a cease and desist letter to *TheDirty.com*" and demanded that

the site remove the article about Trump and Clifford (Cohen warrant, p. 39).

OCT. 12, 2011: Cohen denied the rumors about Trump and Clifford's affair. He stated to *E! News* that, "[t]he totally untrue and ridiculous story... emanated from a sleazy and disgusting website... The Trump Organization and Donald J. Trump will be bringing a lawsuit... Trump and the Trump Organization would like to thank and commend Stormy Daniels and her attorneys for their honest and swift actions" (Cohen warrant, p. 39).

MAR. 18, 2015: Trump announced plans to form a presidential exploratory committee in advance of the 2016 election (*POLITICO*).

JUNE 16, 2015: Trump announced his bid for the presidency at his New York skyscraper. At this time, Cohen "continued to work at the Company [the Trump Organization] and did not have a formal title with the campaign." However, Cohen still "had a campaign email address and, at various times, advised the campaign, including on matters of interest to the press, and made televised and media appearances on behalf of the campaign" (*The Guardian*; Cohen criminal information, pp. 11-12).

IN AUG. 2015: In a meeting reportedly arranged by Cohen, Trump met with Pecker and Cohen at Trump Tower in Manhattan (Trump has been identified in previous federal court filings as "at least one other member of the campaign" and as "Individual-1"). Pecker offered to "help with [Trump's] campaign, saying that he would act as the 'eyes and ears' for the campaign by looking out for negative stories about [Trump] and alerting [Cohen] before the stories were published." This early warning system was designed to "[assist] the campaign in identifying such stories so they could be purchased and their publication avoided." During the meeting, Pecker also committed "to publish negative stories about [Trump's] competitors for the election." (statement of facts, p. 3; AMI non-prosecution agreement, p. 4; Cohen criminal information, p. 12; Cohen sentencing memo, p. 12; *The Fixers*, pp. ix-xi, 317; *The Wall Street Journal*; *CNN*). *The Enquirer* ultimately published, during the primary season alone, "more than sixty stories attacking [Trump's] opponents, the Clintons most of all, followed by Cruz" (*The Fixers*, p. 161). *National Enquirer* executives also allegedly shared pre-publication copies of articles and cover images related to Trump and his political opponents with Cohen throughout the campaign (*The Washington Post*).

IN OR ABOUT Oct. or Nov. 2015: Pecker "learned that a former Trump Tower doorman [Dino Sajudin]... was trying to sell information regarding a child that [Trump] had allegedly fathered out of wedlock." Pecker subsequently directed AMI to negotiate and sign "an agreement to pay [Sajudin] $30,000 to acquire exclusive rights to the story" (statement of facts, pp. 3-4; *The Fixers*, pp. xi, 145).

<u>Nov. 15, 2015</u>: AMI reportedly "entered into a source agreement with Sajudin" whereby, as Pecker directed, Sajudin "would get paid $30,000 if the *Enquirer* published a story based on his information" (*The Fixers*, p. 146).

<u>Nov. 30, 2015</u>: In a memo to Pecker, Dylan Howard, then the chief content officer at AMI, reportedly detailed his team's efforts to confirm Sajudin's story, which included having Sajudin take a polygraph examination. Two former AMI employees told *The New Yorker* that "they believed that Cohen was in close contact with A.M.I. executives while the company's reporters were looking into Sajudin's story, as Cohen had been during other investigations related to Trump. 'Cohen was kept up to date on a regular basis,' one source said" (*The Fixers*, p. 146; *The New Yorker*).

<u>Early Dec. 2015</u>: Sajudin reportedly completed the lie detector test that AMI had arranged for him. During the lie detector test, "Sajudin said that he'd heard Trump had fathered the child from other employees and from residents of Trump World Tower." The private investigator who had conducted the test reported to the *Enquirer* that Sajudin was "being truthful." Sajudin reportedly requested payment from the *Enquirer* immediately thereafter and stated that he would take his story elsewhere if they did not comply (*The Fixers*, pp. 146-7; *The New Yorker*).

<u>Early Dec. 2015</u>: The *Enquirer* reportedly still saw credibility issues with Sajudin even after he passed the lie detector tests, so one of the paper's reporters contacted

Trump's assistant to corroborate the story. Sometime following the call between the reporter and Trump's assistant, Cohen found out about the story. He then contacted Howard and urged him not to move forward with publishing Sajudin's account. Howard reportedly stated that "He is furious" to one of the other editors following his call with Cohen (*The Fixers*, pp. 146-7).

EARLY DEC. 2015: AMI bought Sajudin's story "without fully investigating his claims, but [Pecker] directed that the deal take place because of his agreement with [Trump and Cohen]." Specifically, an editor with the *Enquirer*, Barry Levine, instructed the company's general counsel, Cameron Stracher, to draft a new source agreement whereby the *Enquirer* was to pay Sajudin $30,000 in full before publication. "In return for the $30,000, Sajudin agreed that he wouldn't disclose his story or his agreement with [AMI] to any third parties. 'In the event Source breaches this provision, Source shall be liable to AMI and shall pay to AMI... the sum of $1,000,000,' the contract said." (statement of facts, pp. 3-4; *The Fixers*, p. 148).

SOMETIME AFTER AMI PAID SAJUDIN: Pecker "ordered the A.M.I. reporters to stop investigating" the veracity of Sajudin's story. "[T]he story died" (*The New Yorker*; *The Fixers*, pp. 148).

SOMETIME AFTER AMI PAID SAJUDIN: "AMI falsely characterized this payment in AMI's books and records, including in its general ledger... When AMI later concluded that the story was not true, [Pecker] wanted to release the Doorman from the agreement. However,[Cohen] instructed [Pecker] not to release the Doorman until after the presidential election, and [Pecker] complied with that instruction because of his agreement with [Trump and Cohen]" (statement of facts, pp. 3-4; *The Fixers*, p. xi).

January 2016 - September 2016

Feb. 1, 2016: Trump finished second in the Iowa caucuses, losing the first Republican state nominating contest to Senator Ted Cruz (R-TX) (Reuters).

Mar. 1, 2016: Trump won seven of the 11 Super Tuesday states in the Republican primary (Reuters).

Apr. 2016: Clifford and her agent, Gina Rodriguez, attempted to sell Clifford's story to media outlets for the second time. On April 7, after receiving rejections from other publications, Rodriguez reached out to Howard at AMI. Howard reportedly rejected the story for the same reason the others had: Clifford had previously publicly denied her involvement with Trump, calling affair rumors "bullshit" after the story surfaced in 2011 (*The Fixers*, pp. 123, 163).

May 7, 2016: Carrie Stevens (a fellow former Playboy model and former friend of McDougal) tweeted, "I usually don't get involved in politics but why Bill Clinton can't [sic] get an extramarital BJ but @RealDonaldTrump can?" Soon after, Stevens sent another tweet with the hashtag "donaldloves-playmates" and McDougal's Twitter handle. At that point, McDougal reportedly realized that the story of her affair would likely become public as Trump's presidential campaign continued and decided to meet with an attorney. She met with Keith Davidson, who was also (separately) representing Clifford at the time, in the hopes of asserting "control of the narrative." According to their retainer agreement, Davidson was contracted to assist McDougal with selling her story about her "interactions with Donald Trump" and any "confidentiality agreements" arising out of it (*The Fixers*, pp. 162–163; Cohen criminal information, pp. 12-13).

JUNE 15, 2016: Davidson contacted Howard and attempted to sell McDougal's story to *The National Enquirer,* an AMI publication. In accordance with their August 2015 agreement, Pecker and Howard called Cohen and alerted him to the story's existence. Howard then "began negotiating for the purchase of the story" at "Cohen's urging and subject to Cohen's promise that AMI would be reimbursed" (AMI non-prosecution agreement, p. 4; Cohen criminal information, pp. 12-13; *The Fixers*, p. 164).

IN OR ABOUT JUNE 2016: After initially notifying Cohen about the story, Howard continued to regularly text and call Cohen with further updates. Trump "did not want this information to become public because he was concerned about the effect it could have on his candidacy." Over multiple discussions, Trump and Cohen negotiated with

Pecker about who would purchase McDougal's story (statement of facts, p. 4).

JUNE 20, 2016: Howard reportedly arranged a meeting in Los Angeles with McDougal, Davidson, and two of McDougal's contacts, John Crawford and Jay Grdina. Howard interviewed McDougal about the alleged affair with Trump, but he "sensed her reluctance to come forward." At one point, McDougal reportedly said, "I don't want to be the next Monica Lewinsky." McDougal had brought notes with dates and phone numbers related to the alleged affair, but Howard reportedly claimed that the story needed additional documentation to be worth more than $15,000. McDougal then "suggested that she might have some corroborating materials in a storage locker. She promised to look for them" (AMI non-prosecution agreement, p. 4; *The Fixers*, p. 164).

JUNE 20, 2016: Following the interview, Howard reportedly told Davidson he would update him on whether AMI intended to buy McDougal's story by the end of the day. Davidson agreed to refrain from "shopping McDougal's information to another outlet" in the meantime. After he left Davidson's office, Howard joined "a three-way call with Pecker and Cohen." The group reportedly agreed that AMI would not offer McDougal a deal yet (*The Fixers*, pp. 164–165).

SOMETIME BETWEEN JUNE 20 and June 27, 2016: Cohen reportedly informed Trump of McDougal's meeting with Howard (*The Fixers*, p. 165).

JUNE 27, 2016: Trump reportedly called Pecker to ask whether he could bury McDougal's story (*The Fixers*, p. 166).

JULY 7, 2016: The lead investigative producer for *ABC News*, Rhonda Schwartz, reportedly met with McDougal, Davidson, and Grdina at the Beverly Wilshire hotel for an all-day interview (*The Fixers*, p. 166).

OVER SEVERAL WEEKS following July 7, 2016: McDougal and Schwartz reportedly continued to meet. During this time, "ABC News entered into a confidentiality agreement with Davidson that barred the outlet from publicizing any of the information McDougal provided, unless or until she agreed to do the interview" (*The Fixers*, p. 166).

SOMETIME AFTER JULY 7, 2016: Davidson, likely hoping to secure a better deal for McDougal than the unpaid arrangement with *ABC News*, reportedly alerted Howard to a (phony) ABC News plan to air an interview with McDougal on primetime television. Sources claim that Howard passed the information along to Pecker, who alerted Cohen, who informed Trump (*The Fixers*, pp. 167–168).

JULY 19, 2016: Trump won the official GOP presidential nomination with 1,237 delegates (NBC News).

IN OR AROUND JUNE 2016: After discussing AMI's purchase of McDougal's story with Trump and Cohen, Pecker signed off on the deal. He did so on the condition that "the Trump Organization would reimburse AMI" (statement of facts, p. 4).

JULY 29, 2016: Howard reportedly extended a loose offer to Davidson for McDougal's story (*The Fixers*, p. 168).

FIRST WEEK IN AUG. 2016: Davidson and AMI reportedly negotiated an agreement to purchase McDougal's story (*The Fixers*, p. 168).

ON OR AROUND AUG. 5, 2016: AMI entered into an agreement to acquire the "limited life rights" to the story of McDougal's alleged affair with Trump for $150,000. AMI also committed to feature McDougal on "two magazine covers and publish over one hundred magazine articles authored by her. Despite the cover and article features to the agreement, its principal purpose, as understood by those involved, including [Cohen], was to suppress [McDougal's] story so as to prevent it from influencing the election" (statement of facts, p. 4; Cohen criminal information, p. 13; AMI non-prosecution agreement, p. 4; *The Fixers*, pp. 168, 192).

ON OR AROUND AUG. 10, 2016: AMI sent $150,000 to Davidson "in cooperation, consultation, and concert with, and at the request and suggestion of one or more members or agents of a candidate's 2016 presidential campaign, to ensure that a woman did not publicize damaging allegations about that candidate before the 2016 presidential election and thereby influence that election." As court filings later revealed, "AMI falsely characterized this payment in AMI's books and records, including in its general ledger. The AMI CEO agreed to the deal after discussing it with both [Trump] and [Cohen], and on the understanding from [Cohen] that [Trump] or the Trump Organization would reimburse AMI." (statement of facts, p. 4; AMI non-prosecution agreement, p. 4).

<u>Aug. – Oct. 2016</u>: Clifford reportedly participated in talks with multiple outlets including *Good Morning America* and *Slate* for her account of the alleged Trump affair. Jacob Weisberg, editor of *Slate*, claimed to have spoken with Clifford several times during this period. Clifford reportedly told Weisberg that, using lawyers as intermediaries, "Trump had negotiated to buy her silence." Weisberg claimed that Clifford also sent him photos of "an unfinished draft contract in which pseudonyms had been used." However, Clifford then reportedly "cut Weisberg off," and he did not pursue the story (*The Fixers*, p. 238; *Slate*; *The New York Times*; Cohen warrant, p. 40).

<u>Aug. 2016 – Sept. 2016</u>: Pecker agreed to assign the rights to the non-disclosure portion of AMI's agreement with McDougal to Cohen in exchange for a $125,000 payment. During this period, Cohen also "incorporated a shell entity called 'Resolution Consultants LLC' for use in the transaction." (Cohen criminal information, pp. 13-14; AMI non-prosecution agreement, p. 4).

<u>Sept. 2016</u>: In a recorded conversation, Trump and Cohen discussed reimbursing AMI for its purchase of McDougal's story and obtaining the rights to the story from AMI. Cohen told Trump that he planned to open a company to facilitate this transfer and that he had discussed the matter with the Trump Organization CFO, Allen Weisselberg. In response to Cohen's overview of the plan, Trump asked, "So what do we got to pay for this? One fifty?" Trump initially proposed paying AMI in cash, but after Cohen disagreed with that approach he mentioned paying by check (statement of facts, p. 5).

<u>Sept. 30, 2016</u>: Following his discussions with Cohen, Pecker signed an assignment agreement "in which AMI agreed to transfer its rights to [McDougal's] account to [Cohen's] shell company for $125,000." Pecker delivered the agreement to Cohen "along with an invoice from a shell corporation incorporated by the consultant [separate from Cohen's shell entity] for the payment of $125,000, which falsely stated the payment was for an 'agreed upon 'flat fee' for advisory services'" (statement of facts, p. 5; AMI non-prosecution agreement, p. 5; Cohen criminal information, pp. 13-14).

<u>Sept. 30, 2016</u>: Resolution Consultants LLC was created in Delaware. Cohen reportedly used his own name for the corporate formation documents (*The Fixers*, p. 237).

October 2016 - December 2016

<u>Early Oct. 2016</u>: Before Cohen had paid the $125,000 reimbursement, Pecker "consulted with AMI's general counsel and then told [Cohen] that the deal to transfer the rights to [Cohen's] shell company was off." During the conversation with Cohen, Pecker told Cohen that he "should tear up the assignment agreement. [Cohen] did not tear up the agreement, which was later found during a judicially authorized search of his office" (statement of facts, p. 5; Cohen criminal information, pp. 13-14; *see also* AMI non-prosecution agreement, p. 5). Additional detail from Cohen's defense sentencing memo: "Michael himself did not make the payment to Woman-1 [McDougal] called for by the agreement reached between Corporation-1 [AMI] and Woman-1, but participated in planning discussions with Client-1 [Trump] and the Chairman and CEO of Corporation-1 relating to the payment made by Corporation-1, including obtaining the commitment of Client-1 to repay Corporation-1. As the matter unfolded, the contract was profitable for Corporation-1, and Client-1's failure to reimburse Corporation-1 was ultimately not contested by Corporation-1" (Cohen defense sentencing memo, pp. 18-19).

<u>Oct. 7, 2016</u>: The 2005 "Access Hollywood" tape of Trump saying "Grab 'em by the pussy" became public (*The Washington Post*).

<u>Oct. 8, 2016:</u>[1] The very next day, Rodriguez, Davidson, and Howard reportedly began discussions about AMI purchasing Clifford's story. They appear to have believed it

was "more marketable [then] than it had been when Rodriguez first pitched Howard in April, before the "Access Hollywood" tape placed Trump's treatment of women in the national spotlight" (*The Fixers*, p. 174).

Oct. 8, 2016, *as sourced from* The Fixers *(facts shown in the order they appeared)*:

- Afternoon: Davidson texted Howard that "Trump is fucked." Howard responded, "Wave the white flag. It's over people!" (*The Fixers*, p. 174).
- A few hours later in the afternoon: Davidson emailed Rodriguez, asking if she had "heard from [Clifford] lately?" (*The Fixers*, p. 174).
- Around 30 minutes later: Howard texted Rodriguez to follow up on her client, asking her "to send him a pitch so he could elevate it to his boss, [Pecker]." He added that Pecker would "likely pay." Rodriguez then emailed Howard the pitch, which included "a brief description of her client's [Clifford's] claims" (*The Fixers*, p. 174).
- After 7:20 pm ET: "Cohen had a conference call with Hicks and Trump, followed by a call with Hicks alone. Hicks had heard from another campaign aide" that there was another tape, "this one of Trump cavorting with prostitutes in Moscow during a trip there for the Miss Universe pageant in 2013. Hicks had been told that *TMZ* might have access to the tape, and she knew that Cohen was very close to Harvey Levin, the gossip outlet's founder. Hicks asked Cohen to let her know if he heard anything from Levin. She also

impressed on him... that the campaign's messaging was that Trump's remarks on the "Access Hollywood" were merely "locker room talk" (*The Fixers*, p. 175; *see also* Cohen warrant, p. 41).

- After Cohen's call with Hicks: "Cohen, Pecker, and Howard exchanged a series of calls after Cohen got off the phone with Hicks. Cohen lobbied Pecker to buy Daniels's [Clifford's] story." During these calls, Cohen sought to convince Pecker to purchase and not publish the story, as he had done with McDougal's account in a practice known as "catch-and-kill" (*The Fixers*, p. 175).

- Less than an hour after Rodriguez sent her pitch of Clifford's story to Howard: Howard texted Rodriguez: "'How much for [Clifford]?'" She replied "'250k,'" and they negotiated it down to "'120.'" Howard then told Rodriguez that "he'd be back in touch by the following morning" (*The Fixers*, pp. 175–176).

- "Minutes after signing off with Rodriguez": Howard texted Pecker: "Woman wants 120k" and Pecker replied "'We can't pay 120k.'" Howard then said "'Ok. They'd need to handle. Perhaps I call Michael and advise him and he can take it from there, and handle.'" Pecker responded, "'Yes good idea'" (*The Fixers*, p. 176).

- After AMI decided not to purchase Clifford's story: Howard and Davidson communicated. Howard agreed "to contact Cohen (again) to vouch for Davidson." This was because Davidson was anxious about negotiating with Cohen after

a previously tense interaction in September.
Howard and Cohen communicated again.
Howard told Cohen, "'Be nice'" to Davidson.
Howard then texted Pecker "to let him know that
Cohen had agreed to handle the story and leave
American Media out of it." He continued:
"'Spoke to MC. All sorted. Now removed. No
fingerprints. I'll recap with you face to face.'"
Pecker replied "'Great work Thx'" (*The Fixers*, p.
177).

- 9:13 pm GMT: Howard texted Cohen "'Keith will
  do it. Let's reconvene tomorrow'" (*The Fixers*, p.
  177; *see also* Cohen warrant, p. 42).
- "Past 2 [am]" GMT: Cohen texted Howard,
  "Thank you." A few minutes later he sent
  another text to Howard with "the name of his
  shell company, Resolution Consultants" (*The
  Fixers*, p. 177).

OCT. 8, 2016, *as sourced from Cohen warrant*:

- 7:20 pm: "At approximately 7:20 p.m., Cohen
  received a call from [Hope] Hicks. Sixteen
  seconds into the call, Trump joined the call, and
  the call continued for over four minutes." Based
  on toll records, "this was the first call Cohen had
  received or made to Hicks in at least multiple
  weeks" (Cohen warrant, p. 41; *see also The Fixers*,
  p. 175).
- About 7:34 pm: "Approximately ten minutes after
  the [7:20 pm ET] call ended, Hicks and Cohen

spoke again for about two minutes" (Cohen warrant, p. 42; *see also* The Fixers, p. 175).

- At some point during the 7:20 pm and 7:34 pm calls (no distinction is made between them in *The Fixers*), Hicks and Cohen communicated about a rumor that "Hicks had heard from another campaign aide" that there was another tape, "this one of Trump cavorting with prostitutes in Moscow during a trip there for the Miss Universe pageant in 2013. Hicks had been told that *TMZ* might have access to the tape, and she knew that Cohen was very close to Harvey Levin, the outlet's founder. Hicks asked Cohen to let her know if he heard anything from Levin. She also impressed on him... that the campaign's messaging was that Trump's remarks on the *Access Hollywood* tape were merely 'locker room talk'" (*The Fixers*, p. 175).)

- At 7:39 pm (immediately after the Hicks-Cohen call ends): Cohen called Pecker for 30 seconds (Cohen warrant, p. 42).

- Approximately 4 minutes later (about 7:43 pm): Cohen called Pecker again, and they spoke "for more than a minute" (Cohen warrant, p. 42).

- 3 minutes after the Cohen-Pecker call ends (about 7:47 pm): Howard called Cohen. They spoke "for approximately a minute" (Cohen warrant, p. 42).

- 7:56 pm: Cohen called Hicks for 2 minutes (Cohen warrant, p. 42).

- 7:58 pm: Pecker called Cohen for 2 minutes (Cohen warrant, p. 42).

- 8:03 pm: Cohen called Trump for 8 minutes (Cohen warrant, p. 42).
- 8:39 pm: Howard called Cohen for 4 minutes (Cohen warrant, p. 42).
- 8:57 pm: Howard called Cohen for 6 minutes (Cohen warrant, p. 42).
- 9:13 pm: Howard texted Cohen "'Keith will do it. Let's reconvene tomorrow'" (Cohen warrant, p. 42; *see also The Fixers*, p. 177).

OCT. 9, 2016:

- At some point this day: Rodriguez reportedly told "Howard that she had another offer for [Clifford's] story, this one for $200,000, a lie meant to prod the deal along" (*The Fixers*, p. 177).
- 3:31 am: Cohen texted Howard: "'Thank you'" (Cohen warrant, p. 43).
- 3:39 am: Howard texted Cohen and Davidson: "'Resolution Consultants LLC. is the name of the entity I formed a week ago. Whenever you wake, please call my cell'" (Cohen warrant, p. 43).

OCT. 10, 2016: "[Cohen] negotiated a deal with [Davidson] to secure [Clifford's] silence and prevent disclosure of the damaging information in the final weeks before the presidential election. Under the deal that [Davidson] negotiated, [Clifford] would be paid $130,000 for the rights to her account" (statement of facts, p. 6).

- 10:58 am: Howard texted Cohen and Davidson: "Keith/Michael: connecting you both in regards to that business opportunity. Spoke to the client this AM and they're confirmed to proceed with the opportunity. Thanks. Dylan. Over to you two" (statement of facts, p. 6; Cohen warrant, p. 43).
- Howard also reportedly "checked in with Rodriguez" (*The Fixers*, p. 177).
- 12:25 pm: Davidson texted Cohen: "Michael – if we are ever going to close this deal—In my opinion, it needs to be today. Keith" (Cohen warrant, p. 43).
- Immediately after: Cohen and Davidson spoke on the phone for 3 minutes (Cohen warrant, p. 43).
- During this call, Cohen and Davidson reportedly negotiated the price point for the story: "Cohen wanted to buy the story, but he balked at [Clifford's] six-figure demand... Davidson said $130,000 was as low as Rodriguez and [Clifford] were willing to go." Davidson cited a competing offer, which didn't actually exist (*The Fixers*, pp. 177-178).
- On or about Oct. 10, 2016: Davidson and Clifford signed a "side letter agreement" to a "confidential settlement agreement and mutual release" signed under two pseudonyms: "Peggy Peterson" and "David Dennison." The side letter agreement provided the "true name and identity" of the signatories, but only Peterson was identified in the document (as Clifford); the Dennison identifier and associated signature lines were left blank. A federal investigator later hypothesized

that "Davidson sent Cohen this partially-signed
'side letter' in order to facilitate the closing of a
deal between Davidson's client and Cohen or
Cohen's client" (Cohen warrant, pp. 43-44).

BETWEEN OCT. 10 and OCT. 28, 2016: During a meeting in
Trump's office, Trump allegedly told Cohen "that he had
spoken to a couple of friends, and it is 130,000, it is not a lot
of money, and we should just do it, so go ahead and do it."
Trump then reportedly directed Cohen and Weisselberg
(who Cohen later testified was also present in the meeting)
to "go back to Mr. Weisselberg's office and figure this all out"
(Cohen testimony, p. 38; *see also* Cohen testimony, p. 26).

AT SOME POINT between Oct. 10, 2016 and Oct. 27, 2016:
"[Trump] directed [Cohen] to delay making a payment to
[Clifford] as long as possible. He instructed [Cohen] that if
they could delay the payment until after the election, they
could avoid paying altogether, because at that point it would
not matter if the story became public. As reflected in emails
and text messages between and among [Cohen], [Davidson],
and [Howard], [Cohen] attempted to delay making payment
as long as possible" (statement of facts, p. 6).

OCT. 13, 2016: Cohen began taking "steps to complete a
transaction with Davidson, including attempting to open an
account from which Cohen could transfer funds to Davidson" (Cohen warrant, p. 44).

- 8:54 a.m.: Cohen texted Pecker "I need to talk to you." (Cohen warrant, p. 44).
- 9:06 a.m.: Pecker texted Cohen: "I called please call me back." After this message, Pecker and Cohen appear to have moved their communications onto Signal (Cohen warrant, p. 44).
- 9:23 am: Cohen emailed a set of documents "from the Secretary of State of Delaware indicating that Cohen had formed a limited liability company called 'Resolution Consultants LLC' on September 30, 2016" to a First Republic Bank employee. The body of the email asked the employee to "call me" (Cohen warrant, p. 45).
- 10:44 am: Cohen called the First Republic employee and told him "that he needed an account in the name of 'Resolution Consultants' opened immediately." The account was never opened, however, because Cohen failed to complete the requisite paperwork (Cohen warrant, p. 45).

<u>OCT. 17, 2016</u>: Cohen reportedly dissolved Resolution Consultants and set up a new company, Essential Consultants LLC, 2 minutes later. It appears that Cohen used the same registered agent in Delaware for both companies (*The New York Times*; *The Fixers*, p. 237).

- That afternoon: *The Wall Street Journal* editor Ashby Jones reportedly shared a tip he had received on the hush money payments. Per Jones, a "Los Angeles lawyer with the initials K.D.—the source didn't want to volunteer more—was traversing the country, paying hush money to women who'd been romantically involved with Donald Trump" (*The Fixers*, p. 188).

- At some point on this day: "Davidson emailed Cohen and threatened to cancel the… 'settlement agreement' by the end of the day if Cohen did not complete the transaction." Davidson followed that up with "a second email later in the day that stated in part, 'Please be advised that my client deems her settlement agreement canceled and void'" (Cohen warrant, p. 45-46).
- 4:00 p.m.: Cohen called Davidson. They "spoke for over five minutes" (Cohen warrant, p. 46).
- 4:43 p.m.: Howard texted Cohen: "'I'm told they're going with DailyMail. Are you aware?' One minute later, Cohen responded: 'Call me.'" (Cohen warrant, p. 46).

<u>Oct. 18, 2016</u>: A "thinly sourced article" posted on *The Smoking Gun* website reported the alleged affair between Clifford and Trump. The story received scant attention from mainstream media; Clifford did not respond publicly (*The Washington Post*).

<u>Oct. 25, 2016</u>: Cohen, Davidson, Howard, and Pecker had several text exchanges and calls "apparently concerning a transaction involving Clifford" (Cohen warrant, p. 47)

- 6:09 p.m.: "Howard sent Cohen a text message stating: 'Keith calling you urgently. We have to coordinate something on the matter he's calling you about or its [sic] could look awfully bad for everyone.' One minute later, Davidson sent Cohen a text message stating 'Call me.' Cohen and Davidson called each other several times over the next half hour but appear not to have connected" (Cohen warrant, p. 47)

- 6:42 p.m.: "Cohen and Davidson spoke for about eight minutes" (Cohen warrant, p. 47).
- 7:11 p.m. Cohen and Davidson "spoke for another two minutes" (Cohen warrant, p. 47; *see also* Cohen criminal information, pp. 14-15).

AT SOME POINT before Oct. 26, 2016: "Ultimately, with pressure mounting and the election approaching, [Trump] agreed to the payoff and directed [Cohen] to proceed. [Cohen] discussed the deal with [Trump and Weisselberg]. [Trump] did not want to make the $130,000 payment himself, and asked [Cohen] and [Weisselberg] to find a way to make the payment. After discussing various payment options with [Weisselberg], [Cohen] agreed he would make the payment. Before making the payment, [Cohen] confirmed with [Trump] that [Trump] would pay him back" (statement of facts, p. 6).

OCT. 26, 2016: "[S]hortly after speaking with [Trump] on the phone, [Cohen] opened a bank account in Manhattan in the name of Essential Consultants LLC, a new shell company he had created to effectuate the payment. He then transferred $131,000 from his personal home equity line of credit ('HE-LOC') into that account" (statement of facts, p. 7).

- 8:26 a.m.: "Cohen called Trump and spoke to him for approximately three minutes" (Cohen warrant, p. 47)
- 8:34 a.m.: "Cohen called Trump again and connected for a minute and a half" (Cohen warrant, p. 47)
- 9:04 a.m.: Cohen "emailed an incorporating service to obtain the corporate formation documents" for Essential Consultants LLC (Cohen warrant, p. 47-48; Cohen criminal information, p. 15).
- Between 11:00 a.m. and 1:00 p.m.: Cohen opened an account for Essential Consultants LLC at the First Republic Bank in Manhattan. After opening the account, Cohen "drew down $131,000 from the fraudulently obtained HELOC [home equity line of credit, also held by Cohen at First Republic Bank]," and requested that it be deposited into the Essential Consultants account he had just opened (Cohen warrant, p. 48; Cohen criminal information, p. 15).
- 4:15 p.m.: A First Republic Bank employee confirmed that "the funds had been deposited into the Essential Consultants account" (Cohen warrant, p. 49).

Oct. 27, 2016: At around 10:01 a.m., Cohen "completed paperwork to wire $130,000 from the Essential Consultants account" to Davidson's attorney-client trust account at City National Bank in Los Angeles. On the paperwork, Cohen "falsely indicated that the 'purpose of wire being sent' was 'retainer.'" This payment amounted to a contribution to the

Trump campaign "in excess of the limits of the Election Act, which aggregated $25,000 and more in calendar year 2016" since it was made "in cooperation, consultation, and concert with, and at the request and suggestion of one or more members of the campaign... to ensure that she [Clifford] did not publicize damaging allegations before the 2016 presidential election and thereby influence that election" (Cohen warrant, p. 50; *The New York Times*; Cohen criminal information, pp. 15, 19).

Oct. 28, 2016: Cohen reportedly called Trump and updated him on the situation. The same day, Cohen and Clifford reportedly signed "a contract that effectively promise[d] Ms. Clifford money in exchange for not talking about the alleged affair with Mr. Trump. Mr. Trump's name [did] not technically appear on the document." (*The Fixers*, p. 183; *The New York Times*).

Nov. 1, 2016: Davidson sent Cohen "copies of the final, signed confidential settlement agreement and side letter agreement." After he confirmed delivery of the paperwork, Davidson reportedly "wired the money to [Clifford's] account" (Cohen criminal information, p. 15; *The Fixers*, p. 183).

- 7:05 p.m.: Cohen called Trump but "it appears they did not connect. Cohen then called a telephone number belonging to Kellyanne Conway, who at the time was Trump's campaign manager. They did not connect." (Cohen warrant, p. 52).

- 7:44pm: Conway returned Cohen's call. They spoke for "approximately six minutes" (Cohen warrant, p. 52).

Nov. 4, 2016: Four days before the general election, *The Wall Street Journal* published an article about the $150,000 hush money deal between McDougal and AMI. The article referenced Clifford only briefly, "reporting that she was considering sharing her story with ABC News but abruptly disappeared on the network before doing so" (*The New York Times*; *The Wall Street Journal*).

- Between 4:30 and 8:00 p.m.: "Cohen communicated several times with Howard, Pecker, and Davidson" (Cohen warrant, p. 53).
- 8:51 p.m.: "Cohen sent Howard a message, stating: 'She's [McDougal] being really difficult with giving Keith a statement. Basically went into hiding and unreachable.' One minute later, Howard responded: 'I'll ask him again. We just need her to disappear.' Cohen responded, 'She definitely disappeared but refused to give a statement and Keith cannot push her.'" (Cohen warrant, p. 53).
- 8:55 p.m.: "Howard responded to Cohen's text: 'Let's let the dust settle. We don't want to push her over the edge. She's on side [sic] at present and we have a solid position and a plausible position that she is rightfully employed as a columnist'" (Cohen warrant, p. 53).

<u>Nov. 8, 2016</u>: Trump and Pence were elected president and vice president of the United States (NBC News).

<u>Dec. 2016</u>: Pecker met with Trump "privately in Trump Tower in Manhattan." During their conversation, Trump "thanked [Pecker] for handling the stories of [Sajudin] and [McDougal], and invited [Pecker] to the Inauguration." Before the meeting, Cohen reportedly asked Pecker "to urge Trump to pay Cohen more money," especially given that Trump "hadn't yet repaid his fixer for the Stormy Daniels deal." Pecker apparently so urged Trump, but "Trump was unmoved. 'You don't know how much money he's got,' Trump said" (statement of facts, pp. 7; *The Fixers*, p. 197).

January 2017 - Present

<u>Jan. 20, 2017</u>: Trump was inaugurated as the 45th President of the United States (statement of facts, pp. 7-8).

<u>Jan. 2017</u>: Cohen and Weisselberg "met to discuss how [Cohen] would be reimbursed for the money he paid to ensure [Clifford's] silence," which later court filings charac-terized as "seeking reimbursement for election-related expenses." Weisselberg asked Cohen to come to the meeting with "a copy of a bank statement for the Essential Consul-tants account showing the $130,000 payment." Accordingly, Cohen presented Weisselberg with said statement reflecting the $130,000 payment made to keep Clifford "silent in advance of the election, plus a $35 wire fee." In handwriting, Cohen added another $50,000 onto the statement as a "claimed payment for 'tech services'... related to work [he]

had solicited from a technology company during and in connection with the campaign." Weisselberg "grossed up" that initial $180,035 reimbursement request to $360,000 "so that [Cohen] could characterize the payment as income on his tax returns, instead of a reimbursement." Cohen "would be left with $180,000 after paying approximately 50% in income taxes." On top of the now $360,000 payment, Weisselberg "added an additional $60,000 as a supplemental year-end bonus," bringing the total payment to $420,000. Weisselberg "memorialized these calculations in handwritten notes on the copy of the bank statement that [Cohen] had provided." After finalizing the payment amount, Trump, Weisselberg, and Cohen "then agreed that [Cohen] would be paid the $420,000 through twelve monthly payments of $35,000 over the course of 2017. Each month, [Cohen] was to send an invoice to [Trump] through Trump Organization employees, falsely requesting payment of $35,000 for legal services rendered in a given month of 2017 pursuant to a retainer agreement. At no point did [Cohen] have a retainer agreement with [Trump] or the Trump Organization" (statement of facts, pp. 7-8; Cohen criminal information, pp. 16-17; PBS and *USA Today*).

IN COHEN'S MEMOIR *DISLOYAL: A Memoir; The True Story of the Former Personal Attorney to President Donald J. Trump*, he states:

> When we sat down, he [Allen Weisselberg] started to explain how Trump was going to make me 'whole' on the Daniels payment. First, the $130,000 would be doubled, grossed up as he described it, to make up for the taxes I

would have to pay on that money, meaning the starting sum would be $260,000." (*Disloyal* p. 298)

"So that's two-sixty, plus the hundred, and the Boss wants to do another sixty, to make the total four-twenty," Allen said. (*Disloyal* p. 299)

"So here's what we'll do," he [Trump] said. "We'll use the number Allen came up with. What's the number again?"

"Four hundred and twenty thousand," I said.

"Wow, that's a lot," he said. "We can use this as a retainer for the work you will be doing for me privately. Allen, you can pay Michael $35,000 for each month of the year. Michael, you will send Allen an invoice each month. This is okay with you, right?"

"Sure, Boss," I said. "I'm really honored." (*Disloyal* p. 301)

He'd get the tax deduction for legal fees, almost certainly a criminal offense if any mortal lied on their tax returns about a business expense of nearly half a million dollars, a reality that I would come to understand in time. (*Disloyal* p. 302)

As I thought about the arrangement, Trump was actually making money on the deal, by way of his tax cheat, and he had my legal services free for the year. (*Disloyal* p. 302)

JAN. 2017: Cohen left the Trump Organization and "began holding himself out" as Trump's personal attorney (Cohen criminal information, p. 1).

<u>Jan. 2017</u>: During another visit to Trump Tower, Trump allegedly thanked Pecker for "buying [McDougal's] story and burying it" (*The Fixers*, p. 197).

<u>Early Feb. 2017</u>: Trump and Cohen "met in the Oval Office at the White House and confirmed this repayment arrangement" (statement of facts, p. 8).

<u>Feb. 14, 2017</u>: Cohen "emailed the Controller of the Trump Organization [Jeffrey McConney] the first monthly invoice, which stated: 'Pursuant to the retainer agreement, kindly remit payment for services rendered for the months of January and February, 2017.' The invoice requested payment in the amount of $35,000 for each of those two months. [Weisselberg] approved the payment, and, in turn, [McConney] sent the invoice to the Trump Organization Accounts Payable Supervisor [Deborah Tarasoff] with the following instructions: 'Please pay from the Trust. Post to legal expenses. Put 'retainer for the months of January and February 2017' in the description.' Accordingly, the Supervisor "printed out [the] invoice and marked it with an accounts payable stamp and the general ledger code '51505' for legal expenses. The Trump Organization maintained [the invoice] as records of expenses paid." The Supervisor then "recorded [the] payment in the Trump Organization's electronic accounting system, falsely describing it as a 'legal expense' pursuant to a retainer agreement for a month of 2017." Later court filings note that "[i]n truth and fact, there was no such retainer agreement" and Cohen's invoices "were not in connection with any legal services he had provided in 2017." The Trump Organization "maintained a digital entry

for [the] expense, called a 'voucher,'" which "like vouchers for other expenses, became part of the Trump Organization's general ledgers." Having taken these steps, the Supervisor then prepared a check with an attached check stub "for approval and signature." The first check to Cohen for $70,000 was reportedly signed the same day by Weisselberg and Donald Trump Jr. "as trustees. The check stub falsely recorded the payment as 'Retainer for 1/1-1/31/17' and 'Retainer for 2/1-2/28/17.' (statement of facts, pp. 8-9; Cohen criminal information, p. 17; *The Fixers*, pp. 209–210; *POLITICO*; *The New York Times*; CNN; *ABC News*).

MAR. - DEC., 2017: Cohen "submitted ten similar monthly invoices by email to the Trump Organization for the remaining months in 2017. Each invoice falsely stated that it was being submitted '[p]ursuant to the retainer agreement,' and falsely requested 'payment for services rendered' for a month of 2017." As was the case for the January - February 2017 invoice, there "was no such retainer agreement and [Cohen] was not being paid for services rendered in any month of 2017." Upon receipt of each invoice, McConney forwarded them to the Trump Organization Accounts Payable Supervisor, who followed the same process outlined in the entry above to record and pay the expenses (statement of facts, pp. 8-9).

MAR. 17, 2017: Donald Trump Jr. and Weisselberg signed a $35,000 check to Cohen that "was also paid from the Trust." As for the prior month's payment, "The check stub falsely recorded the payment as 'Retainer for 3/1-3/31/17'" (statement of facts, p. 9; *The New York Times*).

APR. 2017: "The remaining nine checks, corresponding to the months of April through December of 2017, were paid by [Trump] personally. Each of the checks was cut from [Trump's] bank account and sent, along with the corresponding invoices from [Cohen], from the Trump Organization in New York County to [Trump] in Washington, D.C. The checks and stubs bearing the false statements were stapled to the invoices also bearing false statements. [Trump] signed each of the checks personally and had them sent back to the Trump Organization in New York County. There, the checks, the stubs, and the invoices were scanned and maintained in the Trump Organization's data system before the checks themselves were detached and mailed to [Cohen] for payment" (statement of facts, pp. 9-10).

MAY 23, 2017: Trump himself signed a $35,000 dollar check to Cohen from his personal account. Trump ultimately signed six of the publicly available checks to Cohen, though later court filings revealed that he signed nine checks in total (*The New York Times*; statement of facts, pp. 9-10).

SUMMER 2017: Trump "invited [Pecker] to White House for a dinner to thank him for his help during the campaign" (statement of facts, p. 7).

JUNE 2017: Trump personally paid and signed a check to Cohen (statement of facts, pp. 9-10).

<u>July 2017</u>: Trump personally paid and signed a check to Cohen (statement of facts, pp. 9-10).

<u>Aug. 1, 2017</u>: Trump personally paid and signed a $35,000 dollar check to Cohen, which later became public (*The New York Times*).

<u>Sept. 12, 2017</u>: Trump personally paid and signed a $35,000 dollar check to Cohen, which later became public (*The New York Times*).

<u>Oct. 18, 2017</u>: Trump personally paid and signed a $35,000 dollar check to Cohen, which later became public (*The New York Times*).

<u>Oct. 20, 2017</u>: The Department of Justice (DOJ) granted special counsel Robert Mueller "authorization to investigate Cohen, among others, and to follow leads related to his creation and use of Essential Consultants" as Mueller deepened his investigation into the Trump campaign's possible collusion with Russia (The Fixers, p. 221).

<u>Circa Late October 2017</u>: Davidson claims to have received "an unusual inquiry" from a client manager at his bank in Los Angeles asking about the source and purpose of the wire transfer he had made to Clifford the previous year. In response, Davidson reportedly "told the bank that the payment had originated with Essential Consultants, and

that it was for a legal settlement." He then reportedly called Cohen to report the conversation. Cohen was reportedly "concerned that someone pretending to be a bank employee had tried to get Davidson to divulge the nondisclosure agreement" but "didn't seem to grasp the potential peril" that the Mueller investigation was behind the inquiry. Cohen allegedly "did, however, secretly record their phone call" (The Fixers, p. 221).

Nov. 21, 2017: Trump personally paid and signed a $35,000 dollar check to Cohen, which later became public (*The New York Times*).

Dec. 5, 2017: Trump personally paid and signed the final $35,000 dollar check to Cohen, which later became public (*The New York Times*).

Jan. 12, 2018: News broke that Cohen had allegedly arranged a deal to pay Clifford $130,000 to keep her silent during the 2016 campaign. In response, Cohen released a statement addressed to The Wall Street Journal claiming, "These rumors have circulated time and again since 2011. President Trump once again vehemently denies any such occurrence as has Ms. Daniels." Cohen also forwarded The Journal a two-paragraph statement signed by "Stormy Daniels" denying the affair. A White House official separately stated, "These are old, recycled reports, which were published and strongly denied before the election" (*The Wall Street Journal*; *The New York Times*; see also *The New York Times*).

J<small>AN</small>. 17, 2018: *In Touch* published the transcript of its previously-quashed 2011 interview with Clifford (*The Washington Post*).

J<small>AN</small>. 18, 2018: *The Wall Street Journal* reported that Cohen had used "a private Delaware company," Essential Consultants LLC, to make the $130,000 payment to Clifford (*The Wall Street Journal*).

J<small>AN</small>. 22, 2018: Government watchdog organization Common Cause filed an FEC complaint alleging that Cohen's payment to Clifford had violated campaign finance laws. (Cohen warrant, p. 55).

J<small>AN</small>. 30, 2018: During an interview on *Jimmy Kimmel Live*, Clifford neither confirmed nor denied her alleged affair with Trump and "strongly hint[ed] that she is subject to an NDA." Hours before Clifford's interview, Davidson reportedly drafted a second denial statement at the behest of "Cohen and company." The statement reportedly asserted that Clifford was not denying the affair "because [she] was paid 'hush money,'" but because "it never happened." Clifford allegedly signed the document "without complaint," but changed her handwriting "as if in subtle protest." When Kimmel questioned whether Clifford had actually signed the denial, she responded, "I don't know, did I? That doesn't look like my signature, does it?" (*The Washington Post*; *The Fixers*, pp. 242-243).

FEB. 8, 2018: In response to an inquiry from the FEC, one of Cohen's attorneys sent a letter stating, "In a private transaction in 2016, before the U.S. presidential election, Mr. Cohen used his own personal funds to facilitate a payment of $130,000 to Ms. Stephanie Clifford. Neither the Trump Organization nor the Trump campaign was a party to the transaction with Ms. Clifford, and neither reimbursed Mr. Cohen for the payment directly or indirectly." (Letter to the FEC Office of Complaints Examination).

FEB. 13, 2018: In a statement to *The New York Times,* Cohen claimed that "Neither the Trump Organization nor the Trump campaign was a party to the transaction with Ms. Clifford. The payment to Ms. Clifford was lawful, and was not a campaign contribution or campaign expenditure by anyone." (Cohen warrant, p. 56).

ON OR ABOUT FEB. 14, 2018: *The New York Times* asked Cohen "whether Trump had reimbursed him, whether he and Trump had made any arrangements at the time of the payment, or whether he had made payments to other women. Cohen stated in response, 'I can't get into any of that'" (Cohen warrant, p. 56).

FEB. 15, 2018: Likely believing that Cohen's comments to *The New York Times* had nullified her NDA, Clifford's agent told *AP News* that "Everything is off now, and Stormy is going to tell her story" (AP News).

<u>FEB. 16, 2018</u>: The *New Yorker* published a story featuring details of McDougal's alleged affair with Trump based on "an eight-page, handwritten document" created by McDougal and provided to the magazine by Crawford. McDougal granted an interview for the piece but "expressed surprise" that the magazine had obtained her notes. During her interview, McDougal "declined to discuss her relationship with Trump for fear of violating the agreement she had reached with [AMI]." In an email to AMI's general counsel soon after the article dropped, McDougal's lawyer reportedly asserted that while "McDougal was not contractually required to keep quiet," her client would "consider entering into a fresh nondisclosure agreement if [AMI] was willing to pay her more money. If not, she'd grant more interviews" (*The New Yorker; The Fixers*, pp. 248-250).

<u>FEB. 22, 2018</u>: Cohen reportedly initiated secret arbitration proceedings following Clifford's media engagements (*The Fixers*, p. 251).

<u>FEB. 27, 2018</u>: An arbitrator reportedly "found that Ms. Clifford had violated the [NDA] agreement" and issued a restraining order against Clifford (*The New York Times)*.

<u>MAR. 6, 2018</u>: Clifford filed a lawsuit "asserting that the nondisclosure agreement that accompanied the $130,000 was void because Mr. Trump never signed it." The complaint revealed the arbitration proceedings Cohen had initiated in an effort to silence Clifford, as well as the terms

of the contract Clifford had signed on Oct. 28, 2016 (*The New York Times*).

MAR. 7, 2018: Sarah Huckabee Sanders, the White House press secretary, asserted that "there was no knowledge of any payments from the president" and "he has denied all these allegations." The same day, Clifford's attorney, Michael Avenatti (who had replaced Davidson at this point), publicly and explicitly asserted "that [Clifford] had a sexual relationship with Trump" (*The New York Times*; *The Washington Post*).

MAR. 9, 2018: Avanetti provided ABC News with a set of emails that he claimed contained communications between Cohen and First Republic Bank surrounding the 2016 payment to Davidson, who was still Clifford's attorney at the time. *NBC News* separately broke the news that Cohen had used his Trump Organization email for the exchange. Cohen responded by downplaying the emails as "corroborat[ing] all my previous statements." He went on to describe how the payment was made, stating, "The funds were taken from my home equity line and transferred internally to my L.L.C. account in the same bank." Cohen also brushed aside the revelation that he had used his Trump Organization email to coordinate the transaction, stating "I sent emails from the Trump Org email address to my family, friends as well as Trump business emails. I basically used it for everything. I am certain most people can relate" (NBC News).

<u>MAR. 14, 2018</u>: *The Wall Street Journal* published a story highlighting the role that Jill Martin, the Trump Organization's assistant general counsel, played in the arbitration at the request of Eric Trump. Per the *Journal*'s article, Avenatti supplied the outlet with documents Martin had signed, "for the first time [tying] President Donald Trump's flagship holding company to the continuing effort to silence [Clifford]" (*The Fixers*, pp. 263-265; *The Wall Street Journal*).

<u>MAR. 16, 2018</u>: Trump sought "$20 million in damages from [Clifford] for allegedly [breaking the] nondisclosure agreement 20 times. A lawyer for Cohen's limited liability company, Essential Consultants, made the claim in papers filed in federal court" (*The Washington Post*).

<u>MID-MARCH 2018</u>: Two weeks after Clifford sued Trump and Essential Consultants, McDougal reportedly brought "a case against [AMI] in the same Los Angeles court" (*The Fixers*, p. 268).

<u>MAR. 25, 2018</u>: Clifford was interviewed on *60 Minutes* (60 Minutes; CBS News).

<u>MAR. 26, 2018</u>: Clifford amended her lawsuit against both Trump and Cohen to sue Cohen for defamation, which she claimed had occurred when Cohen put out his February 2018 statement about the $130,000 payment. The lawsuit argued that Cohen's statement had caused Clifford "hatred, contempt, ridicule, and shame, and discouraged others from

associating or dealing with her" and that she "ha[d] suffered damages in an amount to be proven at trial according to proof, including but not limited to, harm to her reputation, emotional harm, exposure to contempt, ridicule, and shame, and physical threats of violence to her person and life" (NPR).

APR. 5, 2018: Trump delivered his first public remarks about the alleged Clifford affair and ensuing hush money payment. When asked by a reporter if he knew about the payment to Clifford, Trump responded "No." In response to another question asking why Cohen had made the payment, Trump answered "You'll have to ask Michael Cohen. Michael is my attorney." Trump also claimed that he did not know the source of the money for the payment (*The New York Times*).

APR. 9, 2018: As part of a probe by the U.S. attorney's office in Manhattan, the FBI raided Cohen's Rockefeller Center office, Park Avenue hotel room, and home. Federal investigators reportedly seized eight boxes of documents and millions of electronic files including business records, emails, and bank records related to a payment to Clifford from Cohen's office, among other matters. Cohen called Trump that day to inform him of the raid. "In a return call, Trump told [Cohen] to 'stay strong'" (statement of facts, p. 10; *The New York Times*; *The Fixers*, p. 286).

APR. 15, 2018: Reports became public that the U.S. attorney's office in Manhattan was investigating possible bank fraud in connection with Cohen's payment to Clifford, which he had made using his home equity credit line (*The Wall Street Journal*).

MID-APRIL 2018: ROBERT "BOB" Costello offered to represent Cohen after Costello's law partner, Jeffrey Citron, connected Costello with Cohen. Citron and Cohen reportedly knew each other through their children, who attended the same school (*The Fixers*, p. 289; statement of facts, p. 10).

APR. 17, 2018: Clifford and her attorney released a composite sketch of the man she claimed had threatened her in a Las Vegas parking lot. Clifford's attorney offered a $100,000 reward for information that would lead to the man's apprehension (*The Washington Post*).

APR. 18, 2018: AMI reached a settlement agreement with McDougal, freeing McDougal to publicly discuss her alleged affair with Trump. McDougal's original suit claimed that she had been misled into signing the contract that sold AMI the rights to her story about Trump; the suit also alleged that Cohen had been secretly involved in the negotiations between AMI and McDougal's lawyer. The settlement agreement foreclosed the possibility of pretrial discovery, which could have revealed emails and other evidence beyond what was found in the FBI's April 9 raid (*The New York Times*).

<u>Apr. 21, 2018</u>: Early in the morning, Costello sent the
following email to Cohen summarizing a phone call
Costello had with Giuliani: "I just spoke to Rudy Giuliani
and told him I was on your team. Rudy was thrilled and said
this could not be a better situation for the President or you.
He asked me if it was ok to call the President and Jay
Sekelow [*sic*] and I said fine. We discussed the facts, Jay
Goldberg's stupid remarks etc. he said I can't tell you how
pleased I am that I can work with someone I know and trust.
He asked me to tell you that he knows how tough this is on
you and your family and he will make sue [*sic*] to tell the
President. He said thank you for opening this back channel
of communication and asked me to keep in touch. I told him
I would after speaking to you further." Later that day,
Costello emailed Cohen again: "I spoke with Rudy. Very
Very Positive. You are 'loved'... Rudy said this communication channel must be maintained... Sleep well tonight, you
have friends in high places" (*The Fixers*, pp. 295-296; statement of facts, pp. 10-11).

<u>Apr. 21, 2018</u>: As some speculated whether Cohen would
"flip and begin cooperating with government investigators
against Trump, the president tweeted that "most people will
flip if the government lets them out of trouble, even if it
means lying or making up stories. Sorry, I don't see Michael
doing that." He described Cohen as a "fine person with a
wonderful family" (statement of facts, p. 10; *Twitter*).

<u>Apr. 26, 2018</u>: Trump admitted that Cohen had represented
him in dealing with Clifford in an interview on *Fox &
Friends*, stating, "He represents me, like with this crazy

Stormy Daniels deal, he represented me" (*The New York Times*).

<u>APR. 30, 2018</u>: Clifford filed a defamation lawsuit against Trump in Manhattan federal court. The suit focused on a tweet Trump had sent on April 18, 2018 related to the sketch of the man who allegedly threatened Clifford in 2011 (*The Wall Street Journal*).

<u>MAY 2, 2018</u>: During a *Fox News* interview, Rudolph Giuliani (Trump's new lawyer) acknowledged and described Trump's repayments to Cohen for the hush money. Giuliani stated that "they funneled it [the $130,000 payment to Clifford] through a law firm, and the president repaid it" (*The New York Times*).

<u>MAY 3, 2018</u>: Trump tweeted that he did pay Cohen a monthly retainer, but reiterated that the payments had "nothing to do with the campaign" (*The New York Times*).

<u>ON OR ABOUT JUNE 14, 2018</u>: "[Costello] emailed [Cohen] a news clip discussing the possibility of [Cohen] cooperating, and continued to urge him not to cooperate with law enforcement, writing, 'The whole objective of this exercise by the [federal prosecutors] is to drain you, emotionally and financially, until you reach a point that you see them as your only means to salvation.' In the same email, [Costello], wrote, 'You are making a very big mistake if you believe these 'journalists' are writing about you. They want you to

cave. They want you to fail. They do not want you to persevere and succeed'" (statement of facts, p. 11).

JULY 2, 2018: "My wife, my daughter and my son have my
first loyalty and always will," Cohen told ABC News's
George Stephanopoulos. "I put family and country first"
(ABC News). Stephanopoulos wrote that "Cohen strongly
signaled his willingness to cooperate with special counsel
Robert Mueller and federal prosecutors in the Southern
District of New York—even if that puts President Trump in
jeopardy."

JULY 24, 2018: *CNN* released an audio tape of Trump and
Cohen discussing what appears to be the plan to buy the
rights to McDougal's story. In the recording, Cohen explicitly mentions what appears to be the plan to set up a shell
company to execute the payment, stating "I need to open up
a company for the transfer of all of that info regarding our
friend David" (CNN; *The Washington Post*).

JULY 25, 2018: Trump tweeted a response to the tape and
suggested it was doctored by Cohen: "What kind of a lawyer
would tape a client? So sad! Is this a first, never heard of it
before? Why was the tape so abruptly terminated (cut) while
I was presumably saying positive things?" (*POLITICO*).

JULY 26, 2018: Press reports continued to circulate that
Cohen might be "flipping" on Trump and could cooperate
with the investigation (*CNN*).

<u>Aug. 21, 2018</u>: Cohen pleaded guilty in Manhattan federal court to charges including campaign finance violations and criminal tax evasion. Cohen told the judge that Trump had directed him to arrange the hush money payments, which he claimed were intended to prevent Clifford and McDougal from speaking publicly about their alleged affairs with Trump (statement of facts, p. 12; *The New York Times*; Cohen Plea press release).

<u>Aug. 22, 2018</u>: At 8:44 am ET, Trump tweeted: "If anyone is looking for a good lawyer, I would strongly suggest that you don't retain the services of Michael Cohen!" At 9:21 am ET, he tweeted again: "I feel very badly for Paul Manafort and his wonderful family. 'Justice' took a 12 year old tax case among other things applied tremendous pressure on him unlike Michael Cohen he refused to 'break'—make up stories in order to get a 'deal.' Such respect for brave man!" (*Twitter*; statement of facts, p. 11).

<u>Aug. 22, 2018</u>: Trump claimed that the payments to Clifford and McDougal were legal because they "came from me" rather than his campaign. "They weren't taken out of campaign finance, that's the big thing," he told *Fox & Friends* (*USA Today*).

<u>Sept. 20, 2018</u>: AMI privately signed a non-prosecution agreement protecting the company from criminal charges out of the SDNY U.S. Attorney's Office. In exchange, AMI agreed to "cooperate fully" with investigators and fully disclose all information related to the hush money

payments. In the agreement, AMI admitted "'[a]t no time during the negotiation or acquisition of [McDougal's] story did AMI intend to publish the story or disseminate information about it publicly.' Rather, AMI admitted that it made the payment to ensure that [McDougal] 'did not publicize damaging allegations' about [Trump] 'before the 2016 presidential election and thereby influence that election'" (statement of facts, p. 11; AMI non-prosecution agreement).

DEC. 7, 2018: Federal prosecutors released Cohen's sentencing memo. In its summary of Cohen's crimes, the memo endorsed Cohen's claims that Cohen had carried out both hush money payments "in coordination with and at the direction of" Trump (Cohen sentencing memo, pp. 2-4, 13-15).

DEC. 12, 2018: Prosecutors released the details of the non-prosecution agreement with AMI, revealing the extent of AMI's involvement in the hush money payments and corroborating many aspects of Cohen's story. Among the key revelations was that "AMI's principal purpose in entering into the agreement was to suppress the model's story so as to prevent it from influencing the election"—indicating that the payments were likely campaign-related. (*The New York Times*; AMI non-prosecution agreement).

DEC. 12, 2018: Cohen was sentenced to three years in prison for a litany of financial crimes committed while he was in Trump's employ. Cohen was also sentenced the same day in a separate case for making false statements to Congress (*The Washington Post*; DOJ press release).

J<small>AN.</small> 10, 2019: Congressional Democrats announced that Cohen had agreed to testify before the House Oversight and Government Reform Committee on February 7 (*The Washington Post*).

J<small>AN.</small> 11, 2019: Avenatti announced that he and Clifford would attend the Cohen hearing on February 7 (*POLITICO*).

J<small>AN.</small> 23, 2019: Cohen postponed his February 7 appearance before Congress after reportedly receiving "threats against his family" from Trump and Giuliani. (*USA Today*).

F<small>EB.</small> 5, 2019: Clifford dropped her defamation claim against Cohen. Avenatti stated "We asked that the minor defamation claim be dismissed and it was because the court sided with us and against Cohen" (*The Washington Post*).

F<small>EB.</small> 27, 2019: Cohen testified publicly against Trump before the House Oversight and Government Reform Committee. (Cohen's testimony can be found here.) When asked if Trump's organization had made other hush money payments during the campaign, Cohen claimed that Pecker had sent money to other individuals under similar circumstances—and that "not all of them had to do with women" (*The New York Times*; *POLITICO*).

MAR. 7, 2019: Cohen sued the Trump Organization for breach of contract and sought reimbursement for $1.9 million in legal fees incurred after Cohen began cooperating with federal prosecutors. The complaint also claimed that the Trump Organization was responsible for paying the nearly $2 million penalty imposed after Cohen pleaded guilty (*The New York Times*).

JUNE 19, 2019: In testimony during Trump's first impeachment investigation, Hicks said that during the 2016 campaign she had never spoken with Trump or Cohen about any payment to Daniels. She further testified that she not aware of any "hush money agreement" until the *Wall Street Journal*'s reporting on Nov. 4, 2016 (*transcript of Hicks' testimony*, pp. 47, 151-152, 179-180, 266-267).

JULY 18, 2019: Court documents were unsealed that publicly revealed the communications among Trump, Hicks, Cohen, and several AMI executives in the days following the "Access Hollywood tape release in 2016. The documents also appeared to show that "Cohen learned around the same time that Clifford had been considering going public with her claim that she had sex with Trump... at least some of these communications concerned the need to prevent Clifford from going public, particularly in the wake of the Access Hollywood story" (CNBC).

AUG. 1, 2019: Manhattan DA Cyrus R. Vance Jr. subpoenaed the Trump Organization for documents related to the Clifford hush money payments (*The New York Times*).

<u>MAY 21, 2020</u>: Due to the coronavirus pandemic, Cohen was released from federal prison to serve the remainder of his sentence at home (*AP News*).

<u>JULY 9, 2020</u>: Federal marshals took Cohen back into custody after he "refused the conditions of his home confinement." Probation officers had reportedly asked Cohen to agree to a set of conditions including "no engagement of any kind with the media, including print, TV, film, books, or any other form of media/news" for the remainder of his home confinement. Cohen reportedly refused and was brought to a federal detention facility (*The New York Times*).

<u>JULY 23, 2020</u>: A federal judge ordered Cohen's return to home confinement after finding that his re-imprisonment amounted to a retaliatory act undertaken by the government. During the hearing, the judge stated "I cannot believe fairly that it was not in purpose... to stop his exercise of First Amendment rights." Cohen had planned to publish a tell-all book about Trump during his confinement (*USA Today*).

<u>JULY 31, 2020</u>: The 9th U.S. Circuit Court of Appeals upheld a lower court ruling dismissing Clifford's 2018 libel lawsuit against Trump (*POLITICO*).

<u>APR. 13, 2021</u>: The Federal Election Commission found "reason to believe that the violation of the [Federal Elections Campaign] Act by AMI and Pecker" in connection with the

payments to McDougal and Clifford "was knowing and willful," based primarily on factual admissions AMI made in its non-disclosure agreement with the DOJ (FEC factual and legal analysis, p. 16) (*see also* May 17, 2021 entry below).

APR. 26, 2021: The FEC voted to dismiss a 2018 and a 2019 complaint against Cohen for his role in the Clifford payments. The commissioners found that since "the public record is complete with respect to the conduct at issue in these complaints, and Mr. Cohen has been punished by the government of the United States for the conduct at issue in these matters... pursuing these matters further was not the best use of agency resources" (FEC statement of reasons).

MAY 6, 2021: In a split decision that fell along partisan lines, the FEC voted against investigating charges that Trump and his Committee had violated campaign finance laws in the process of making the 2016 Clifford payment and subsequent Cohen reimbursements. The dissenting commissioners noted: "We voted to support OGC's recommendations to find reason to believe that Trump and the Committee knowingly and willfully accepted an excessive contribution from Cohen and a prohibited corporate or excessive contribution from the Trump Organization, that the Committee knowingly and willfully filed false disclosure reports, and that the Trump Organization knowingly and willfully made a corporate or excessive contribution through its reimbursements to Cohen. There is ample evidence in the record to support the finding that Trump and the Committee knew of, and nonetheless accepted, the illegal contributions at issue here;" "the Commission's Office of the General Counsel ('OGC') recommended finding reason to believe that Cohen and the Trump Organization made, and Trump and Donald J. Trump for President, Inc. (the 'Committee') accepted and failed to report, illegal contributions." (FEC statement of reasons).

<u>MAY 17, 2021</u>: The FEC reached a settlement with AMI after the commission concluded that the company (allegedly at the direction of Trump and Cohen) had "knowingly and willfully" violated campaign finance laws through its payments to McDougal. AMI acknowledged the violations and agreed to pay a $187,500 fine, but did not admit to "knowingly and willfully" committing them (*The Wall Street Journal*; *The New York Times*) (*see also* April 13, 2021 entry).

<u>Nov. 12, 2021</u>: In Cohen's civil suit against the Trump Organization, a Manhattan state court ruled that the company was not required to reimburse Cohen for the millions of dollars in legal fees that Cohen sought. In a statement to CNN, the Trump Organization called the decision an "incredible victory" (*Forbes*).

<u>Nov. 22, 2021</u>: Cohen's three-year prison sentence, which had largely been served in home confinement, ended (AP News).

<u>DEC. 17, 2021</u>: Cohen filed a civil rights lawsuit against Trump and several other DOJ officials, seeking damages for alleged First, Fourth, and Eighth Amendment violations

related to his re-confinement in federal prison the prior year (*Law&Crime*).

Nov. 14, 2022: A Trump-appointed judge dismissed Cohen's civil rights lawsuit (*Law&Crime*; Cohen v. U.S. et al. decision).

Nov. 15, 2022: In a 5-0 decision, a New York state appeals court revived Cohen's previous lawsuit seeking legal fee reimbursements from the Trump Organization. The court found that the presiding judge had incorrectly dismissed the case, opening a path for Cohen to sue the Trump Organization again (*Reuters*; Cohen v. Trump Organization LLC).

Nov. 21, 2022: Reports emerged that Manhattan DA Alvin Bragg planned to revive his office's criminal investigation into the Clifford hush money payment. Bragg's predecessor had examined the payment as possible grounds for a criminal indictment years before, but his office later reportedly decided that the surrounding legal theories were too risky to pursue the matter further (*The New York Times*).

Jan. 30, 2023: Bragg convened a grand jury in Manhattan to hear evidence related to the Clifford hush money payment (*The Washington Post*).

Jan. 30, 2023: Pecker reportedly met with prosecutors from Bragg's office (CNN; *The New York Times*).

<u>FEB. 2, 2023</u>: Jeffrey McConney, the Trump Organization's controller, reportedly appeared before the Manhattan grand jury hearing evidence related to the hush money payment (CNN).

<u>SOMETIME AFTER THE</u> grand jury was impaneled and before Mar. 1, 2023: Howard, Davidson, and Deborah Tarasoff, the Trump Organization's accounts payable supervisor, testified before the grand jury (*The New York Times*).

<u>MAR. 1, 2023</u>: Kellyanne Conway reportedly met with prosecutors from Bragg's office, likely to discuss the ongoing hush money investigation (MSNBC).

<u>MAR. 6, 2023</u>: Hicks reportedly met with prosecutors from Bragg's office (MSNBC).

<u>MAR. 9, 2023</u>: Bragg invited Trump to testify before the grand jury, according to one of Trump's lawyers (AP News).

<u>MAR. 13, 2023</u>: Cohen reportedly testified before the grand jury (*The Washington Post*).

<u>MAR. 15, 2023</u>: An attorney for Clifford stated that Clifford had met with Manhattan prosecutors and agreed to "make herself available as a witness, or for further inquiry if needed" (CBS News).

<u>Mar. 18, 2023</u>: In a Truth Social thread, Trump claimed that he would be arrested the following Tuesday, March 21, 2023. In a tweet, GOP House Majority Leader Kevin McCarthy separately announced that "he would direct House committees to investigate" Bragg and his office. McCarthy stated that Bragg's potential prosecution of Trump is "an outrageous abuse of power by a radical DA who lets violent criminals walk as he pursues political vengeance against President Trump," and that he planned to direct "relevant committees to immediately investigate if federal funds are being used to subvert our democracy by interfering in elections with politically motivated prosecutions." Following these posts, Bragg wrote in an internal email to his staff that his office would "not tolerate attempts to intimidate our office or threaten the rule of law in New York" (Truth Social; see also Truth Social; *POLITICO*; CNN).

<u>Mar. 19, 2023</u>: Trump commented on the Manhattan investigation in another series of *Truth Social* posts, claiming that Bragg was funded by billionaire George Soros and that he had no evidence of criminal wrongdoing on Trump's part (See, for example, Truth Social and Truth Social).

<u>Mar. 20, 2023</u>: Costello appeared before the Manhattan grand jury as a witness on behalf of Trump. Throughout the day, Trump continued to post about the investigation on *Truth Social* (PBS; Truth Social; see also Truth Social)

<u>Mar. 20, 2023</u>: Congressional Representatives Jim Jordan, James Comer, and Bryan Steil (chairmen of the House Judi-

ciary, Oversight, and Administration committees, respectively) sent a letter requesting that Bragg testify before Congress, calling the Trump investigation an "unprecedented abuse of prosecutorial authority" and a "politically motivated prosecution." When asked about the letter, McCarthy stated that the congressmen were "just 'asking questions.'" A spokesperson for Bragg responded to the letter the same day, stating, "We will not be intimidated by attempts to undermine the justice process, nor will we let baseless accusations deter us from fairly applying the law" (Jordan, Steil & Comer first letter; CNN).

<u>Mar. 23, 2023</u>: Bragg's office released a formal response to Jordan, Comer, and Steil's request. Leslie Dubeck, general counsel for the DA's office, told the chairmen that "they lacked a 'legitimate basis for congressional inquiry'" but also said, "request[ed] an opportunity to meet and confer with committee staff to better understand what information the DA's office can provide that relates to a legitimate legislative interest and can be shared consistent with the District Attorney's constitutional obligations." (Manhattan DA Letter; CNN). The same day, Trump posted an image of himself "holding a baseball bat alongside a picture of Bragg's head" on *Truth Social*. The post was later deleted. In two other *Truth Social* posts, Trump called Bragg a "SOROS BACKED ANIMAL [sic]" and levied what appeared to be criticism of those calling for peaceful protest: "OUR COUNTRY IS BEING DESTROYED, AS THEY TELL US TO BE PEACEFUL!" (*The Washington Post*; *The New York Times*; Truth Social; Truth Social).

MAR. 24, 2023: Trump explicitly referenced the possibility of violence surrounding his possible arrest, posting on *Truth Social* that the "potential death & destruction in such a false charge could be catastrophic for our Country" (Truth Social).

MAR. 25, 2023: Jordan, Comer, and Steil sent a second letter to Bragg, saying that the potential criminal indictment of Trump "implicate[d] substantial federal interests." That evening, Bragg tweeted a response to the chairmen, stating "We evaluate cases in our jurisdiction based on the facts, the law, and the evidence. It is not appropriate for Congress to interfere with pending local investigations. This unprecedented inquiry by federal elected officials into an ongoing matter serves only to hinder, disrupt and undermine the legitimate work of our dedicated prosecutors. As always, we will continue to follow the facts and be guided by the rule of law in everything we do" (Jordan, Steil & Comer second letter; CNN; Twitter).

MAR. 25, 2023: Dubeck sent former prosecutor Mark Pomerantz a letter instructing him, "as a former employee and attorney of the DA's office, to not provide any information or materials relating to your work in the DA's office in response to [the Committee's] request" (Dubeck letter to Pomerantz; *POLITICO*).

MAR. 27, 2023: Pecker reportedly testified before the Manhattan grand jury for the second time (*The New York Times*).

<u>Mar. 27, 2023</u>: In a letter to Jordan and the Judiciary Committee, Pomerantz informed them that he would not comply with their request that he testify voluntarily, explaining that he had previously received instructions from the DA's office "to not provide any information of materials in response to [the Committee's] request" (Pomerantz letter to Judiciary Committee; *POLITICO*).

<u>Mar. 30, 2023</u>: The Manhattan grand jury voted to indict Trump on 34 felony counts of falsifying business records in the first degree under New York Penal Law §175.10 (Manhattan DA indictment).

<u>Mar. 31, 2023</u>: Bragg's office sent a response to the second letter (March 25th letter) to Jordan, Comer, and Steil informing them that the office filed charges against Donald Trump after the grand jury indictment and that "Congress has no warrant for interfering with individual criminal investigations much less investigations conducted by a separate Sovereign." Dubeck also detailed how Bragg's office spends its limited federal funding and wrote to the Chairs that "[w]e trust you will make a good-faith effort to reach a negotiated resolution before taking the unprecedented and unconstitutional step of serving a subpoena on a district attorney for information related to an ongoing state criminal prosecution" (Bragg second letter to Congress).

<u>Apr. 4, 2023</u>: Trump surrendered to New York law enforcement in Manhattan and was arraigned in a criminal court hearing there. During the arraignment hearing,

Trump pleaded not guilty to all 34 felony counts of falsifying business records charged in the DA's indictment. Judge Juan Merchan warned both Trump and the DA's office during the hearing not to make any public statements that could "incite violence, create civil unrest or jeopardize the safety or well-being of any individuals" and to "not engage in words or conduct which jeopardizes the rule of law, particularly as it applies to these proceedings in this courtroom." The indictment and accompanying statement of facts were unsealed that afternoon (Arraignment hearing transcript; CNN).

APR. 4, 2023: Trump returned to Florida after the arraignment. Later that evening, he hosted a gathering at Mar-a-Lago, during which he gave a speech and stated: "I never thought anything like this could happen in America, never thought it could happen. The only crime that I have committed is to fearlessly defend our nation from those who seek to destroy it... It's an insult to our country." In his remarks he also referred to Justice Merchan as a "Trump-hating judge" and to Bragg as a "criminal" (CNN; *New York Post*).

APR. 6, 2023: Jordan subpoenaed Pomerantz in an effort to compel Pomerantz's testimony before the House Judiciary Committee after he "turned down a request to voluntarily cooperate with" the congressional investigation of Bragg's office. In the subpoena, Jordan ordered Pomerantz to sit for a deposition before the Committee on April 20 at 10:00 am (CBS News).

<u>APR. 11, 2023</u>: Bragg sued Jordan seeking a temporary restraining order to block the subpoena for Pomerantz's testimony as well as any future subpoenas issued to him or other members of the DA's office. The lawsuit alleged that the congressional investigation of Bragg's office was a "brazen and unconstitutional attack" and a "transparent campaign to intimidate and attack" Bragg. The lawsuit was filed in federal court in the Southern District of New York. That afternoon, U.S. District Judge Mary Kay Vyskocil denied Bragg's request for a temporary restraining order. She ordered that Bragg serve the complaint on Jordan by 9:00 pm that evening, and that Jordan file a response to Bragg's complaint by April 17. Judge Vyskocil also scheduled a hearing on Bragg's complaint for 2:00 pm on April 19 (*Bragg v. Jordan*; Judge Vyskocil's April 11, 2023 order; *The New York Times*).

<u>APR. 12, 2023</u>: Trump sued Cohen in federal court in the Southern District of Florida requesting $500 million in damages for Cohen's alleged "breaches of fiduciary duty, unjust enrichment, conversion, and breaches of contract." Trump's lawyer also requested a jury trial on the matter (*Trump v. Cohen*; *POLITICO*; *NBC News*).

<u>APR. 17, 2023</u>: Rep. Jordan filed an opposition to DA Bragg's lawsuit against him, the House Judiciary Committee, and Pomerantz. Jordan writes in the document, "the Constitution's Speech or Debate Clause gives him, the committee, and Pomerantz immunity from the lawsuit, and thus Bragg's motion should be denied." (Jim Jordan files opposition to Manhattan DA suit). In the opposition, Jordan also claims

that Trump's investigation "could be politically motivated" and that the committee is considering legislation that "would prohibit the use of federal forfeiture funds to investigate a current or former President" as well as legislation "that would expressly allow current and former Presidents and Vice Presidents to remove any criminal actions against them from state to federal court." (*POLITICO*)

Apr. 17, 2023: Pomerantz submitted a response and a declaration supporting the Alvin Bragg complaint and joined Bragg in asking the judge to block the subpoena for his testimony, saying he was "not involved in the decision to seek an indictment" of Trump since he resigned more than a year before the indictment was returned (CNN).

Apr. 17, 2023: Twenty-one individuals, including four former Republican members of Congress filed an amicus brief supporting Manhattan DA Alvin Bragg's motion for "injunctive relief to quash a subpoena in the case he filed against House Judiciary Chair Rep. Jim Jordan." The brief states that "Congress has no authority to interfere with an ongoing criminal prosecution, particularly one brought by a state prosecutor. That calculus does not change just because the defendant whom a grand jury indicted happens to be a former President of the United States. Nor does it change when Members of Congress attempt to characterize their unlawful interference as 'oversight.'" The authors also wrote that the subpoena issued by Jordan, "Threatens attorney work product privilege; Threatens the law enforcement privilege; Threatens grand jury secrecy; and Threatens the public interest and deliberative process privileges" (*Democracy 21*).

<u>Apr. 19, 2023</u>: Federal Judge Vyskocil ruled that Republican House members have a constitutional right to subpoena and question former prosecutor Pomerantz. The Manhattan DA's office responded by saying, "We respectfully disagree with the District Court's decision," and requested that the subpoena be paused while the ruling was appealed. The request was denied. DA Bragg's lawyers argued that because Pomerantz has already appeared on "60 Minutes" and written a book about his time working on the Trump investigation, questioning him would be about interfering with the investigation over gaining information from Pomerantz. Rep. Jordan's lawyers asserted that the subpoena is about inspecting the use of federal funds for local investigations and the prospect of future legislation (*The New York Times*).

<u>Apr. 19, 2023</u>: DA Bragg and former prosecutor Mark F. Pomerantz both appealed to the U.S. Court of Appeals after Judge Vyskocil's ruling, and were granted a temporary stay of Pomerantz's questioning (*The New York Times*).

<u>Apr. 25, 2023</u>: The Manhattan DA's office filed a request with Justice Juan Merchan to restrict Trump's access to materials from his criminal case, and his ability to post the evidence online (*The New York Times*).

<u>Apr. 27, 2023</u>: Trump's attorneys filed a request for a bill of particulars. A bill of particulars is a written itemization of the claims and/or alleged facts brought against a defendant, which a defendant will usually request when the charges or claims are unclear. The idea is that the defendant needs proper notice of the charges so that they can prepare an adequate defense. Here, Trump's request inquired into the legal basis for felony charges of falsification of business records. (*The Washington Post*; NBC News)

<u>May 4, 2023</u>: Trump requested removal to the federal Southern District of New York. His request was based on 28 U.S.C. §1442 (a)(1), which requires removal in state criminal cases against federal officers when the alleged criminal conduct occurred while the defendant was a federal officer and under the "color of his office." Because the state crimes which Trump allegedly committed are superseded by federal election laws with some of the same elements, Trump argued that the federal preemption doctrine applied here. Under that doctrine, Trump argued, only federal prosecutors could bring charges against him for that alleged conduct. Trump also stated in the filing that criminal charges against a former president of the United States were "unprecedented in our nation's history," further compelling the judge to remove the case to the Southern District of New York.

<u>May 8, 2023</u>: Justice Merchan ruled, as part of a protective order, that Trump may not post any discovery materials on "any news or social media platforms, including, but not limited, to Truth Social, Facebook, Instagram, WhatsApp,

Twitter, Snapchat, or YouTube, without prior approval from the Court" (CNN).

MAY 16, 2023: Bragg rejected Trump's request for a bill of particulars, arguing that he already has enough relevant information. "The 15-page, 34-count indictment and 13-page statement of facts fully inform defendant of the nature of the charges against him," said Assistant District Attorney Becky Mangold. Nevertheless, Bragg released a list of statutes that may serve as Trump's underlying crime to justify the felony enhancement.

MAY 23, 2023: In a hearing, Justice Merchan established the ground rules for the protective order (see May 8, 2023), and explained, "It's certainly not a gag order," as Trump is allowed to publicly discuss the case. The judge set the commencement of the trial for March 25, 2024."

JULY 19, 2023: U.S. District Court Judge Alvin Hellerstein granted the DA's motion to remand the case back to state court (see May 4, 2023). Judge Hellerstein ruled that Trump failed to establish that the alleged conduct had any connection to his official duties as president, and that Trump had failed to raise a colorable immunity defense. The court wrote, "The evidence overwhelmingly suggests that the matter was a purely personal item of the President—a cover-up of an embarrassing event. Hush money paid to an adult film star is not related to a President's official acts. It does not reflect in any way the color of the President's official duties." In the same order, Judge Hellerstein also denied

Trump's claim that federal election law preempts New York's state jurisdiction, explaining "The mere fact that Trump is alleged to have engaged in fraudulent conduct with respect to a federal election is not a basis for preemption."

Sept. 29, 2023: Trump filed omnibus motions to dismiss the indictment, raising seven distinct arguments: (1) pre-indictment delay; (2) the records in question are not records of a business enterprise but rather records of Trump personally and his revocable trust; (3) the indictment lacked a viable object offense to justify the first-degree falsification of records; (4) insufficient evidence of an intent to defraud; (5) selective prosecution; (6) statute of limitations violations; and (7) multiplicity, i.e., that the indictment charges the same crime in different counts. In his omnibus filing, Trump also sought that DANY provide additional particulars to its case, asked to inspect the grand jury minutes and for a hearing on alleged violations of grand jury secrecy, and argued that DANY was not complying with its discovery obligations.

Nov. 9, 2023: The DA's office filed its opposition to Trump's omnibus motions. In responding to each specific argument, DA Bragg also made the broader point that the court must reject Trump's request for special treatment because he is a presidential candidate: "like any other defendant whose argument for dismissal are meritless, this defendant's motions should be denied, and this prosecution should proceed to trial."

<u>Feb. 15, 2024</u>: Justice Merchan held a hearing on the omnibus motions and gave his preliminary ruling from the bench before issuing a written order later that day. He denied Trump's various motions to dismiss and set the case for trial on March 25, 2024. The court sided with Trump on two issues: (1) precluding the prosecution from arguing that the falsification of other companies' business records—those of AMI or Cohen—constituted the other crime required for first-degree falsification of records; and (2) allowing Trump to review grand jury minutes but declining to hold a hearing for any alleged violation of grand jury secrecy.

<u>Feb. 22, 2024</u>: The DA's office filed a motion to restrict Trump from making extrajudicial statements about the case, essentially requesting a narrowly tailored gag order to prohibit Trump from making statements intended to threaten, intimidate or harass jurors, prosecutors, witnesses, or court staff. The DA's office also filed a motion for a protective order limiting disclosure of jurors' names and addresses.

Also on Feb. 22, each party filed motions *in limine* to address evidentiary issues in advance of trial. The DA's office filed eight motions, which can be grouped into three categories: (1) excluding specific witnesses and evidence ; (2) excluding improper legal arguments; and (3) admitting evidence of Trump's prior bad acts, known as "*Molineux*" evidence in New York (or "404(b)" in federal practice). Trump filed 16 motions *in limine*, which can be grouped into three categories: (1) excluding specific evidence and witnesses; (2) excluding evidence and argument about his intent to defraud and what constitutes an "enterprise" under the definition of business records; and (3) housekeeping matters.

FEB. 29, 2024: Trump and the DA's office each filed oppositions to the other side's motions *in limine.*

MAR. 4, 2024: Trump filed a response to the DA's motion for a narrowly tailored gag order prohibiting his extrajudicial prejudicial statements.

THAT SAME DAY, Trump filed a response regarding the DA's motion for a protective order limiting disclosure of juror information.

MAR. 7, 2024: The court granted the DA's request for a protective order regarding juror information but expanding the scope as Trump had requested to include the entire legal teams, not just the attorneys.

MAR. 7, 2024: Trump asked the court to adjourn trial pending the U.S. Supreme Court's decision on presidential immunity in the Jan. 6 federal election interference criminal prosecution against Trump.

<u>Mar. 8, 2024</u>: Following Trump's motion to adjourn trial, filed two weeks after the deadline for pretrial motions had passed, the court ordered the parties to seek permission before filing additional motions.

That same day, Trump filed a letter seeking permission for his motion to dismiss the indictment, or alternatively preclude Cohen and Daniels from testifying while adjourning the trial for at least 90 days, based on alleged discovery violations committed by the DA's office.

<u>Mar. 10, 2024</u>: Trump filed a letter seeking permission to file a motion to vacate the court's March 8 order requiring permission to file a motion.

Also on March 10, Trump sought permission to file a motion for public proceedings, namely "(1) unsealing and public access to all pleadings, orders, and written communications that have involved the Court and the parties, including communications sent by letter and substantive email, and (2) simultaneous public access of all future pleadings, orders, and written communications except to the extent redactions are required by the protective order or law."

<u>Mar. 11, 2024</u>: Trump filed a notice that he would not be asserting a "formal advice-of-counsel defense" but would intend to elicit evidence and make arguments regarding the "presence, involvement, and advice of lawyers."

Mar. 12, 2024: The DA's office responded in opposition to Trump's motion for public proceedings

Mar. 13, 2024: The DA's office filed its opposition to Trump's motion for adjournment based on presidential immunity.

Mar. 14, 2024: The DA filed an initial response to Trump's March 8 motion regarding alleged discovery violations, denying any violations but acknowledging that a recent document production by the U.S. Attorney's Office justified a 30-day adjournment.

Mar. 15, 2024: Regarding the alleged discovery violations, the court granted a 30-day adjournment, gave the DA's office until March 18 to respond in full, and scheduled a hearing for March 25.

Mar. 18, 2024: The court issued rulings denying most of Trump's motions *in limine* and granting most of those by the DA's office, including that Trump cannot rely on a "presence of counsel" defense.

That same day, the DA's office filed its two briefs in response to Trump's motion alleging discovery violations. One brief focused on the U.S. Attorney's Office recent document production, arguing that the 30-day adjournment granted on March 15 was sufficient to give Trump a "meaningful opportunity" to review the limited universe of new and relevant documents before trial. The second brief focused on what it described as Trump's "grab-bag of meritless discovery arguments," harshly criticizing the defense's gamesmanship and encouraging the court to proceed to trial.

ALSO ON MARCH 18, Trump filed a motion for further adjournment based of prejudicial pretrial publicity (March 18, 2024)

MAR. 25, 2024: At the hearing regarding alleged discovery violations, Justice Merchan rejected Trump's arguments and set trial for April 15.

MAR. 26, 2024: The court denied Trump's motion to vacate its March 8 order requiring permission to file motions.

ALSO ON MARCH 26, the court effectively denied Trump's motion for public proceedings, noting that court filings, orders and other correspondence not subject to the court's May 8, 2023, protective order were already accessible to the public.

THAT SAME DAY, Justice Merchan also issued a gag order, prohibiting Trump from making statements about counsel in the case other than the District Attorney, members of the court's staff, and the family members of any counsel or staff member, if those statements are made with the intent to materially interfere with the case.

MAR. 28, 2024: The DA's office filed a letter asking the court to clarify or confirm that its March 26 gag order contemplated family members of Justice Merchan and DA Bragg.

MAR. 29, 2024: Trump filed a response to DANY's letter to clarify the gag order, stating that the order's current terms do not apply to Merchan's or Bragg's family members and disagreeing with extending them in that fashion.

APR. 1, 2024: The DA's office filed a supplemental brief in support of its March 28 letter requesting clarification of the March 26 gag order. Trump filed a further opposition to DANY's motion to clarify the gag order. Trump's opposition also stated that he had submitted to the court that day "a pre-motion letter seeking leave to file a [judicial] recusal motion based on change of circumstances and newly discovered evidence."

LATER THAT DAY, the court granted DANY's motion, amending the March 26 gag order to include the family members of Justice Merchan and DA Bragg; and formally putting Trump on notice that he will forfeit his statutory right to access juror names if he engages "in any conduct that threatens the safety and integrity of the jury or the jury selection process."

CAST OF CHARACTERS

I n this chapter, we provide a brief guide to key people in the *Manhattan case, including the judge, the district attorney's prosecution team, Trump's defense team, as well as individuals identified in the statement of facts. This cast of characters is intended to provide readers with a brief explanation of each individual's role in this matter. This includes both well-known and obscure persons.*

KEY WITNESSES IN THE CASE

STEPHANIE CLIFFORD (**also known as Stormy Daniels**)— Clifford is identified as "Woman 2" in the statement of facts. Clifford claims she had a sexual relationship with Trump while he was married. According to the statement of facts, AMI CEO David Pecker learned of Clifford's allegations in October 2016, shortly after an "Access Hollywood" audio of Trump discussing lewd acts was aired. Clifford was subsequently paid $130,000 to keep her story out of the press prior to the 2016 presidential election.

MICHAEL COHEN—COHEN is identified as "Lawyer A" in the statement of facts. Cohen was Trump's personal lawyer and facilitated the "catch and kill" scheme on his behalf. In late October 2016, Cohen set up a shell company to pay Clifford hush money. He transferred $131,000 from a home equity loan to a bank account for the shell company and then paid Clifford's lawyer $130,000. Trump paid Cohen back in a series of checks between February and December 2017—that is, during Trump's first year in office. Those checks are central to the Manhattan DA's case, as Trump allegedly falsified business records in New York to cover up the purpose of the monies paid to Cohen. In 2018, Cohen pleaded guilty to eight charges, with the Department of Justice (DOJ) explaining that the hush money payments made to Clifford and McDougal were "intend[ed] to influence the 2016 presidential election."

KELLYANNE CONWAY—CONWAY was Trump's campaign manager before serving as assistant and senior counselor to the president from 2017-2020. Conway was allegedly in contact with Cohen the day of the hush money payment to confirm its logistics. Cohen wrote in his memoir that Trump "didn't take" his call that the transaction was a success but instead his "old pal" Conway "called and said she'd pass along the good news."

ROBERT COSTELLO—COSTELLO is identified as "Lawyer C" in the statement of facts. In April 2018, Costello allegedly approached Cohen and offered to serve as a "back channel of communication" between Cohen and Trump. Costello allegedly followed up in emails claiming Cohen was still in good standing with Trump.

KEITH DAVIDSON—DAVIDSON, Clifford's lawyer, is identified as "Lawyer B" in the statement of facts. He allegedly negotiated the hush money agreement with Cohen, including the $130,000 payment to Clifford.

RUDOLPH GIULIANI—GIULIANI, Trump's personal attorney, is "Lawyer D" in the statement of facts. In an email on or about April 21, 2018 to Michael Cohen, Robert Costello ("Lawyer C") allegedly claimed he "had a close relationship with" Giuliani, adding: "[T]his could not be a better situation for the President or you." Costello was allegedly attempting to convince Cohen not to cooperate with authorities at the time. In an email that same day, Costello allegedly wrote: "I spoke with [Giuliani]. Very Very Positive. You are 'loved'. . . [Giuliani] said this communication channel must be maintained. . . Sleep well tonight, you have friends in high places."

HOPE HICKS—HICKS worked for Ivanka Trump at the Trump Organization prior to working as the Trump campaign's press secretary in the 2016 election. Between January 2017 and March 2018, she served in Trump's administration as White House director of strategic communications then as communications director, before returning between March 2020 and January 2021 as an assistant and counselor to the president. Hicks allegedly participated in a conference call with Cohen and Trump on Oct. 8, 2016. Records also show Hicks spoke with Cohen "several times" before and after calls with AMI. Hicks has testified she had no knowledge of the Clifford matter other than what she learned from reporters.

DYLAN HOWARD—HOWARD is identified as the "AMI Editor-in-Chief" in the statement of facts. In or about June 2016, Howard allegedly discussed with Cohen that a woman (Karen McDougal, "Woman 1") claimed that "she had a sexual relationship with [Trump] while he was married." Howard updated Cohen "regularly about the matter over text message and by telephone."

JEFFREY MCCONNEY—MCCONNEY is identified as the "TO Controller" in the statement of facts. Cohen allegedly sent his first invoice to McConney on or about Feb. 14, 2017. McConney then forwarded the invoice to Tarasoff, writing: "Post to legal expenses. Put 'retainer for the months of January and February 2017' in the description." McConney allegedly forwarded Cohen's other invoices to Tarasoff, and each invoice was marked as if it was for "legal expenses."

KAREN MCDOUGAL—MCDOUGAL, a former Playboy model, is identified as "Woman 1" in the statement of facts. McDougal alleges that she had sexual relations with Trump while he was married. In or about June 2016, senior AMI officials discussed McDougal's allegations with Cohen. AMI subsequently paid $150,000 to McDougal and received the exclusive rights to her story as part of the exchange. In a conversation recorded around September 2016, Trump discussed with Cohen how they could acquire the rights to McDougal's story. Trump asked: "So what do we got to pay for this? One fifty?" Although AMI initially agreed to transfer the rights to her story to a shell company set up by Cohen, AMI backed out of the deal. AMI did not release McDougal from the non-disclosure agreement until after the 2016 presidential election.

DAVID PECKER—PECKER is identified as AMI's chairman and chief executive officer (the "AMI CEO") in the statement of facts. AMI publishes the *National Enquirer* and other tabloids. In August 2015, Pecker attended a meeting with Trump and Cohen at Trump Tower in midtown Manhattan. During that meeting, Pecker agreed to act as the "eyes and ears" of the Trump campaign—that is, Pecker agreed to participate in Trump's "catch and kill" scheme. Pecker helped Cohen and Trump identify any problematic sources who came forward prior to the 2016 election with sordid details from Trump's past. In fall 2015, Pecker facilitated a payment of $30,000 to a doorman at Trump Tower who claimed that Trump was the father to a baby born out of wedlock. In 2016, AMI also paid $150,000 to Karen McDougal, a former *Playboy* model, to prevent her from sharing her story about a sexual encounter with Trump. AMI entered into a non-prosecution agreement with the DOJ, admitting that the payment to McDougal was intended to ensure she did not "publicize damaging allegations about" Trump "before the 2016 presidential election and thereby influence that election."

DINO SAJUDIN—SAJUDIN is the Trump Tower "Doorman" discussed in the statement of facts. In late 2015, as part of the "catch and kill" scheme, AMI paid Sajudin $30,000 to prevent him from going public with an allegation that Trump fathered a child out of wedlock. As part of the agreement, AMI acquired the "exclusive rights" to Sajudin's story. According to the Manhattan DA's office, AMI "later concluded that the story was not true," but Cohen "instructed" Pecker "not to release" Sajudin from the agreement "until after the presidential election." Pecker "complied with that instruction because of his agreement with" Trump and Cohen—again demonstrating the "catch and kill" scheme was solely intended to prevent negative stories about Trump from coming to light prior to the 2016 presidential election.

DEBORAH TARASOFF—TARASOFF is identified as "TO [Trump Organization] Accounts Payable Supervisor" in the statement of facts. At the direction of other Trump Organization officials, Tarasoff allegedly prepared the checks used to reimburse Cohen and also falsely recorded those checks as "legal expenses" in the organization's bookkeeping.

DONALD TRUMP—TRUMP IS THE "DEFENDANT" in both the indictment and the statement of facts. Trump declared his candidacy in June 2015. Just two months later, in August 2015, he met with Cohen and Pecker at Trump Tower in midtown Manhattan to formulate their "catch and kill" scheme. During his first year in office, Trump allegedly repaid Cohen for the hush money paid to Clifford. Those checks, which were cut between February and December

2017, are the heart of the 2016 election interference case. Trump and his associates allegedly created falsified business records in New York to cover up the true purpose of the checks. According to the statement of facts, Trump "instructed" Cohen "that if they could delay the payment until after the election, they could avoid paying altogether, because at that point it would not matter if the story became public." Trump's alleged instructions suggest that he was only concerned with keeping Clifford's testimony from the public prior to the presidential election because he knew it would likely harm his chances. Trump ultimately agreed that Cohen should pay Clifford the hush money just days prior to the election. Trump denies all wrongdoing.

Allen Weisselberg—Weisselberg, the former chief financial officer of the Trump Organization, is identified as "TO CFO" in the statement of facts. Trump allegedly instructed Cohen and Weisselberg to find a way to pay Clifford the $130,000 in hush money. Weisselberg allegedly arranged for Trump to reimburse Cohen from his trust and personal bank account in a series of checks cut throughout 2017. Weisselberg also allegedly helped Cohen cover up the true purpose of these monies, making it appear as regular taxable income. The Manhattan DA's office claims Weisselberg "memorialized these calculations in handwritten notes" on a "copy" of a "bank statement" that was produced by Cohen. Weisselberg was a key figure in the Manhattan DA's investigation of the Trump Organization and testified at trial. In August 2022, he pleaded guilty to 15 charges brought during the Manhattan DA's investigation into the Trump Organization. As part of his plea deal, Weisselberg served five months in prison. In March 2024, Weisselberg pleaded guilty to two additional charges of lying under oath during Trump's civil fraud case in New York.

THE JUDGE

JUSTICE JUAN MERCHAN—JUAN Manuel Merchan is an acting New York Supreme Court justice[1] who is presiding over the case. Merchan was born in Bogotá, Colombia and moved to Queens, New York at the age of 6. He graduated from Baruch College with a business degree in 1990, and later Hofstra University, where he earned his law degree in 1994. Merchan began his legal career as an assistant district attorney in Manhattan specializing in financial fraud cases. Five years later, he started working in the state attorney general's office. In 2006 Mayor Michael Bloomberg appointed Merchan to be a family court judge in the Bronx. In 2009, he was promoted to his current position as an acting State Supreme Court justice. Merchan often takes on financial cases and oversees a Manhattan mental health court where he has given defendants the opportunity to seek treatment with supervision rather than serving prison sentences.

Merchan has been involved in several high-profile cases during his tenure as a New York Supreme Court justice. Most recently, he presided over the Trump Organization's criminal tax fraud jury trial in which the company was found guilty on 17 counts and fined $1.6 million. During that case, he accepted finance chief Allen Weisselberg's guilty plea and sentenced him to 5 months in jail in exchange for his testimony against the Trump Organization. Other notable trials that Merchan has presided over include the "Soccer Mom Madam" case, in which a suburban mom ran a call girl ring for wealthy New Yorkers on the Upper East Side, as well as a high-profile case in which a man raped and murdered his ex-girlfriend because, according to him, he was cursed by a witch doctor.

Colleagues of Merchan describe him as a fair, thoughtful, and no-nonsense judge who maintains control of his courtroom. Manhattan defense attorney Ron Kuby called him "a serious jurist, smart and even tempered." And Nicholas Gravante, Weisselberg's lawyer in the Trump Organization tax fraud case, said Merchan "was mindful of the role my colleagues and I played as advocates, treating us with the utmost respect both in open court and behind closed doors." He went on to characterize Merchan as "practical, efficient, a real 'listener,' well-prepared and a man who kept his word."

Pretrial proceedings thus far reveal Merchan's skepticism toward some of the Trump team's arguments. At a hearing in mid-February, Merchan promptly denied Trump's motions to dismiss the case and scheduled jury selection to begin on March 25th. Trump's lawyer Todd Blanche protested saying, "the fact that President Trump is now going to spend the next two months working on this trial instead of campaigning is something that shouldn't happen in this country" to which Merchan asked, "What's your legal argument? That is not a legal argument."

THE MANHATTAN DA'S PROSECUTION TEAM

ALVIN BRAGG—BRAGG is the 37th Manhattan District Attorney. Elected in November 2021, he is a Democrat and the first Black person to lead the Manhattan District Attorney's office. Before that, he had a distinguished career as a federal prosecutor and deputy New York attorney general.

Bragg's early life was spent in Harlem, New York, where he was born to a social services worker and a teacher. His educational journey took him to Harvard for both his undergraduate and law degrees, where he emerged as a leader among his peers and contemplated a career in prosecution after observing its impact during his work with a federal judge.

His path to becoming district attorney involved defeating eight other candidates on a progressive platform. Bragg's campaign and policy positions resonated with the progressive prosecutorial movement that seeks to reform the criminal justice system by reducing reliance on incarceration for minor offenses and investing in communities to increase public safety. Despite his progressive stance, Bragg's nuanced policies, informed by his experiences growing up in Harlem, defy simple categorization.

Upon assuming office, Bragg faced immediate challenges and controversies, particularly related to his policy of seeking jail time only for the most serious offenses and his initial hesitance in the Trump investigation. However, he maintained that the investigation into Trump's activities was ongoing, focusing on hush money payments and tax fraud involving Trump's company and CFO Weisselberg.

Bragg has brought together an experienced team of assistant and executive district attorneys to prosecute the case. This team, drawn from diverse legal backgrounds, includes specialists in white-collar-crime and fraud cases.

SUSAN HOFFINGER—HOFFINGER is the executive assistant district attorney and chief of the investigation division, boasts a robust history in white-collar criminal cases, both in prosecution and defense. She is a "leader on the team" and has previously worked on significant tax fraud, securities fraud, and other financial misconduct cases, including co-leading DANY's prosecution of Trump's business.

CHRISTOPHER CONROY—CONROY brings 27 years of experience at the Manhattan DA's office, including time in DANY's frauds and major economic crimes bureaus, and as former chief of the investigations division under Bragg's predecessor, having overseen major cases involving U.S. sanctions violations and falsification of business records. He has been assigned to the case longer than any other team member.

JOSHUA STEINGLASS—STEINGLASS, a 25-year DANY veteran, is one of Bragg's "most experienced trial lawyers." He is currently Bragg's senior trial counsel on the case as he was in DANY's case against the Trump Organization, alongside Hoffinger and others. As assistant DA, he prosecuted members of the Proud Boys for attacking protesters outside the Metropolitan Republican Club in Manhattan as well as leading the investigation into the New York subway homicide of Jordan Neely. Steinglass has already developed a reputation in the case against Trump as one who plays no games, a "fiery" advocate in court, willing to "fiercely" argue the state's case.

MATTHEW COLANGELO—COLANGELO is senior counsel and has a career that spans law, government and the public interest sector, with roles in the NAACP Legal Defense & Educational Fund and the Department of Justice. He joined the team at the end of 2022, bringing a "wealth of economic justice experience combined with complex white-collar investigations," and prior to serving as DOJ acting associate attorney general, he led the New York Attorney's general civil inquiry into Trump.

REBECCA MANGOLD—MANGOLD, an assistant district attorney in the major economic crimes bureau, comes from a private law background with significant experience in financial fraud investigations. She led negotiations with UBS Real Estate Securities Inc. and Bank of America, resulting in the recovery of $850 million for investors related to the subprime mortgage crisis. She joined DANY in 2022 after years in private practice. She clerked in the District of New Jersey from 2011 to 2013.

TRUMP'S DEFENSE TEAM

TODD BLANCHE—BLANCHE is a prominent attorney known for representing high-profile clients. He has a background as a federal prosecutor and a distinguished career in white-collar criminal defense and has been involved in significant legal battles. He has played a central role in Trump's legal team since April 2023: during the former president's arraignment on federal charges related to the mishandling of classified documents, as co-counsel in the Jan. 6 federal case, and is also "the maestro of the defense team" preparing for the Bragg trial.

Before joining Trump's legal team, Blanche served as an

assistant U.S. attorney in the Southern District of New York for close to a decade, where he honed his skills in prosecuting complex cases. He worked at Cadwalader, Wickersham & Taft, an elite New York law firm, departing to focus on representing Trump in the Bragg case. Blanche also represented Paul Manafort, Trump's 2016 presidential campaign manager, and Igor Fruman, an associate of former Trump personal lawyer Rudy Giuliani.

EMIL BOVE—BOVE is a partner at Blanche Law serving on Trump's legal team. He previously worked for nine years as an assistant U.S. attorney in the Southern District of New York where he focused on national security cases. Todd Blanche has described him as "an expert in white collar and CIPA-related litigation," and at Blanche Law he has represented "clients in white-collar criminal and regulatory defense matters, internal investigations, and complex commercial disputes involving civil litigation and arbitration."

SUSAN NECHELES—NECHELES is recognized as one of New York's elite lawyers, representing individuals and corporations across a breadth of government and regulatory investigations as well as at trial. She is a former assistant district attorney in Kings County, New York, and served as the president of the New York Council of Defense Lawyers. A registered Democrat as of 2023, Necheles has played a key role in defending Trump and his businesses. She co-led the defense of the Trump Organization in DA Bragg's 2022 prosecution (with heated exchanges with Assistant DA Steinglass), and her firm received $465,000 from Trump's PAC in the first six months of 2023.

Necheles is an "understated tactician," and her role in the case has been described as the "research person." But she will likely play a key role in advancing the defense case at trial. In the late 1990s, she was counsel to the late Venero Mangano, also known as "Benny Eggs," the underboss of the Genovese crime family. In 2010 she represented New York State Senate Majority leader Pedro Espada (D) in a corruption case that former New York Governor Andrew Cuomo called "the most outrageous abuse of public office I have ever seen." More recently she represented Jeremy Reichberg, a former fundraiser for Mayor Bill de Blasio of New York, who was convicted of bribing New York Police Department officials.

4

KEY STATUTES

Where the previous chapters lay out the key facts, this chapter offers the reader what is the major backbone of the entire case: the law. We lay out the four main relevant statutes, beginning with Falsifying Business Records in the First Degree (New York Penal Law § 175.10), the offense with which DANY charged the former president. We include selected statutory text for sentencing for that crime, under New York's Penal Law (§ 70.00).

Falsifying Business Records in the First Degree requires an "intent to defraud [which] includes an intent to commit another crime or to aid or conceal the commission thereof." That brings us to the remaining statutes we excerpt: three such "other," or "predicate," crimes that DANY will argue to the jury Trump allegedly intended to commit or aid or conceal. They are: Conspiracy to Promote or Prevent Election (New York Election Law § 17-152); violations of the Federal Election Campaign Act (52 U.S.C. § 30109(d)(1)(A); § 30116; § 30118); and violations of New York Tax Fraud Acts (New York Tax Law §§ 1801(a)(3) and 1802).

To further assist readers, we excerpt from Justice Juan Merchan's analysis in his Feb. 15, 2024 decision and order *regarding how these four statutes allegedly apply. We situate his passages next to each relevant statute to highlight the controlling explication of the law for the trial.*

Falsifying Business Records in the First Degree

New York Penal Law § 175.10:

A person is guilty of falsifying business records in the first degree when he commits the crime of falsifying business records in the second degree, and when his intent to defraud includes an intent to commit another crime or to aid or conceal the commission thereof.

Falsifying business records in the first degree is a class E felony.

JUSTICE MERCHAN'S ANALYSIS OF § 175.10:

"Intent to defraud" is not defined within that section [PL § 15.00]. However, courts in the First Department have interpreted this culpable mental state broadly. *See People v. Kase*,76 AD2d 532 [1st Dept 1980], *aff'd*,53 NY2d 989 [1981]; *People v. Sosa-Campana*, 167 AD3d 464 [1st Dept 2018]; *Khahl*, 73 AD3d at 509...

Intent to defraud is not constricted to an intent to deprive another of property or money. In fact, "intent to defraud" can extend beyond economic concern. *People v. Headley* 37 Misc3d 815, 829 [Sup Ct, Kings County 2012]; *People v. Schrag*, 147 Misc 2d 517 [Rockland County Ct. 1990]. "Nor is there any requirement that a defendant intend to conceal the commission of *his own* crime; instead, 'a person can commit First Degree Falsifying Business Records by falsifying records with the intent to cover up a crime committed by somebody else.'" People's Opposition at pg. 22, *citing to People v. Dove*, 15 Misc3d 1134(A), *judgment aff'd*, 85 AD3d 547 [1st Dept 2011]; *People v. Fuschino*, 278 AD2d 657 [3rd Dept 2000]...

The term "business records" is defined in PL § 175.00 as "any writing or article, including computer data or a computer program, kept or maintained by an enterprise for the purpose of evidencing or reflecting its condition or activity." PL § 175.00(2). The definition for "business records," is not a narrow one as there are a wide array of factors that courts consider...

Falsifying Business Records in the First Degree requires that a defendant have the intent to commit "another crime or to aid or conceal the commission there-of." Thus, the statute does not require a defendant to actually be convicted of the "other crime," but merely that he *intend* to commit another crime. *People v. McCumiskey* 12 AD3d 1145 [2004]. This element of PL § 175.10 is satisfied so long as the Defendant intended to commit *or* conceal the "other crime." *People v. Houghtaling*, 79 AD3d 1155 [3d Dept 2010]. The focus here is on the element of *intent*. [Emphasis in original.]

Conspiracy to Promote or Prevent Election

New York Election Law § 17-152:

Any two or more persons who conspire to promote or prevent the election of any person to a public office by unlawful means and which conspiracy is acted upon by one or more of the parties thereto, shall be guilty of a misdemeanor.

JUSTICE MERCHAN'S Analysis of NYEL § 17-152:

Defendant's argument that N.Y. Election Law § 17-152 is not an object offense under PL § 175.10 fails. Specifically, Defendant claims that because the allegation is that he tampered with the 2016 *presidential* election, then N.Y. Election Law § 17-152 is not applicable because its application is limited to elections for "public office," a term which Defendant claims does not include federal elections. [Emphasis in original.]

New York Election Law § 1-102, titled "Applicability of Chapter," explicitly states "[T]his chapter shall govern the conduct of *all* elections at which voters of the state of New York may cast a ballot for the purpose of electing an individual to any party position or nominating or electing an individual to any federal, state, county, city, town or village office..." (emphasis added [by Justice Merchan]). It is clear from the text of § 1-102 that the New York Election Law applies to ballots cast for any election. including federal. The "principal objective of the Election Lew is to give the electorate a full and fair opportunity to express its choice among the candidates presented." *Limpert v. Brandt*, 165 AD3d, 1469 [3d Dept 2018] *citing to Reda v. Mehile*, 197 AD.2d 723 [1993]. This Court is hard pressed to find and indeed cannot, that federal elections are not included in the statute's principal objective.

...[The] argument, that N.Y. Election Law § 17-152 is preempted by federal law, is also unsuccessful. As Judge Hellerstein reasoned in *People v. Trump*, 2023 WL 4614689 [S.D.N.Y 2023] when he was presented with the same argument by this Defendant, N.Y. Election Law § 17-152 'does not fit into any of the three categories of state law that FECA preempts.' *People v. Trump*, 2023 WL 4614689 at 11.

This Court agrees and follows Judge Hellerstein's decision. Since FECA does not affect the states' rights to pass laws concerning voter fraud and ballot theft, there is no preemption by FECA in this matter. *Id.*

Federal Election Campaign Act

52 U.S.C.§ 30109(d)(1)(A):

(d) Penalties; defenses; mitigation of offenses

(1) (A) Any person who knowingly and willfully commits a violation of any provision of this Act which involves the making, receiving, or reporting of any contribution, donation, or expenditure—

(i) aggregating $25,000 or more during a calendar year shall be fined under title 18, or imprisoned for not more than 5 years, or both; or

(ii) aggregating $2,000 or more (but less than $25,000) during a calendar year shall be fined under such title, or imprisoned for not more than 1 year, or both.

52 U.S.C. § 30116(a)(1)(A):

(a) Dollar limits on contributions

(1) Except as provided in subsection (i) and section 30117 of this title, no person shall make contributions—

(A) to any candidate and his authorized political committees with respect to any election for Federal office which, in the aggregate, exceed $2,000....

52 U.S.C. § 30118(a):

(a) In general it is unlawful for any national bank, or any corporation organized by authority of any law of Congress, to make a contribution or expenditure in connection with any election to any political office, or in connection with any primary election or political convention or caucus held to select candidates for any political office, or for any corporation whatever, or any labor organization, to make a contribution or expenditure in connection with any election at which presidential and vice presidential electors or a Senator or Representative in, or a Delegate or Resident Commissioner to, Congress are to be voted for, or in connection with any primary election or political convention or caucus held to select candidates for any of the foregoing offices, or for any candidate, political committee, or other person knowingly to accept or receive any contribution prohibited by this section, or any officer or any director of any corporation or any national bank or any officer of any labor organization to consent to any contribution or expenditure by the corporation, national bank, or labor organization, as the case may be, prohibited by this section.

JUSTICE MERCHAN'S Analysis of FECA:

The People disagree that a FECA violation cannot satisfy the "other crime," element and submit that Defendant's reliance on *Witherspoon* is misplaced. The People stress that *Witherspoon* expressly limited its holding to the construction of the phrase "any crime" within the context of CPL Section 160.59. This Court agrees and further finds that CPL section 160.59(3)(f) has no application to the issue presented before this Court...

This Court finds that there was legally sufficient evidence presented to the Grand Jury of the Defendant's intent to violate FECA. It is a crime under FECA for any person to make contributions to any candidate seeking election to federal office, and his authorized political committees, which exceeds $2,000 during a single calendar year.

Tax Fraud Acts

New York Tax Law §§ 1801(a)(3) and 1802:

§ 1801. Tax fraud acts. (a) As used in this article, "tax fraud act" means willfully engaging in an act or acts or willfully causing another to engage in an act or acts pursuant to which a person...

(3) knowingly supplies or submits materially false or fraudulent information in connection with any return, audit, investigation, or proceeding or fails to supply information within the time required by or under the provisions of this chapter or any regulation promulgated under this chapter....

§ 1802. Criminal tax fraud in the fifth degree. A person commits criminal tax fraud in the fifth degree when he or she commits a tax fraud act. Criminal tax fraud in the fifth degree is a class A misdemeanor.

JUSTICE MERCHAN's Analysis of New York Tax Law:

This Court disagrees that the alleged New York State tax violation is of no consequence because the State of New York did not suffer any financial harm. This argument does not require further analysis.

PART II

A GUIDE TO PRETRIAL, TRIAL, AND SENTENCING

In Chapter 5, we explain the pretrial proceedings—the key rulings by the court to prepare and present the case to a jury, as well as the jury selection process and the likely composition of the jury.

Chapter 6 covers trial proceedings from opening statements to the prosecution and defense cases.

When all of that concludes, the jury will be instructed on the law and on how to apply it, and Chapter 7 presents the likely jury instructions.

In Chapter 8, we assess post-trial outcomes, addressing sentencing. We explain why we think conviction and a sentence of incarceration are likely, although Trump must of course be considered innocent until proven guilty.

5

FROM INDICTMENT TO JURY SELECTION

This essay is excerpted from "A Complete Guide to the Manhattan Trump Election Interference Prosecution," which was published by Norm Eisen, Andrew Warren and Siven Watt in Just Security on March 27, 2024. The numbering and content have been modified since its original publication. As in the original, answers are numbered for ease of reference.

INTRODUCTION

1. Is the Case Weak or Strong?

From an outside perspective, it appears that DANY has built a robust case along a narrowly-tailored theory of prosecution: falsifying business records to conceal criminal conduct that hid damaging information during the 2016 presidential campaign. Despite the historical significance of being the first indictment of a former president, the core allegations of falsifying business records are routine. As we detail below, the Manhattan DA has brought many of these cases over the years, including for covert payments made to benefit political campaigns. Thus, while having a former president as the defendant may be novel, prosecuting this type of conduct is not.

Despite early and ongoing skepticism of DANY's case that met and followed the indictment, we view it as strong because prosecutors will likely establish with relative ease three of the four corners of the alleged crimes. Those three are the "catch and kill" scheme, the payment to Daniels to bury the story of the affair, and the paper trail of reimbursements and records that mischaracterized and concealed the nature of the hush payment. As one commentator wrote, "the spine of the case is the paper trail of the money, [and] Bragg will be bringing the receipts to trial."

The fourth corner of the scheme is Trump's intent to commit or conceal another crime, as the law requires for the charges to be elevated to the felony first-degree falsification of business records. DANY will have to prove that Trump intended to commit or conceal campaign finance violations (state or federal) or tax violations. Proving this intent will be more difficult than proving the objective facts (as it almost always is), but as discussed in more detail below, DANY appears to have the upper hand.

Some observers and the defendant—who denies all wrongdoing—have criticized the case. That includes characterizing it as unlikely to succeed because it is too political or legally convoluted. But as the editor has previously written, those criticisms are misplaced. Ultimately, barring any major surprises at trial, DANY will likely be able to convince a unanimous jury of the 34 charges. We explain below (Questions 27, 28, and 33) much more about why, including why Trump's defenses will likely fail.

Others have criticized DANY for being too slow to charge the alleged misconduct, which dates from 2016 and 2017. But it took several years for the evidence of possible wrongdoing fully to emerge. An initial subpoena to Trump was issued by Bragg's predecessor in 2019, and Trump fought it for years, including multiple trips to the U.S. Supreme Court. After Bragg was elected in 2022, he first successfully prosecuted the Trump Organization, along with its CFO Allen Weisselberg, for a criminal financial scheme. He simultaneously evaluated the instant case and brought it a little more than a year after taking office and within the statute of limitations. That is not an inordinate delay, as Justice Merchan already has ruled.

Others claim the charges brought against Trump—for falsifying New York business records—are unusual. Not so. They are in Bragg's words, the "bread and butter" of his office's "white collar work." DANY's record of prosecuting felony falsification of business goes far beyond prosecuting Trump businesses. When Bragg first charged Trump in April 2023, he stated that in his 14 months in office he had already prosecuted 117 felony counts of falsifying business records against 29 individuals and companies. During the 10 years from March 2013 to March 2023, the office prosecuted 437 such cases. Moreover, DAs across the state of New York frequently charge defendants with felony falsification of business records. Reports in April 2023 stated, "Data shows 9,794 cases involving state penal law 175.10, or falsifying business records in the first degree, have been arraigned in both local and superior New York state courts since 2015."

Previous Just Security analysis found that use of the statute is "commonplace and has been used by New York district attorneys' offices across the state to hold to account a breadth of criminal behavior from the more petty and simple to the more serious and highly organized." In fact, an additional Just Security analysis found that falsification of business records has previously been charged, as here, in the context of political campaign violations, some of which were "important" and "closely analogous." Take for instance former New York State Assemblyman Clarence Norman who was convicted in 2005 of falsifying business records in connection with campaign finance violations following two separate trials. Some years later, in 2018, Richard Brega, a transportation executive, pleaded guilty to one count of felony falsifying business records for his misrepresenting to the New York State Board of Elections the source of funds that he funneled into a county executive campaign. That same year Richard Luthmann was arraigned for multiple felony charges including falsifying business records and election law violations after he impersonated New York political figures on social media in an attempt to influence campaigns in 2015 and 2016; he subsequently pleaded guilty. These cases, as the editor of this book wrote for *The New York Times*, show that Bragg "is not navigating uncharted waters."

PRETRIAL PROCEEDINGS AND LOGISTICS

2. What Happened on Removal?

First, DANY defeated Trump's attempt to litigate the case in federal court. On May 4, 2023, Trump initially removed the case to federal court, claiming that the charged conduct occurred while he was president and was part of his official responsibilities. In support of removal, Trump claimed immunity on the basis that out of constitutional concerns for his duties as president, he placed his business in a trust and hired Cohen to handle his personal affairs to keep his personal affairs separate from his public duties.

Following a June 27, 2023 hearing, on July 19, 2023 U.S District Court Judge Alvin Hellerstein granted DANY's motion to remand the case back to state court. Judge Hellerstein ruled that Trump failed to establish that the alleged conduct had any connection to his official duties as president. To the contrary, the court wrote, "The evidence overwhelmingly suggests that the matter was a purely personal item of the President—a cover-up of an embarrassing event. Hush money paid to an adult film star is not related to a President's official acts. It does not reflect in any way the color of the President's official duties." In denying that Trump had raised a colorable immunity defense,[1] the court explained in the same ruling:

Reimbursing Cohen for advancing hush money to Stephanie Clifford cannot be considered the performance of a constitutional duty. Falsifying business records to hide such reimbursement, and to transform the reimbursement into a business expense for Trump and income to Cohen, likewise does not relate to a presidential duty.

3. What Happened on Preemption?

DANY also defeated Trump's claim that federal election law preempts New York's state jurisdiction. Trump raised this defense as part of his attempt to remove the case, claiming that the charges against him are based on alleged violations of state and federal election laws and are therefore preempted by the Federal Election Campaign Act (FECA). As the editor of this guide explained:

Federal preemption refers to the circumstance where federal law renders a state law unenforceable. The Supremacy Clause of the United States Constitution makes federal law 'the supreme Law of the Land.' As a result, when there's some irreconcilable conflict between state and federal law (conflict preemption), when Congress' legislation of an area of law is sufficiently pervasive (field preemption), or even when Congress just says so (express preemption), the federal law wins and the state law is unenforceable.

Rejecting Trump's argument, Judge Hellerstein found, "The Indictment does not intrude on FECA's domain." The judge found that the case centered on document falsification, and that collateral impact of the kind presented here on a federal election failed to constitute a sufficient basis for federal preemption of state criminal charges. After a lengthy analysis of applicable cases and other authorities, he concluded that the "mere fact that Trump is alleged to have engaged in fraudulent conduct with respect to a federal election is not a basis for preemption." Trump ultimately chose to abandon his appeal of Hellerstein's ruling.

4. What Happened on Motions to Dismiss?

DANY's next significant pretrial victory was largely defeating Trump's various motions to dismiss after the case returned to state court.

In September 2023, Trump filed omnibus motions to dismiss the charges, which DANY opposed in November (Trump replied in support weeks later). Trump raised several grounds to dismiss: (1) pre-indictment delay; (2) the records in question are not records of a business enterprise but rather records of Trump personally and his revocable trust; (3) the indictment lacked a viable object offense to justify the first-degree falsification of records; (4) insufficient evidence of an intent to defraud; (5) selective prosecution; (6) statute of limitations violations; and (7) multiplicity, i.e., that the indictment charges the same crime in different counts. In his omnibus filing, Trump also sought that DANY provide additional particulars to its case, asked to inspect the grand jury minutes and for a hearing on alleged violations of grand jury secrecy, and argued that DANY was not complying with its discovery obligations.

On Feb. 15, Justice Merchan announced from the bench during a pretrial hearing that he had denied Trump's motion to dismiss. Later that day, he issued an order in which Trump lost on all but a few points. While "broadly advancing" DANY's theory of the case, the court found:

- There were "legitimate reasons" for the delay in bringing the case, namely the preceding federal investigation and a lawsuit that Trump initiated over a subpoena for tax records.

- The invoices, checks, and general ledger entries underlying the 34 counts are business records of an "enterprise," as that term is broadly defined to include any person or group engaged in an organized activity for which records are kept. The payments made to Cohen "'exemplify the intermingling of the Trump Organization's business records and Defendant's purportedly personal expenses.'"

- There were three viable "object offenses"— violations of FECA; violations of New York election law; and violation of New York tax law—

and there was sufficient evidence of each presented to the grand jury. However, the court sided with Trump in finding that there was insufficient evidence to support Trump's intent to falsify business records outside of the Trump Organization. The Court explained it was not deciding whether Trump knew about the falsification of AMI's and Cohen's records but rather that was "not convinced that this particular theory fits into the 'other crime' element" of the law, but instead is "intertwined and advances" the election and tax crimes.

- There was no evidence of selective prosecution because DANY had previously charged other defendants with the same falsification of records offenses, and because Trump failed to show he was treated any differently than other defendants for whom there was probable cause of committing that crime.

- There was no statute of limitations violation. Although the charges were brought more than the usual five-year statute of limitations for falsification of records, an executive order issued by the Governor of New York during COVID tolled the five-year period as a matter of law.

- There was no violation for multiplicity because each count is based on a separate false entry that legally supports a different crime.

Additionally, the court granted Trump's motion to inspect grand jury minutes, precluded DANY from advancing falsification of business records as the possible "other crime" for felony purposes, and precluded DANY from introducing any new or different "other crime" theories. The court also denied Trump's request for a hearing on grand jury secrecy, did not require DANY to produce a bill of particulars, and declined to strike DANY's certificates of compliance with its discovery obligations.

For now, Trump cannot relitigate the denial of his motions to dismiss, unless and until he is convicted of these crimes and appeals the conviction. In terms of evidence and argument at trial, as discussed at Question 16, Trump filed motions *in limine* seeking to limit how DANY could prove the object offenses and that Trump's personal and trust records constitute business records. On the former, he lost on all but a few minor points, and on the latter, the court made clear that it had already rejected those arguments. At the same time, DANY sought to block Trump from introducing evidence of the legal defenses the court had already rejected, and the court agreed with DANY on that matter.

Trump could again raise on appeal the validity of the indictment and other issues, but that would be after trial and following a possible conviction.

Other pending motions are addressed below at Question 6 (motions to dismiss and adjourn based on discovery violations), Question 15 (limiting Trump's extrajudicial statements), and Question 35 (motions to dismiss and adjourn based on presidential immunity).

5. Didn't a Former Prosecutor Quit the Case and Criticize It?

Justice Merchan's ruling on the motions to dismiss was also notable because it resolved legal questions that had been raised by a former prosecutor on the case after he resigned.

- In a book he released just weeks before the indictment, Former Special Assistant District Attorney Mark Pomerantz questioned whether felony falsifying business records charges could be supported by an intent to commit other crimes. Pomerantz, who had not worked at DANY prior to this case, helped lead the investigation into Trump until early 2023, an investigation he referred to as "the Zombie case" because it "opened and shut so many times."

- According to Pomerantz, DANY's concern was the theory of criminality relied on untested legal strategies—creating a "gnarly legal question" about whether the court would dismiss the charges on a technicality.

- Pomerantz's "zombie" comment has been cited "countless" times by the defense, including in support of Trump's now rejected argument that DANY has failed to establish predicate crimes necessary to bring felony charges. DA Bragg, commentators including one of the authors of this essay, and now Justice Merchan have strongly disagreed.

- The judge dismissed Trump's arguments that the prosecution failed to establish an intent to commit violations of state and federal law in recognizing three object crimes, federal campaign finance law, state election law and state tax law.

- In denying Trump's motions to dismiss, Justice Merchan also rejected efforts to utilize the Pomerantz book to argue selective prosecution.

- The court noted that in pressing this argument, Trump had "relie[d] primarily on the comments of" Pomerantz to establish that his book had pressured Bragg to bring a "zombie case." The court made short shrift of the allegation as "strain[ing] credulity." DANY's own opposition (pp. 52-55), surreply (pp. 3-4) and public statements to the allegation have made clear that prior to 2023, at the time Pomerantz was adamant that DANY bring charges, the case was not ready. "I bring hard cases when they are ready," DA Bragg said in retort to Pomerantz's book.
- Pomerantz himself later said that there was "nothing in this book that should prejudice this prosecution. The book has nothing to do with the facts and the law on which a case has to be decided. So, the book is meaningless—it doesn't provide any kind of defense."

6. Why Was the Original March 25, 2024 Start of the Trial Delayed Until April 15?

Jury selection was slated to begin on March 25, 2024, but the trial was postponed when a large volume of documents was produced by federal prosecutors in response to a subpoena by Trump. On March 15, 2024, the court adjourned the case for 30 days—at least until April 15—to address alleged discovery violations that Trump raised. The court scheduled a hearing for March 25 to address the discovery issues. At the hearing, Justice Merchan decided in favor of DANY and ruled that no further delays were in order. He set jury selection to begin on April 15.

On March 8, Trump had filed a letter with the court

seeking permission to file a motion to dismiss the indictment, or alternatively preclude Stormy Daniels and Michael
Cohen from testifying, and adjourn the trial for at least 90
days, as a result of DANY's alleged discovery violations.[2]
The gist of Trump's motion was that DANY "engaged in
widespread misconduct" involving (1) "attempts to suppress"
the production of voluminous materials by the United
States Attorney's Office for the Southern District of New
York (USAO-SDNY); (2) eleventh-hour productions of
discoverable information related to Cohen and Daniels; (3)
untimely notice of a rebuttal expert; and (4) unnecessary
redactions.

On March 4, USAO-SDNY produced over 73,000 pages
of materials to Trump, and it then produced another 31,000
pages on March 13. These productions occurred in response
to a subpoena Trump had issued to USAO-SDNY in January
2024. Trump contended that the last-minute production of
such a large volume of discovery material requires, at a
minimum, an adjournment of trial to give Trump and his
team sufficient time to review these records. Although
USAO-SDNY, not DANY, produced these materials, Trump
argued that Bragg's office is responsible for the late production, in part, because it obstructed Trump from obtaining
these records by contesting subpoenas Trump issued in
2023.

Trump also asserted a discovery violation for DANY
producing a small volume of materials regarding Cohen and
Daniels over the past month. The materials contain
impeachment materials against both witnesses, including
information pertaining to a documentary about Daniels
that NBCUniversal announced on March 7 was to be
released on March 18, one week before the scheduled trial
date. Trump claimed DANY acted in bad faith in not

disclosing this information earlier and argued that, in combination with the USAO-SDNY production, the court should dismiss the indictment. If the court did not dismiss the case, Trump asked for the court to preclude all of Cohen's and Daniels' testimony, essentially reasserting arguments from his motions *in limine* about barring Cohen and Daniels that were rejected as discussed at Question 16.

Trump also sought to preclude certain testimony from an expert witness named Adav Noti. DANY disclosed Noti as a rebuttal witness to Trump's intent to call former Federal Elections Commissioner Bradley Smith, as well as to testify about agreements between Cohen, AMI, and Pecker with other federal agencies concerning election law violations. Trump's motion claimed DANY's notice of Noti was untimely as it occurred after the deadline for motions *in limine* and that the subject of those agreements was improper. As discussed at Question 16, Smith's testimony was allowed but sharply curtailed by the judge in ruling on the motions *in limine*, and we anticipate that Merchan will allow similarly curtailed rebuttal testimony from Noti. For the remainder, Trump is essentially reasserting arguments from his motions *in limine* that were rejected.

On March 14, DANY submitted an initial response to Trump's motion, agreeing to a 30-day adjournment and asking until March 18 to respond in full. DANY explained the timing of the USAO-SDNY production was largely Trump's fault and that, based on its current but ongoing review on production, all but a few hundred pages of the 73,000 page production (as of that time) were irrelevant.

In its March 15 ruling, the court gave DANY until March 18 to respond and ordered the parties by March 21 to submit a detailed timeline of events related to the document requests and productions. On March 18, DANY filed its opposition to Trump's motion vis-à-vis USAO-SDNY's production, arguing that there was no discovery violation, that there were only "an estimated 270 documents" that were relevant and new (related to Cohen) in the March 13 production of approximately 31,000 pages, which could easily be reviewed within the 30-day adjournment already granted, and were in any case mostly "inculpatory." DANY noted facts that suggest USAO-SDNY was dilatory. For instance, data from Cohen's phone was sought in January and February 2023 but the USAO-SDNY "declined" to turn over the information "because it would be unduly burdensome." DANY also noted that its review was ongoing and it was "still in the process of determining how many relevant, undisclosed documents were within the information sources the USAO previously declined to provide." That said, DANY contended the responsibility lay with Trump's "own inexplicable and strategic delay," not DANY or USAO-SDNY, "independent prosecutorial" entities operating in "good faith."

DANY also filed a separate opposition to Trump's other discovery arguments on untimely production of discoverable information related to Cohen and Daniel, and untimely notice of a rebuttal expert. DANY argued that Trump's "grab-bag of meritless discovery arguments" is nothing but the latest tactic in trying to delay his trial and evade accountability. They stated, "Enough is enough. These tactics by defendant and defense counsel should be stopped." Trump's motion focused on alleged discovery violations from summer 2023 and should be procedurally barred, DANY said, and, in any case, lacks merit. On the NBCUniversal documentary, DANY made clear that it acted diligently, and repeatedly reached out to the production company, issuing a subpoena on Feb. 6, which was responded to on March 1, and handed over to the defense on the next business day, March 4. Responding to Trump's allegation that DANY worked with Daniels to "hide" the release of her upcoming documentary and time its release to impact the jury pool, DANY stated that it was totally "false and nonsensical." Neither DANY nor Daniels controlled the release date of the documentary, and, quite contrary to concealing the documentary, DANY turned it over to Trump soon after receiving it. In any case, so long as there is not bad faith involved, DANY argued it was under no "duty to seek out and disclose information concerning a private contract between a potential witness and a publisher," but did so anyway, in the interests of openness.

And finally, making short work of Trump's argument that notice of disclosure of expert Noti was untimely or "strategically timed" to fall after Trump's deadline to respond to motions *in limine*, DANY made clear that Trump had consented to a March 1 deadline for such notice. DANY also said the issue was likely mooted by the court's ruling on a pretrial motion limiting the scope of former FCC Commissioner Smith, whom Trump intends to call (discussed at Question 16).

At the March 25 hearing, the court agreed with DANY's arguments, rejected Trump's requested relief, and set trial for April 15. From the beginning of the hearing, Justice Merchan appeared skeptical of Trump's claims of prosecutorial misconduct. He immediately questioned Trump's attorneys about their claims coming on the eve of trial, noting that they waited until two months before trial to request the documents and then failed to raise the issue with the court at the Feb. 15 hearing. The court engaged in a contentious back-and-forth with Trump's attorney about whether documents in USAO-SDNY's possession are under

DANY's custody and control. Justice Merchan said, "You are literally accusing the Manhattan DA's office and the people assigned to this case of prosecutorial misconduct… and you don't have a single [case] citation to support that allegation that the USAO is under the DA's control." He also said the defense has alleged "incredibly serious, unbelievably serious" allegations of misconduct against the prosecutors and had accused "me of being complicit in it" without factual or legal support, which was "disconcerting." The court found DANY "went so far above and beyond" in producing evidence that "it's odd that we're even here taking this time."

The judge also questioned the parties about the universe of relevant documents in USAO-SDNY's over-150,000-page production. DANY estimated there were approximately 300 relevant documents, "almost exclusively cumulative and in our view inculpatory." Trump's lawyers claimed there were "thousands and thousands" after initially not satisfactorily answering the court's questions. Ultimately, the court concluded, "The defendant has been given a reasonable amount of time to prepare" and ordered the trial to begin with jury selection on April 15.

At the end of the hearing, Trump's attorney asked to file a motion to delay the trial because of pretrial publicity. The court said it would allow the motion and give DANY one week to respond, before concluding with, "That's fine. See you all on the 15th."

THE COURTHOUSE

7. Can the Public Watch?

Like with all criminal trials, and as guaranteed by the Constitution, the court is open to the public. However, the trial will not be televised, as New York prohibits audio-visual coverage of trials and other court proceedings that involve witness testimony.

The trial will occur at the Manhattan Criminal Court-house, at 100 Centre Street, courtroom 59, located on the 15th floor. The trial will be open to the public, including jury selection. Due to limited space, the court used overflow courtrooms for earlier proceedings where people could watch remotely. Expect the court to do the same for trial.

8. How Does the Press Get Access to the Court?

To be eligible to receive a temporary press credential, an applicant must be a member of the media who will be covering the trial, in person, either for the duration or on a day-by-day basis.

Applicants need to submit a copy of a valid U.S. Government-issued photo ID along with a letter, on letterhead, from the organization where the coverage will appear. Free-lance reporters must have an accredited news organization or agency affirmatively ensure that they are employing the applicant to cover the trial. The letter along with a legible copy of the valid ID may be scanned and emailed to publicinformation@nycourts.gov.

Members of the media who already possess a valid NYPD Working Press Card with their photo on it, not a reserve/pool card, or a New York State Unified Court System SECURE Pass, do not need to apply for this card.

Use of laptops, tablets, iPads, iPhones, and the like inside the courtroom during the trial is at the sole discretion of the presiding judge.

VENUE

9. Will Trump Try to Move the Trial to a Different County in New York?

On April 8, 2024, Trump's attorney Blanche asked for a change of venue, citing jury fairness concerns. Under New York Criminal Procedure Law (NY CPL) § 230.20, the appellate division (not the trial court) hears and decides a motion to change venue. This is rarely granted, especially when much of the press coverage is caused by the defendant himself. Indeed, the venue change was summarily denied the same day by Associate Justice Lizbeth González of the Appellate Division, First Department (which as we explain below hears venue motions).

10. What Happens if There is a Change of Venue?

Under NY CPL § 230.20, there are two options. One is for the trial to be sent to another court in another county. The other option is that the trial stays in the current county but the jury pool is expanded to include jurors from contiguous counties. In choosing between the two options, the appellate court "shall consider, among other factors, the hardship on potential jurors and the potential depletion of a county's qualified juror list that may result from an order expanding the jury pool."

11. What's the Legal Standard?

To grant a venue change, the appellate court must be satisfied that there is "reasonable cause to believe that a fair and impartial trial cannot be had" in the county where the case is pending.

A "pretrial change of venue for the purpose of protecting the right to a fair trial is an extraordinary remedy reserved for the rarest of cases." People v. Boss, 261 A.D.2d 1, 701 N.Y.S.2d 342 (N.Y. App. Div. 1999). "[S]ubstantial foundation... must be laid in order for the motion to be successful." McKinney, NY CPL § 230.20.

Motions to change venue often focus on the jury pool, arguing that the publicity in the case would cause the defendant to have an unfair trial. Essentially, the issue is "whether the jury panel was unduly tainted as a consequence of a barrage of publicity such that the jurors could not fairly deliberate on the question of the defendant's guilt." McKinney, NY CPL § 230.20. Changing venue "is a means of preventing" a trial from being "dominated by a 'wave of public passion' (Irvin v. Dowd, 366 U.S. 717, 728, 81 S.Ct. 1639, 6 L.Ed.2d 751),... overwhelmed by press coverage (Murphy v. Florida, 421 U.S. 794, 798, 95 S.Ct. 2031, 44 L.Ed.2d 589),... conducted in a 'carnival atmosphere' (Sheppard v. Maxwell, 384 U.S. 333, 338, 86 S.Ct. 1507, 16 L.Ed.2d 600)." People v. Boss, 261 A.D.2d 1, 701 N.Y.S.2d 342 (N.Y. App. Div. 1999).

There is "no bright-line test which requires change of venue based solely on fact that fixed percentage of veniremen have expressed preconceived opinion about [the] case; rather, what is required is examination of totality of circumstances to determine whether pretrial publicity has so permeated community as to render it impossible to obtain fair and impartial trial." McKinney, NY CPL § 230.20 citing People v. Ryan, 151 A.D.2d 528, 542 N.Y.S.2d 665 (N.Y. App. Div. 1989).

Relevant considerations are whether the publicity is accurate as to the facts or instead of such a "sensational character as to excite local popular passion and prejudice." McKinney, NY CPL § 230.20. With a change of venue motion in mind, during voir dire defense counsel should "specifically inquire [of jurors] about what they learned about the case from the media, when they learned about the case and whether those reports influenced the jurors' opinions about the case." *Id*. Defense counsel will likely ask the court for individualized questioning of prospective jurors. *Id*.

In this case, there will be an issue as to whether any unfairness allegedly caused to Trump by pretrial publicity can be mitigated by a change of venue. There is a strong public policy however not to incentivize a defendant to forum shop by causing the very publicity he is complaining about. Additionally, it is unlikely that jurors in other boroughs have heard about Trump less, given the global nature of the coverage.

12. Can Trump Change the Venue by Claiming That Justice Merchan is Biased?

Probably not. Judicial bias can be used to support a motion for a change of venue, and courts have identified the lack of judicial bias as a reason for denying a change. See People v. McClary, 150 A.D.2d 631 (N.Y. App. Div. 1989). However, for a party claiming judicial bias, the "correct procedure to obtain relief sought would be for [the] defendant to move for [the] trial judge to disqualify himself. People v Blake, 133 A.D.2d 549, 520 N.Y.S.2d 92, 1987 N.Y. App. Div. LEXIS 50085 (N.Y. App. Div. 4th Dep't 1987)." McKinney, NY CPL § 230.20.

13. When Does Trump Need to File a Motion to Change Venue?

Typically a party will move to change venue based on juror fairness after jury selection. A party can try to change venue before jury selection, but pre-voir dire motions are very difficult to win. They are "almost never granted[;] the motion bears a significantly heavy burden." McKinney, NY CPL § 230.20. The publicity must have created "a deep and abiding resentment" in the county in which the prosecution is pending. People v. Boudin, 90 A.D.2d 253, 457 N.Y.S.2d 302 (N.Y. App. Div. 1982). Usually, a defendant seeking a change of venue will use the jury selection process to build an evidentiary record to show that he cannot obtain a fair trial.

Trump may file a motion to change venue before jury selection and then, if the court denies the motion, renew the motion after jury selection using examples from the selection process to support his motion.

14. Will the Trial Be Stayed While Trump Seeks a Venue Change?

Not automatically. But under NY CPL § 230.30(1), Merchan "may, in his discretion and for good cause shown, order that the trial... be stayed" for no longer than 30 days "from the issuance of such order." "Such an order may be issued only upon an application made in writing and after reasonable notice and opportunity to be heard has been accorded the other party." NY CPL § 230.30(2). If Merchan had denied the application, Trump could not renew his application "to any other such justice."

If Merchan had ordered a stay, "no further proceedings may be had" before him until Trump's motion is determined by the appellate division or if Trump fails to file a motion by the deadline. NY CPL § 230.30(2). In this case, Trump's venue motion was denied by the First Department, so there will be no stay.

OTHER PRETRIAL MATTERS

15. Is There a Gag Order in Place?

Yes. On March 26, 2024, the court imposed a narrowly tailored gag order that prohibited Trump from making or directing others to make public statements about witnesses, counsel other than DA Bragg or their families, court staff or their families, and jurors. The penalties for violation of a gag or any other order of the court can include fines and even confinement. The gag order closely tracked the one adopted by the DC Circuit in the federal election interference case against Trump, here with the additional protection for jurors. On April 1, following Trump's social media posts attacking Justice Merchan's daughter, the court amended its March 26 order, at the request of DANY, to include the family members of Merchan and DA Bragg, and formally put Trump on notice that he will forfeit his statutory right to access juror names if he engages "in any conduct that threatens the safety and integrity of the jury or the jury selection process."

The court's March 26 order granted in substantial part a pretrial motion filed by DANY in February 2024, which contended that Trump's "[a]dvocacy of revenge and retribution against perceived opponents" justifies such an order. The motion cataloged Trump's long history of verbally attacking people involved in legal proceedings against him and his allies, offering examples from this case, the DC federal criminal prosecution, the Georgia state prosecution, the NY civil fraud case, and the prosecution of Roger Stone.

In granting the motion, Justice Merchan rejected Trump's argument that as the presumptive Republican nominee for president, he needs to be able to respond to political attacks and "criticize these public figures." The judge found that Trump's history of extrajudicial statements "went far beyond defending himself against 'attacks' by 'public figures,'" and included "threatening, inflammatory, denigrating" statements targeting local officials, prosecutors, court staff, and juror "performing their civic duty." The court concluded that these types of statements "undoubtedly risk impeding the orderly administration" of the court, with no less restrictive means to guard against that risk short of a limited gag order.

Within days of Justice Merchan's March 26 gag order, DANY filed a pre-motion letter asking the court to clarify or confirm that its order contemplated family members of Justice Merchan and DA Bragg. DANY later filed a supplemental brief in support of its March 28 letter requesting clarification and asked the court revisit and grant its Feb. 22 request to expressly warn Trump that he would forfeit any statutory right he may have to access juror names if he continued harassing or disruptive conduct. Trump opposed, arguing that the current order did not include the family members of Merchan or Bragg.

The court's order, as amended, is consistent with New

York and U.S. Supreme Court law, which in order to protect the administration of justice, allow a court to restrict a party's extrajudicial speech that is "substantially likely to have a materially prejudicial effect" or that presents a "'reasonable likelihood' of a serious and imminent threat" to the integrity of the trial.

In Trump's New York civil fraud trial, Manhattan Supreme Court Justice Arthur Engoron implemented a narrow gag order prohibiting Trump from commenting about court staff in response to the ex-president's repeated criticisms of one of Engoron's clerks. A New York appellate court upheld the decision. In the D.C. prosecution, the federal appellate court largely upheld district court Judge Tanya Chutkan's gag order prohibiting Trump from comments about known witnesses.

The gag order, as amended, compliments a protective order from May 2023 in which Justice Merchan granted DANY's motion to prohibit Trump from disclosing on social media any discovery the defense received from the prosecution as well as barring disclosure of names and identifying information of DANY's personnel, other than sworn member of law enforcement, assistant district attorneys and expert and fact witnesses (other than summary witnesses). As we go to press, Trump has filed an Article 78 proceeding against the judge in the First Department challenging the gag order.

16. What Motions *in limine* Did the Parties File, and How Did the Court Rule?

Both parties filed on February 22, 2024 a series of motions *in limine*, the purpose of which is to address evidentiary issues and other trial logistics in advance of trial. The parties filed their opposition briefs on February 29. On March 18, the court granted most of DANY's motions and denied most of Trump's. As the editor described, the rulings were a "disaster for Trump and a home run for the DA" and "[p]robably a signal that trial will proceed in April."

Below we summarize each of the filings and the court's decisions.

a. State of New York's motions *in limine*, Trump's Opposition, and the court's rulings

DANY filed eight motions *in limine*, which we've grouped into three categories.

1. Category 1: Exclude specific evidence and witnesses (4 motions)

- DANY moved to exclude testimony from Bradley Smith, a former Federal Election commissioner, about federal election law, including whether the hush money payments would have violated federal election law. Expert testimony is admissible to help juries understand facts but not the law; the judge has the exclusive authority to explain the law. Legal experts are usually disallowed for that reason. In response, Trump claimed Smith will testify as a regulatory expert to help the jury understand the framework of election law. But Trump's response acknowledged that Smith will offer his opinion about Trump's good faith belief that the former President was in compliance with FECA. Experts are generally prohibited from testifying as to the state of the defendant's mind and whether he had the requisite intent, as those are ultimate questions of fact for the jury to decide.

- The court granted in part this motion, agreeing that Smith could not testify about the meaning of federal campaign finance law or whether the alleged conduct constitutes a FECA violation. The court will allow Smith to testify to background information about the Federal Election Commission, including its function, mission, and the generally accepted definition of terms related to this case, including "campaign contribution." In its order, the court warned that it "will monitor this testimony closely to ensure full compliance. Any deviation from this ruling could result in sanctions up to and including the striking of the expert's entire testimony."

- DANY filed two motions that sought to exclude evidence respectively about the Federal Election Commission dismissing complaints against Trump and about the Department of Justice (DOJ) declining to file charges against Trump. Decisions by other civil and criminal agencies about whether to file charges or lawsuits are generally inadmissible because they reflect opinions and legal conclusions based on different (albeit perhaps similar) sets of facts and laws. In response, Trump said he did not intend to offer these unless DANY offers Cohen's and AMI's agreements with prosecutors (discussed below).

- The court granted this motion, writing these decisions are "probative of nothing" and therefore irrelevant, as there are "countless reasons why the FEC and DOJ could have decided not to pursue enforcement against Defendant, all having nothing to do with whether he is guilty of the charges here against him."

- DANY sought to exclude evidence of other prosecutors' statements about Michael Cohen's credibility. DANY was required to disclose these statements to the defense as part of its discovery obligations, but other people's views of a witness's credibility are generally inadmissible. In response, Trump claimed he is entitled to cross Cohen about his lies and inconsistencies, including comments made by federal prosecutors about his lack of truthfulness.

- The court granted the motion, ruling that it is improper to "impeach witnesses through inadmissible hearsay such as the opinions of federal prosecutors." Because it is always permissible to challenge credibility, the court expressly said it would allow "appropriate, good faith impeachment."

2. *Category 2: Exclude improper legal arguments and supporting evidence (3 motions)*

- DANY moved to exclude evidence in support of legal arguments that the court already denied, specifically those raised in Trump's motions to dismiss. Because the court has rejected these legal arguments, any evidence in support would likely be irrelevant and inadmissible. Trump, in response, said the court had not ruled on the admissibility of those defenses and claimed a broad but vague right to cross-examine witnesses about issues dealt with in the court's prior rulings.

- The court granted the motion, precluding Trump from rearguing matters already ruled on raised in his motions to dismiss, including (1) alleged delay in bringing charges; (2) a federal offense is a valid object crime for first degree falsification of business records; (3) NY election law applies to the charged conduct; (4) improper prosecutorial motivation; (5) there was no violation of the statute of limitations; and (6) there were no violations of grand jury secrecy.

- Similarly, DANY filed a motion specifically addressing evidence of selective prosecution in light of Trump's frequent public comments complaining that he has been treated unfairly. The court already rejected this defense as without merit, and any testimony or evidence suggesting selective prosecution would be inadmissible and may improperly suggest a jury nullification argument. In response, Trump said he did not intend to raise this defense but is allowed to introduce evidence suggesting the investigation was "shoddy."

- The court found the issue to be moot because Trump stated he does not intend to argue selective prosecution to the jury. However, the court clarified that Trump is precluded from making arguments or introducing evidence about the indictment being novel, unusual, or unprecedented; pretrial delay; prosecutorial motivations; alleged bias of the judge or court staff; or Pomerantz's views of the case. And the court warned that it "will closely monitor any attempts to circumvent" the court's ruling.

- DANY moved to preclude Trump from improperly raising an advice-of-counsel defense through the testimony of Trump Organization Chief Legal Officer Alan Garten before establishing the legal prerequisites. An advice-of-counsel defense requires that the defendant honestly and in good faith (1) sought legal advice; (2) gave the relevant information to his attorney(s); and (3) followed that advice. As discussed in detail at Question 36, Trump took the position that he would not assert a "formal advice-of-counsel" but would "elicit evidence concerning the presence, involvement and advice of lawyers."

- The court granted the motion, finding that Trump waived the defense and would not allow his "amorphous defense of 'presence of counsel'" —which is "the very defense he has declared he will not rely upon."

3. Category 3: Prior bad acts

DANY sought pretrial determinations to admit three different types of evidence of Trump's prior bad acts. Evidence of prior bad acts is referred to as "*Molineux*" in New York or "404(b)" in federal court (after the corresponding New York case and Federal Rule of Evidence, respectively). It is generally inadmissible to establish a defendant's bad character or criminal propensity. For example, in a case involving a traffic accident, evidence that the defendant received speeding tickets in the past would be inadmissible to suggest that the defendant was speeding at the time of the accident. Also, in a case involving a traffic accident, evidence that the defendant previously battered his wife would also be inadmissible because it is irrelevant to the accident and would be offered only to suggest the defendant is a bad person.

However, prior bad acts evidence is generally admissible to show a defendant's motive, intent, plan, etc. Also, evidence of prior bad acts is generally admissible where those acts are inextricably interwoven with the crime and therefore part of the factual background to help the jury understand what happened (as opposed to telling the jury what the defendant has done in the past).

The three types of bad acts evidence DANY intends to introduce are:

1. Evidence regarding the "catch and kill" scheme, including payments made to Daniels, and two others. They are Dino Sajudin, the doorman who allegedly tried to sell a now debunked story about Trump fathering a child out of wedlock, and Karen McDougal, the former *Playboy* model who allegedly sold her story of an affair with Trump. DANY also alleges that these acts, as well as AMI's publication of negative stories about Trump's opponents, should be considered part of the same overall scheme and are therefore admissible.

- The court agreed with DANY, finding this evidence to be "inextricably interwoven with the narrative of events, that is, the steps that eventually led to the purchasing of information

from, among others, Daniels." However, the court
excluded one piece of evidence, finding that
DANY can introduce evidence related to a
$50,000 reimbursement to Cohen for a
campaign-related expense but cannot elicit that
the purpose of that expense was to "rig an online
poll," as that evidence is unnecessarily
prejudicial.

2. The "Access Hollywood" tape and the public allegations of sexual assault that followed. DANY argued that the
tape is evidence of Trump's intent and motive—which make
it admissible as *Molineaux*. Specifically, the tape and related
facts can show Trump's deep concern about potential harm
to his standing with female voters that allegedly motivated
his hush money payment scheme and the falsification of
business records to conceal it. Trump claimed the tape and
hearsay evidence of sexual assault allegations by three
women are irrelevant and unfairly prejudicial.

- The court ruled that the facts underlying the
  "Access Hollywood" tape are admissible as they
  relate to Trump's "intent and motive for making
  the payment to Daniels and then, attempting to
  conceal them." However, the court ruled that to
  avoid undue prejudice, the tape itself should not
  be played or admitted—just testimony about the
  interview that was caught on tape.
- The court reserved ruling on the admissibility of
  the allegations of assault that followed, pending
  DANY making a further offer of proof so the
  court is in a "better position to properly analyze"
  that evidence.

3. Evidence that Trump discouraged witnesses from cooperating with law enforcement, which DANY argued demonstrates his consciousness of guilt. In response, Trump objected to this evidence as irrelevant and unfairly prejudicial. He also said the court should not determine the admissibility of any such evidence in advance of trial in a blanket pretrial ruling but rather based on the specific evidence sought to be introduced at the time DANY offers it.

- The court explained, "attempting to threaten witnesses, imploring them to testify falsely and offering money to change their testimony could certainly be probative of consciousness of guilt," but it reserved ruling on the motion until it can review the specific evidence being offered.

b. Trump's motions *in limine*, DANY's opposition, and the court's ruling

Trump made 16 motions *in limine*, which we've grouped into three categories.

1. Category 1: Exclude specific evidence and witnesses (10 motions)

- Trump sought to block Michael Cohen from testifying, arguing that he's an admitted perjurer who is inherently unreliable.
- The court denied the motion, explaining there is no basis for excluding a witness because his credibility has been challenged. Credibility is different from admissibility, and the jury will determine whether Cohen is to be believed.

- Trump tried to block Stormy Daniels from testifying, claiming that her story is not relevant, and that she has been inconsistent in her statements.

- The court denied the motion, explaining that Daniels' role "not only completes the narrative of events that precipitated the falsification of business records but is also probative of the Defendant's intent." The court granted Trump's motion to preclude the results of any polygraph tests taken by Daniels.

- Trump filed separate motions to preclude any evidence from or about Dino Sajudin and Karen McDougal, claiming they lack "meaningful similarity" to the charged crimes. However, the statement of facts discusses both as examples of the catch and kill scheme, and as DANY argued there is likely sufficient evidence for a jury to conclude that the payments to Sajudin and McDougal were related to the payments to Daniels that underlie the charges and are part of the same common scheme or plan, as permissible *Molineux* evidence.

- The court denied the motions, finding "the steps taken to secure the stories of Sajudin and McDougal complete the narrative of the ['catch and kill'] agreement." But the court found that testimony from or about Sajudin and McDougal must be limited to the "fact of" what happened and not get into the "underlying details of what allegedly transpired between those individuals and the Defendant."

- Trump wanted to block the Access Hollywood tape as irrelevant and unduly prejudicial. As noted above, DANY filed a motion to admit the tape because it provides context for why Trump was concerned about news leaking of the Daniels affair and his motivation to conceal it.

- As discussed above in the context of DANY's motion to allow this evidence, the court ruled that testimony about the interview caught on tape is admissible but the tape itself is not.

- Trump tried to preclude evidence of the "catch and kill" agreement that dates back to 2015 along with use of the phrase "catch and kill" as inherently pejorative. But as DANY argued, there is nothing unfairly prejudicial about the phrase, which is used as a term of art within the tabloid publishing industry.

- The court denied the motion, finding that the background of the agreement is relevant to the charges.

- Trump wanted to preclude statements made by Rudy Giuliani discussing what Trump knew about the hush money scheme, arguing that Giuliani was not Trump's authorized agent at the time, as required for admission of those out-of-court statements. In response, DANY said it does not intend to admit any statements from Giuliani.

- In light of DANY's representations, the court found the motion moot and did not rule on it.

- Trump sought to block the prosecution from using Cohen's plea agreement or AMI's non-prosecution agreement as evidence of violations of the Federal Election Campaign Act. In response, DANY explained that the agreements are admissible for credibility reasons, whether introduced by the defense or prosecution, and to explain Cohen and Pecker's firsthand knowledge of facts to which they testify.

- The court granted the motion to the limited extent of precluding DANY from arguing that these agreements are probative of Trump's guilt but will allow DANY to introduce them to establish the underlying facts of the agreements.

- Trump wanted to block the admission of notes supposedly made by Trump Organization CFO Allen Weisselberg in January 2017 without first establishing that the notes were in fact made by Weisselberg and are otherwise admissible. DANY contended the notes are admissible as business records, and the prosecution will establish at trial the foundation to establish they are business records.

- The court explained that the notes are likely admissible so long as DANY establishes that they are business records, but it reserved ruling on the motion at this time.

- Trump asked to preclude evidence about the false entries in AMI's corporate books on the basis that the court already ruled that the falsification of AMI's records cannot serve as one of the object crimes of intent. As DANY pointed out, however, the court's ruling on the motion to dismiss expressly contemplated that the prosecution could introduce evidence of false records (by Cohen or AMI) as evidence of intent

to commit/aid/conceal one of the other three
object crimes.

- The court denied the motion, permitting DANY
  to introduce this as evidence in support of any of
  the three permissible theories of intent to
  commit another crime.

*2. Category 2: Exclude evidence and argument about
Trump's intent to defraud (3 motions) and about what
entity constitutes the "enterprise" for under the definition
of business records (1 motion)*

Trump made three motions aimed at limiting or
blocking how DANY can establish Trump's intent to
defraud. For example, Trump claimed that DANY is not
allowed to argue that Trump's attempt to prevent the public
disclosure of damaging information constitutes fraud. The
court denied these motions as "nothing more than a motion
to reargue disguised as a motion *in limine."* It also criticized
Trump's attempt to reargue these motions as "procedurally
and professionally inappropriate and a waste of this Court's
valuable resources."

Trump also moved to preclude DANY from offering
evidence and argument that records from Trump personally
or the Trump Revocable Trust constitute records of a business "enterprise." As discussed at Question 4, and as DANY
pointed out in its opposition, the court "squarely rejected"
this argument in his motions to dismiss. The court agreed,
denying the motion and cautioning Trump not to raise this
argument to the jury.

3. Category 3: Housekeeping (2 motions)

Trump made two housekeeping motions. The first sought to require DANY to prove the admissibility of 94 statements attributed to Trump in books, interviews, and social media posts. DANY pointed out that Trump's statements are admissions of a party opponent, and there is no reason for a pretrial hearing on their admissibility; the court can rule as each is introduced during trial. The court agreed, denying the motion and explaining that, as with all evidence, DANY will be required to lay the proper foundation before introducing any of these statements.

Second, Trump asked for the court to order DANY to provide an updated and pared-down exhibit list, claiming that the current list was in a "state of disarray." DANY responded that it had complied with its obligations and that any confusion or disorganization was a result of Trump's own doing. The court accepted DANY's representations and directed it to continue complying with their discovery obligations.

17. What Discovery Has Trump Turned Over?

The authors have been unable to discern from the public record whether any such production has been made (as of this writing).[3] But the production of discovery would not necessarily be public. The rules of procedure require Trump, like any criminal defendant, to produce essentially all relevant evidence in his possession, including expert opinion evidence; tapes and electronic recordings; photographs and drawings; reports and data concerning physical or mental examinations of any witness; witness inducements; physical evidence; and any witness statements.

18. Does the Criminal Trial of the Trump Organization Business Offer Any Insight Into This Case?

DANY's 2021 indictment and subsequent conviction of two Trump Organization entities and Allen Weisselberg for, *inter alia*, conspiracy, scheme to defraud, grand larceny, tax fraud, and falsifying records provides some useful context for the upcoming trial.

At the heart of the prosecution of the Trump Payroll Corp. and the Trump Organization was whether the corporations were criminally responsible for a 13-year "sophisticated tax fraud scheme" in which Weisselberg and other high-level executives were awarded off-the-books perks and compensation to intentionally conceal information from tax authorities and avoid paying taxes. A critical issue was whether the prosecution could prove beyond a reasonable doubt that executives had carried out criminal acts "*in behalf of*" the corporations.

The five-week trial saw the prosecution and defense agree that Trump Organization "employees had engaged in a lucrative tax fraud scheme... but dr[ew] diametrically opposed conclusions about whether their actions implicated the Trump Organization itself." The prosecution case focused on proving that Weisselberg (and others, including controller Jeffrey McConney) were "high managerial" agents "acting within the scope of their employment" on behalf of the Trump Organization and its many entities. Additionally, the prosecution contended they were also acting "in behalf of the corporations"— amid a corporate environment in which Trump "explicitly sanctioned" tax fraud to the intentional benefit of others.

In contrast, the defense argued that Weisselberg was a rogue actor who had not acted "in behalf" of the Trump Organization but was instead motivated "solely" by personal gain and greed. They argued, "Weisselberg did it for Weisselberg," and thus the prosecution had failed to establish, as Merchan had required necessary, that "there was some intent to benefit the corporation."

Closing arguments lasted two days and mirrored many of the themes throughout trial, particularly on whether Weisselberg had acted with the intent to, at least in part, benefit the Trump Organization. During his three days on the stand, Weisselberg admitted that both he and McConney knew that reductions in salaries via unreported perks would benefit the Trump Organization by lowering its payroll tax obligation, although he testified they never explicitly discussed it—and each side dissected that testimony during summation to make their respective cases.

The jury deliberated for 10 hours before finding the corporations guilty on all 17 counts. At the time of conviction, Bragg said that his successful case against the Trump Organization was only "a chapter"—"[a] case against the corporations"—in his ongoing investigations into Trump's business practices in New York.

This next chapter, while distinct from the 2022 trial, will likely see several similarities, including some of the same lawyers leading the case for each side; Merchan's acumen for dealing with complex financial issues and not allowing the defense to confuse the jury on the law or shoehorn inadmissible evidence into the case; battles over the meaning of essential elements of the charged crimes and whether Cohen was acting for Trump or going rogue; and if there's a conviction, Merchan weighing prosecutors' recommended sentence.

JURY SELECTION

19. Why is This a Jury Trial?

Under NY CPL, a criminal defendant has a right to a jury trial for all felonies and certain classes of misdemeanors. Trump is charged with 34 felonies and therefore has a right to a jury trial. A defendant can waive his right to a jury trial (except for first-degree murder) and have the judge serve as the factfinder (called a "bench trial"), so long as the waiver is in writing and signed by the defendant in open court with the court's approval. NY CPL § 320.10. Trump has not elected and is not expected to elect to have a bench trial.

20. How Many Jurors Will There Be?

In New York, a trial jury consists of 12 jurors, but the court may choose to additionally select and swear up to six alternate jurors. Alternates are selected in case a regular juror is discharged or excused and thus will sit and hear evidence like regular jurors, though will not be involved in deliberations. They must also be drawn in the same manner as regular jurors, they must have the same qualifications (see Question 21), and must be subject to the same examination and challenges (see Question 23). NY CPL § 270.30.

21. Who Can Sit as a Juror?

To qualify as a juror a person must be a U.S. citizen and resident, a resident of Manhattan, at least 18 years old, be able to understand and communicate in the English language, and have no felony convictions. These are referred to as the "juror qualifications."

22. Who Is in the Jury Pool?

The jury pool consists of adult residents of New York County (total population: 1.69 million recorded in the 2020 Census) who meet the juror qualifications.

According to the U.S. Census Bureau, the county is 52.2% female; 45.5% white (non-Hispanic/Latino); 26.2% Hispanic/Latino; 18.7% Black or African-American; 13.3% Asian; and 3.6% mixed race/ethnicity.[4]

As of February 2024, of the approximately 1.1 million registered voters (active and inactive) in New York County (Manhattan), 70.0 percent are registered Democratic and 7.8 percent Republican. In the 2020 presidential election, the county voted for Joe Biden over Trump, 86.7 percent to 12.3 percent. In the 2016 presidential election, the county voted for Hillary Clinton over Trump, 86.6 percent to 9.7 percent.

23. What Is Voir Dire/Jury Selection and How Does It Work?

First, the judge will introduce prospective jurors to the voir dire (or jury selection) process and to the case. Next, the judge as well as parties will examine groups of prospective jurors, before parties make any objections. The process will continue until 12 jurors and up to six alternates are selected.

See generally NY CPL, Article 270; McKinney, NY CPL §
270.15.

a. Judge's Introductory Remarks

The judge will welcome the prospective jurors, identify
the parties and their respective lawyers, and give a brief
introduction to the case. NY CPL § 270.15. The judge will
then explain the jurors' role and the purpose of the selection process—to compile a panel of jurors who can be fair
and impartial in evaluating the evidence and applying the
law as directed by the judge. The judge will also explain to
prospective jurors what the trial process involves (see these
model instructions that guide judges through this process).

b. Questioning Prospective Jurors

The heart of jury selection is the attorneys' questioning
of the jury pool. After introductory remarks by the judge,
prospective jurors will be "sworn to answer truthfully" any
questions asked of them "relative to their qualifications."
Groups of at least 12 prospective jurors will be placed in
the jury "box" and questioned. The court usually leads
with its initial questioning before allowing a "fair opportunity" for counsel for both sides to examine prospective
jurors on any "unexplored matter." The court should not
allow "repetitious or irrelevant, or questions as to a juror's
knowledge of rules of law," and "[i]f necessary to prevent
improper questioning as to any matter, the court shall
personally examine the prospective jurors as to that matter.
The scope of such examination shall be within the discretion of the court. After the parties have concluded their
examinations of the prospective jurors, the court may ask

such further questions as it deems proper." NY CPL §
270.15(1).

Also, "[i]n its discretion, the court may require prospective jurors to complete a questionnaire concerning their
ability to serve as fair and impartial jurors, including but not
limited to place of birth, current address, education, occupation, prior jury service, knowledge of, relationship to, or
contact with the court, any party, witness or attorney in the
action and any other fact relevant to his or her service on
the jury." *Id*. A questionnaire has been discussed by the
judge and counsel but has not yet been agreed as of this
writing.

Generally, defendants have a right to be present during
questioning of prospective jurors, but (unlike during the
actual trial) can freely waive this right. McKinney, NY CPL §
260.20.

c. Challenges to Prospective Jurors

After each group of prospective jurors have been examined, parties (starting with the state) are given the opportunity to object to certain prospective jurors: first through a
"challenge for cause" and then through peremptory challenges. NY PL § 270.15(2).

1. Challenge for Cause

"A challenge for cause is an objection to a prospective
juror and may be made only on the ground that," in so far as
is possibly applicable, 1) the juror does not have the necessary qualifications (as stated in Question 21) to be an eligible
juror; or 2) the juror "has a state of mind that is likely to
preclude" her "from rendering an impartial verdict based
upon the evidence adduced at the trial; or 3) the juror is
related to the defendant, victim, a witness, or counsel, or 4)

the juror "was a witness at the preliminary examination or before the grand jury or is to be a witness at the trial." NY CPL § 270.20(1).

With respect to a challenge for cause, "[a]ll issues of fact or law arising... must be tried and determined by the court." *If* the challenge is allowed, the prospective juror *must* be excluded. NY CPL §§ 270.20(2) & 270.15(2). Note also that a challenge for cause must generally be made before that prospective juror is sworn in as a trial juror. If not, the defendant will be taken to have waived such challenge, unless "based upon a ground not known to the challenging party," in which case a challenge can be made "at any time before a witness is sworn at the trial." NY CPL § 270.15.(4).

Generally, to appeal a trial court's erroneous denial of a party's challenge for cause the party must have exhausted its peremptory challenges by the close of jury selection. NY § CPL 270.20(2); McKinney, NY CPL § 270.15.

"[C]hallenges for cause must be made and determined, and peremptory challenges must be made, within the courtroom but outside of the hearing of the prospective jurors in such [a] manner as not to disclose which party made the challenge. The prospective jurors who are not excluded from service must retain their place in the jury box and must be immediately sworn as trial jurors. They must be sworn to try the action in a just and impartial manner, to the best of their judgment, and to render a verdict according to the law and the evidence." NY CPL § 270.15(2).

Any prospective juror that is excluded will generally be replaced by another prospective juror from the larger jury panel. "If the jury is not selected from the first group of people placed in the jury 'box' and members of the panel remain, the court may fill the 'box' with such number of the remaining people as the court deems appropriate and continue the process until a jury is selected." McKinney, NY CPL § 270.15. "The juror whose name was first drawn and called must be designated by the court as the foreperson, and no special oath need be administered to him or her." NY CPL § 270.15(3).

2. Peremptory Challenges

Following parties' opportunity to challenge for cause, the court must permit peremptory challenges to the remaining prospective jurors. Both sides have a "statutorily guaranteed right to exercise peremptory challenges." DANY must exercise its "peremptory challenges first and may not, after" Trump "has exercised his peremptory challenges, make such a challenge to any remaining prospective juror who is then in the jury box." NY CPL § 270.15(2).

Unlike challenges for cause, a "peremptory challenge is an objection to a prospective juror for which no reason need be assigned. Upon any peremptory challenge, the court must exclude the person challenged from service." NY CPL § 270.25(1). For a class E felony like first-degree falsifying business records, each party must be allowed ten peremptory challenges for the regular jurors and two for each alternate juror to be selected. NY CPL § 270.25(2).

24. What Can We Expect From Jury Selection Here?

a. Juror Demographics

In DANY's prosecution of the Trump Organization, 132 prospective jurors were whittled down to twelve jurors for trial (eight women and four men) and six alternates. Among the twelve were a retired nurse living in East Harlem as well as a retired man from Washington Heights. Among prospective jurors eventually struck were a political consultant for liberal political candidates, a Manhattan doorman, a woman psychiatrist, and a woman from the Manhattan Murray Hill neighborhood who worked at a financial services company.

The jury pool in the federal Carroll litigation was wider than in the impending DANY case, drawing on jurors from across the Southern District of New York (Manhattan, Bronx and several suburban counties). As noted above, the jury pool in DANY's case against Trump will be drawn from New York County (Manhattan) alone. That said and although jurors were anonymized, what we do know of the prospective juror pools and the nine jurors eventually selected in those cases offer insight into potential demographics in the DANY prosecution of Trump.

Jury selection in *Carroll I* consisted of 50 prospective jurors. The final jury consisted of 7 men and 2 women. All but one of the jurors were White. "At least three indicated they moved to the U.S. after growing up in Europe—specifically Germany, Ireland and Spain." The majority were from Manhattan, the Bronx and Westchester County, and their jobs included a property manager, a professional violinist, a retired track supervisor for the New York City Transit Authority, an emergency physician, a publicist, and four other New Yorkers. "Not everyone offered their age, but among those who did, the ages ranged from 26 years old to 60 years old." Similarly, *Carroll II* saw 48 prospective jurors summoned, consisting of a "decent cross-section of New York: people of different ages, races, genders, and social classes." The final jury in *Carroll II* consisted of six men and three women. In *Carroll II*, all jurors indicated that they had registered to vote, as did "many" in the subsequent defamation trial, though in *Carroll II* several had not voted in 2016 and 2020.

b. Duration of Jury Selection

The length of jury selection is difficult to predict. It is highly dependent on the prospective jurors' responses to questions asked, any challenges made by the prosecution or defense, as well as Merchan's ability to keep the ball rolling (which he did in DANY's case against the Trump Organization). Jury selection in both Carroll cases was complete within a day. It took an unexpectedly short three days to empanel 12 jurors in DANY's prosecution of the Trump Organization and an additional day to choose six alternate jurors.

We expect a longer period here as the trial against the Trump businesses did not involve him personally, and jurors are likely to have strong feelings about him one way or the other. It is true that he was the defendant in the civil cases, and jury selection went quickly there. However jury selection in federal court is different from state court, and more jurors are needed in this criminal matter. Moreover, the estimated six-week trial may be problematic for some in the jury pool.

c. Potential Questions and Striking Jurors

The key issue during jury selection is ensuring the right questions are asked of prospective jurors to ensure a fair trial and avoid a mistrial. The recent Feb. 15 hearing before Merchan provided a glimpse into potential questions the prosecution and defense will ask to whittle down their jurors for trial. First, questions are likely to focus (in part) on the political affiliations of prospective jurors. This is an important matter to deal with; juror "political bias" has already led to a mistrial in the New York federal case against Trump ally Timothy Shea. Secondly, questions are expected to mirror, to an extent, those used in the Trump Organization criminal case and federal Carroll cases. Beyond Merchan dismissing the defense's "hybrid approach" suggestion that all prospective jurors be questioned even if they raise their hand to affirm that they believe they could not be fair and impartial, final questions are yet to be settled. We therefore begin by looking at some of the questions asked in those cases and the jurors' responses, before turning to specific questions discussed so far in this case.

DANY's prosecution of the Trump Organization included a 32-part questionnaire and one-on-one questioning. Prospective jurors were questioned in groups, with each side given 30 minutes to ask questions. Many "were not shy about expressing their thoughts," though those eventually picked "were among the least vocal about Trump," but some had "admitted that they had opinions about him and his leadership, but vowed to set aside any personal thoughts and consider only evidence presented during the trial." The six alternate jurors included "several who expressed dislike for Trump, including one who described some of his comments as 'racist' and another who called him 'offensive' and 'degrading.' Merchan allowed them to serve because they said they could be fair and impartial in this case." "It is about whether those feelings about Trump would prevent their ability to be a fair and impartial juror," DANY argued in a conference with Merchan and defense counsel.

Merchan sought to draw a clear line between opinions that were innocuous and those that were disqualifying: merely having an opinion on Trump as a president was not enough, for it bore no relevance to his work as a businessman and his company. In addition to questions about Trump, "prospective jurors were asked several other questions, including about whether they could trust testimony from Mr. Weisselberg when they knew he stood to benefit from taking the stand." Among those struck were individuals whose views were particularly one sided, including a woman who said Trump continued to lie to the American people that he won the 2020 presidential election, another woman who was unapologetically supportive of Trump and his company, a psychiatrist who said she believed Trump exhibited social narcissistic behavior, a Manhattan doorman who said he was leaning to one side, and as well as a political consultant for liberal political candidates who had DA Bragg as a guest on a podcast he hosted.

In both Carroll cases, Judge Kaplan posed all questions to jurors, as is the custom in federal court, with jurors indicating "their answers by either raising their hands or standing." In New York state court, however, after the judge leads the questioning, the parties are each given an opportunity to question the panel. Justice Merchan may seek to utilize this procedure in the DANY case just as he did in DANY's case against Trump's corporations.

In Carroll I, prospective jurors were asked if they believed that the 2020 election was stolen. A few said they did and were ultimately not selected to serve. They were also asked whether they had "ever contributed money or supported a political campaign" for Trump, Obama, Hillary Clinton or Biden. Specific to Trump, prospective jurors were asked whether they had "ever read any books by Mr. Trump?" Or if they had "ever watched 'The Apprentice?'" (A handful indicated they had). Examples of jurors that were not selected in Carroll I included a "retired English teacher who got her news from 'Pod Save America,'... a workplace investigator from Westchester who had attended a Trump rally... [and] a 60-year-old corporate lawyer from Manhattan who answered affirmatively when... asked whether anyone felt that... Trump was being treated unfairly by the courts." The jury selection process in Carroll II was very similar. Questions included whether prospective jurors believed the 2020 election was stolen as well as whether they supported conspiracy theories peddled by QAnon, Oath Keepers, Antifa, and the like. No hands were raised to either. "One woman was excused from service when she said she believed in the #MeToo movement." Around a fifth of prospective jurors were struck for saying they would struggle to decide the case justly and impartially.

In addition to a selection of the questions topics above, the Feb. 15 hearing (see here and here) provided a glimpse into some of the questions the prosecution and defense intend to ask, including:

- Whether jurors support or follow conspiracy theory groups such as QAnon, the Proud Boys, or Antifa.
- Whether jurors believe the 2020 election was stolen, which the prosecution wanted but the defense opposed. Jurors in Carroll were asked this question.
- Thoughts on if Trump is being treated unfairly by the courts, which the defense opposed.
- Whether jurors have a desire to see Trump convicted.
- Whether jurors had read or listened to relevant recent books or podcasts from Mark Pomerantz and Michael Cohen.

- Jurors' bumper stickers and yard sticks.
- Whether jurors have ever read or listened to any of Trump's books and related literature.
- Whether jurors have ever read, watched, or listened to any media involving Trump, which the prosecution took issue with as "too broad to probe bias."
- What media outlets jurors engage with. The prosecution suggested adding conservative shows such as Tucker Carlson, Infowars, Ben Shapiro show, and Alex Jones show, prompting the defense to suggest further outlets. Merchan suggested that a version of the question could be adopted from the prosecution of the Trump Organizations, or dropped altogether.
- Whether jurors are Democrats or Republicans, although the prosecution disagreed and it seems Merchan did too.

25. Will Trump Know the Jurors' Names and Addresses?

Unlike in federal court (including in the Carroll cases), New York state criminal rules do not provide for fully anonymized jurors. For that reason, on Feb. 22, 2024, DANY filed a motion for a protective order emphasizing the necessity of protecting jurors. The motion sought three forms of relief: (1) prohibiting disclosure of prospective and sworn jurors' residential and business addresses except to counsel of record (but not the parties themselves); (2) prohibiting disclosure of jurors' names except to the parties and counsel; and (3) warning Trump that any harassing or disruptive conduct toward jurors could result in forfeiting his access to their names. DANY's motion argued that Trump's "conduct in this and other matters—including his extensive history of attacking jurors in other proceedings—presents a significant risk of juror harassment and intimidation that warrants reasonable protective measures to ensure the integrity of these proceedings, minimize obstacles to jury selection, and protect juror safety."

Trump filed a response on March 4. He largely agreed to the first two requests but suggested the disclosure of names should include the entire legal team, including paralegal and jury consultants. Trump also asked the court not to tell jurors why such precautions were being taken so as not to prejudice him. If jurors asked, Trump suggested a neutral explanation be given so that the jurors were not affected by knowing that Trump's history of conduct justified the precautions.

On March 7, the court granted the protective order on the first two issues but expanded the disclosure of jurors' names to the entire legal teams, as Trump requested. In terms of warning Trump about his statements, the court reserved judgment until it ruled on the gag order. But the court did remind both sides of its prior instructions to refrain from, and encourage their witnesses to refrain from, making any comments that could incite violence, civil unrest, or jeopardize the courtroom proceedings.

On March 26, the court granted DANY's motion for a gag order (see Question 15 above). On April 1, in expanding the gag order to protect family members of the DA and the court, Justice Merchan added an express warning Trump that he would forfeit any statutory right he may have to access juror names if he "engages in any conduct that threats the safety and integrity of the jury or the jury selection process."

6

THE TRIAL

I n this chapter, we cover trial proceedings from opening statements to the prosecution and defense cases. We forecast what to expect at trial, including the key arguments and evidentiary issues.

This essay is excerpted from "A Complete Guide to the Manhattan Trump Election Interference Prosecution," which was published by Norm Eisen, Andrew Warren and Siven Watt in Just Security on March 27, 2024. The numbering and content have been modified since its original publication.

FROM OPENING STATEMENTS TO CLOSING ARGUMENTS

26. What Are the Stages of a Criminal Trial?

N.Y. Crim PL § 260.30 sets out the "order of a jury trial, in general... as follows:

1. The jury must be selected and sworn.

2. The court must deliver preliminary instructions to the jury.

3. The people must deliver an opening address to the jury.

4. The defendant may deliver an opening address to the jury.

5. The people must offer evidence in support of the indictment.

6. The defendant may offer evidence in his defense.

7. The people may offer evidence in rebuttal of the defense evidence, and the defendant may then offer evidence in rebuttal of the people's rebuttal evidence. The court may in its discretion permit the parties to offer further rebuttal or sur-rebuttal evidence in this pattern. In the interest of justice, the court may permit either party to offer evidence upon rebuttal which is not technically of a rebuttal nature but more properly a part of the offering party's original case.

8. At the conclusion of the evidence, the defendant may deliver a summation to the jury.

9. The people may then deliver a summation to the jury.

10. The court must then deliver a charge to the jury.

11. The jury must then retire to deliberate and, if possible, render a verdict."

27. What Can We Expect From Opening Statements?

Opening statements are an opportunity for each side to introduce the case and preview the evidence for the jury. Opening statements are not evidence; they are the attorneys' summaries of what they expect the evidence to show.

a. The Prosecution Opening

For prosecutors, an effective opening statement will inform the jury of what happened—the who, what, where, when and why. It will explain the theory of prosecution— the lens through which it wants the jury to view the evidence. It will preview the evidence: the key witnesses, documents, and other pieces of information that will prove the case. And it should be interesting; effective prosecutors will use the opening to tell the jury a compelling story.

Expect DANY to make the following points in its opening (note that these are all allegations at this point, to be proven or not by the evidence introduced):

- Identifying the central issue of the case: this is a case about campaign corruption and cover up.
- Connect the central issue to the crimes charged: Trump falsified business records in order to conceal hush money paid to Stormy Daniels at the end of the 2016 campaign. Coming on the heels of the Access Hollywood tape, Trump feared another scandal would have affected the campaign so he hid it, and then was involved in faking 34 documents to cover that up. He did all of this with the intent to commit, aid or conceal violations of federal and state election laws and state tax law. We do not anticipate the prosecution getting too much into the weeds of the law, which is more appropriate for closing arguments. But giving a glimpse of the legal

theory at the beginning of the case will help
orient the jury about what DANY must prove.

- Tell the story: Trump, Cohen, and Pecker had a
  meeting in August 2015, two months after Trump
  announced his presidential candidacy in June.
  They agreed to a "catch and kill" arrangement,
  with Pecker to serve as the "eyes and ears" for the
  campaign by looking out for possible negative
  stories about Trump and alerting Cohen to
  suppress publication of the stories. Pecker also
  agreed that AMI would publish negative stories
  about Trump's competition. In late 2015, Pecker
  heard that Trump's former doorman at Trump
  Tower was selling a negative story about Trump,
  and Pecker directed AMI to purchase the rights
  to the story in order to suppress it. AMI paid the
  doorman $30,000, and although they learned the
  story was not true, Cohen instructed Pecker not
  to release the doorman from the deal until after
  the election. Around June of 2016, the editor-in-
  chief of the *National Enquirer* contacted Cohen
  about Karen McDougal, who claimed to have
  had an affair with Trump. Trump was worried
  about the information leaking as it would hurt
  his candidacy. Trump, Cohen, and Pecker
  discussed how to buy McDougal's silence, and
  they ultimately agreed AMI would pay her
  $150,000 to keep quiet, along with giving her
  cover features and a series of articles to be
  published under her name. Trump, Cohen, and
  Pecker agreed that Trump or the Trump
  Organization would reimburse AMI. In a
  recorded conversation, Trump and Cohen

discussed reimbursing AMI and setting up a shell company to effectuate the scheme. (The publisher ultimately backed out of seeking reimbursement and the payment was never made.) In early October 2016, just one month before the election, news broke of an *Access Hollywood* tape in which Trump made highly offensive comments about women. Trump and his campaign team were concerned about the impact on voters, especially women voters. Shortly after the *Access Hollywood* news, Pecker heard that Daniels claimed to have had an affair with Trump. On Pecker's instruction, the editor-in-chief notified Cohen and connected Cohen with Daniels' attorney. Cohen and Daniels' attorney agreed to secure her silence by paying her $130,000 for the exclusive rights to her story. Cohen and Trump talked about this arrangement, and Trump wanted to wait until after the election so he could avoid having to pay Daniels. Ultimately, as pressure mounted and the election approached, Trump agreed to the payoff. Trump and Cohen agreed that Cohen would make the payment and Trump would reimburse him. In late October, just two weeks before the election, Cohen paid Daniels' attorney $130,000 as everyone had agreed. After the election, Trump made arrangements to reimburse Cohen with Allen Weisselberg, the Trump Organization's CFO. Weisselberg and Cohen agreed to a total payment of $420,000. They reached that number by adding $130,000 for the Daniels reimbursement plus $50,000 for a separate reimbursement. To conceal that the payments were reimbursements, they agreed to double that amount to $360,000 so that Cohen could falsely claim the payment was his income —which would incur income tax—leaving Cohen whole after paying the tax. They also agreed to pay Cohen a $60,000 bonus, for a total of $420,000, paid at a rate of $35,000 every month for twelve months. Over the course of a year, Cohen was to submit a false invoice claiming $35,000 per month in legal fees when in fact the funds were the reimbursement to cover up the hush money payment and other expenses. Cohen worked out the details with Weisselberg, and then later met with Trump in the Oval Office to confirm the arrangement. Cohen ended up submitting eleven false invoices—the first one covered two payments—claiming the repayment was for legal expenses. Every month the Trump Organization falsely documented the invoices and the payments in the corporate books as if it were repayment for legal expenses. The first two checks were from Trump's Trust account; the other nine were from Trump's personal account. The payments to Cohen stopped after he received the last $35,000 check.

- Preview the evidence: DANY will give the jury an idea of how it is going to prove that story, specifying key pieces of evidence, including: Testimony from (likely) witnesses such as Michael Cohen, Stormy Daniels, Karen McDougal, David Pecker, and Dino Sajudin (the former doorman). Text messages and emails showing conversations between Trump, Cohen, and others. Business records of the Trump Organization, including the checks, fake invoices, and false ledger entries, all intended to conceal the true nature of the campaign expense of silencing Daniels. Weisselberg's notes showing how a $130,000 reimbursement became $420,000 in payments. Business records of Cohen's shell company, Essential Consultants.

- Prepare the jury for credibility attacks on Cohen and Daniels by fronting inconsistent statements they have made and Cohen's criminal conviction for false statements. Also, inform the jury that the documents will corroborate each of their testimony.

- Preview likely defenses. *See* Questions 27 and 33.

- Introduce different themes, including: Common sense will reveal Trump's motivations: the evidence will show that he knew news of his affair with Daniels could be a major issue for the campaign, so he silenced her and covered it up. Trump created a pressure campaign on Cohen and others not to cooperate with law enforcement, which shows his consciousness of guilt. Trump chose to be involved in every aspect of this scheme and cover-up: the "catch and kill" agreement, the hush money payment, the reimbursement, and the falsification of the records to cover it up.

- Preview the law: Explain there are 34 counts pertaining to the eleven checks, eleven false invoices, and twelve false ledger entries. Outline each of the elements of the crime charged.

Explain the intent to commit, aid or conceal
other laws that escalates the falsification of
records to a felony, preview how that will be
proven, and what the other laws are.

b. The Defense Opening

As with the prosecution opening statement, the defense
opening will introduce the jury to the defense theory of the
case. A major difference, however, is whereas the prosecution is trying to prepare the jury for accepting its theory of
the case and the evidence in support, the defense can
achieve its goal of creating reasonable doubt in two compli-
mentary ways: poking holes in the prosecution's theory, or
offering a different theory altogether.

Expect Trump's team to accomplish the following in its
opening:

- The defense may choose to offer a competing
  theory of the case, such as: Trump's motivation
  was to keep personally embarrassing
  information away from his wife and children; not
  to keep it away from voters. There is nothing
  inherently wrongful about suppressing negative
  information during a campaign. Therefore
  Trump did not have any intent to defraud or
  violate election laws. Nor did Trump have any
  intent to commit or conceal any tax crime, as he
  was not involved in the preparation, filing, or
  payment of Cohen's personal taxes. Because of
  the importance of the intent questions—the trial
  will likely turn on them—we address them at
  length in Questions 16, 41 and 42. Trump was not

involved in the creation of business records other than signing checks for services to his personal attorney, Cohen. Trump might have tried to argue that he relied to some extent on advice from his lawyers but the court ruled that Trump may not "even suggest" the defense in the form Trump was advancing here. *See* Question 35.

- The defense may nest one or more of those theories in contextual facts tending to exonerate Trump: Even before being elected President, Trump was a highly successful businessman and one of the most recognizable people on the planet. Like many celebrities, he is often the target of unscrupulous people trying to take advantage of him for money or other reasons. His presidential candidacy enlarged the target on his back. Like any political campaign, Trump's team had a communications strategy in which they tried to maximize favorable coverage, minimize or eliminate negative coverage, and amplify negative coverage of his opponents. Trump was not intimately involved with this strategy and left it to his political team and allies to handle. Trump had minimal knowledge of and involvement with alleged arrangements with Sajudin, McDougal, and Daniels. Michael Cohen had been an attorney for Trump for years, and Trump routinely paid him money for legal services. Cohen was a "fixer" for Trump, who Trump trusted to handle a variety of issues, often without Trump's knowledge. Like many small business owners, Trump's personal and business accounts were often commingled, which resulted in different entities paying different expenses at different times based on routine business considerations. As the principal owner and CEO of a multi-billion dollar group of companies, Trump was not the person making every operational decision. He relied on his subordinates, including his CFO, accountants, and lawyers, to handle the daily operations.

- Poke holes in the prosecution's evidence. Start with Cohen. Emphasize how he is the prosecution's star witness. Everything starts and ends with Cohen: the alleged catch and kill agreement, the alleged hush money payments, the alleged cover-up, the alleged false invoices. Trump's lawyers may ask the jury to consider as they hear the evidence whether there is any case at all without Cohen. And then they will challenge Cohen's credibility, as a convicted felon and admitted perjurer who has told several different stories about the conduct in question. Consider challenging the credibility of Daniels and other witnesses. Emphasize how the documentary evidence demonstrates the lack of Trump's personal involvement: Trump was not processing the invoices, making the ledger entries, or drawing up the checks. Trump was not the one primarily handling the Trump Organization records that are alleged to be false. And Trump was obviously not the one who submitted Cohen's invoices that the prosecution contends are false.
- Preview the evidence: summarize the witnesses who will testify on Trump's behalf and the

documents and other evidence that will be introduced, and how that (1) supports the defense theory of the case and/or (2) pokes holes in the prosecution's case.

- Consider whether to let the jury know if Trump will testify. This is an important decision for the defense, and they should tell the jury Trump will testify only if they are certain that he will take the stand. They will most likely punt, avoiding a commitment and making the decision at or near the last minute because the decision is a momentous one and they will want to have as much information as possible about how the trial is going before they make it.

- Emphasize reasonable doubt: the many weaknesses in the state's case, including their key witnesses being not credible, the lack of any smoking gun proof, and questionable interpretations of other evidence, provide many different reasons to doubt the prosecution's theory.

- Emphasize that the burden of proof is entirely on the prosecution.

- Humanize Trump: He's a controversial ex-president who speaks his mind, and the prosecution has introduced salacious and unflattering aspects of his private life. The jury does not have to like him, agree with him, or approve of what he has said publicly or done privately. But the jury is not here to judge him for being the perfect candidate or person. The jury is only to determine whether the prosecution has proven beyond any reasonable

doubt that Trump committed the crimes in
question.

- Address affirmative defenses, if any (note that
  some typical defenses such as advice of counsel
  have been precluded as discussed in Question
  35).
- Complicate the case: Whereas the prosecution
  wants to simplify the case and therefore the jury's
  ultimate decision, look for the defense to tell the
  jury that the case is about many issues, and that
  the prosecution is oversimplifying and conflating
  two-and-a-half years of conduct involving
  Trump's personal life, his business, and his
  campaign.

28. What is the Prosecution's Case?

Once we get past the opening statements, DANY's burden
starting with their first witness is to prove that Trump intentionally falsified (or caused the falsification of) business
records and did so with the intent to commit, aid, or conceal
violating federal election law, state election law, or tax fraud.
The question is *how* does the prosecution prove this. While
the parties' witness and exhibit lists are not public, we can
assess the broader contours of the prosecution and defense
cases based on publicly available information.

As discussed at Question 27 regarding opening statements, the prosecution will hammer home the central
theme of election interference: that Trump corrupted the
2016 election to protect his campaign through the hush
money payments and then covered it up. The prosecution's
goal will be to prove the narrative it described in the
opening statement. Daniels, her attorney, McDougal,

Sajudin, Pecker, and possibly others (such as advisors from the Trump campaign) are the key witnesses to establish the full account of the "catch and kill" agreement within which the hush money payment occurred. DANY may of course elect not to call former campaign advisors because of their perceived loyalty to Trump, in which case emails, texts, and memos can fill those parts of the narrative. Other AMI witnesses, such as the *National Enquirer's* editor-in-chief, Dylan Howard, can also supplement the testimony that Pecker will offer (if called). For example, Howard could testify that he was following Pecker's orders in working with Cohen about buying and suppressing stories, even if the editor did not know about an express "catch and kill" agreement between Trump and Pecker.

Expect the prosecution to also call Trump Organization employees who were responsible for record-keeping to explain how the company accounted for the reimbursement payments to Cohen. The records themselves—in particular the 34 checks, invoices, and ledger entries corresponding to each of the 34 counts—are important. But having a person from within the Organization explain those records brings them to life for the jury in a way that introducing them through a law enforcement witness or offering them into evidence without witness testimony does not.

Press reports have suggested the prosecution will not call Weisselberg. On the one hand, he could be a powerful witness to explain the record keeping, corroborate Cohen's testimony, and possibly testify to incriminating conversations he had with Trump. But on March 4, 2024, Weisselberg pleaded guilty to two felony perjury charges for lying during his deposition testimony in July 2020 in connection with the civil fraud trial against Trump. He also admitted lying during his trial testimony but was not charged with that offense. Weisselberg's guilty plea undercuts his credibility as a witness, and DANY may elect not to call him as a witness for that reason let alone whether he can be trusted to tell the truth.

Michael Cohen will be an important witness. Obviously the prosecution cannot call Trump as a witness (because of his 5th Amendment rights), leaving Cohen as the only person with first-hand knowledge of the one-on-one conversations he had with Trump. Expect DANY to elicit from Cohen incriminating communications with Trump, including that the two discussed how Trump would reimburse Cohen in a manner to conceal the nature of the reimbursements. The icing on the cake of Cohen's testimony would be if he had conversations with Trump about whether the hush money payments should have been a campaign expense or the impropriety of having Cohen classify his reimbursement as income. But make no mistake, Cohen's testimony—and thus his credibility—is essential to the prosecution's case.

We address the inevitable attacks on Cohen's credibility in more detail below as part of the defense case. To bolster Cohen's credibility, expect the prosecution to take the initial step of acknowledging his credibility issues from the outset. As noted above, the prosecution should reference this in the opening statement and then, with Cohen on the witness stand, question him about his admitted lies, inconsistent statements, and personal animosity toward Trump. Presenting this information objectively and allowing Cohen to explain it will help the prosecution's credibility by showing they are not hiding anything from the jury and mitigate the impact of the defense attacks to come. Two additional steps the prosecution can take to bolster Cohen are to (1) emphasize how, in spite of his checkered past with telling the truth, he has been consistent in describing the events at issue in this case, and (2) use documents and audio recordings to corroborate his testimony.

29. What is the Defense Case?

Once we get past the opening statements, as with most criminal prosecutions, the defense case has two parts: poking holes in the prosecution's case and offering an alternative narrative. The defense will accomplish the former primarily through cross-examination of the prosecution witnesses and the latter primarily through putting on its own case.

As outlined at Question 27 above, expect Trump to attack the prosecution's case primarily by challenging witness credibility and by highlighting Trump's lack of involvement.

That starts with Cohen. In 2018, he pleaded guilty to tax evasion, making false statements to a financial institution, and campaign finance violations. After he sought a reduction in his 36-month sentence in 2019, federal prosecutors opposed the motion arguing that they had "substantial concerns" about his credibility, noting contradictions between his public comments, including post-sentencing congressional testimony, and his acceptance of responsibility from his guilty plea. The court eventually rejected Cohen's attempt to cut his sentence. While testifying during Trump's civil fraud trial in 2023, Cohen admitted lying under oath during his 2018 guilty plea.

New York Rule of Evidence 6.19 allows Trump to use Cohen's conviction to impeach his credibility, but Rule 6.11 prohibits using extrinsic evidence to impeach a witness on a "collateral" matter, meaning one not directly relevant to issues in the present case. This means that while Trump's attorneys can question Cohen about his inconsistent statements, they likely cannot introduce the court filing in which federal prosecutors questioned his credibility, or any other outside evidence (except for criminal convictions).

While Trump's team will surely attack Cohen as not credible, whether they do so with other potential witnesses such as Daniels, McDougal, and Sajudin is less certain. Sometimes the defense will utilize a strategy of attempting to discredit *any* prosecution witness. Other times, the defense will be selective in challenging witnesses because it (1) highlights the importance and effect of the credibility challenges it chooses to make, and (2) suggests that the testimony of witnesses it chooses not to challenge is not helpful to the prosecution.

In this case, the better strategy appears to be the latter. Based on what we currently know, neither Daniels, McDougal, nor Sajudin is likely to offer evidence that directly incriminates Trump, for example by testifying about his intent. Instead, all three can provide details on the operation of the "catch and kill" agreement. Also, Daniels and McDougal are likely to come off as sympathetic women caught up in Trump's personal and political life. As one former prosecutor commented, "I'll take the credibility and jury appeal of Daniels over the credibility of Trump as a witness any day of the week." Sajudin may inherently be less sympathetic and more likely to be viewed as someone who tried to make a quick buck by selling dirt (and allegedly false dirt at that), but all three witnesses are more involved in the salacious background stories than the core criminal conduct at issue. Trump's best bet may be to highlight the testimony that none of the three offered—the lack of direct, incriminating evidence—rather than attack their credibility.

Minimizing the importance of Daniels and other secondary witnesses dovetails with the expected defense of arguing Trump's limited involvement in the business decisions that underlie the main allegations of misconduct. Through cross-examination, the defense will likely emphasize Trump's absence from critical conversations, emails, and text messages between Pecker, Daniels' lawyer Keith Davidson, Cohen, Weisselberg, Trump Organization Chief Legal Officer Alan Garten, and the other Trump Organization employees who handled accounting, processed invoices and payments, and kept the books. Similarly, expect the defense to emphasize Trump's lack of involvement in the events generating another key body of evidence: the proof of Trump's intent in causing the falsification of books and records included an intent to commit, aid or conceal an election or tax crime. The better that Trump's attorneys do to minimize direct, incriminating evidence of his involvement, the more it makes the prosecution's case dependent on Cohen's testimony.

Emphasizing Trump's limited involvement through its cross-examination of prosecution witnesses also conforms with the defense strategy of offering its own factual narrative. For Trump, as with most criminal defendants, the decision whether to put on an affirmative case often depends on the strength of the prosecution's case. Here, expect Trump to call witnesses and introduce evidence to present a competing narrative, as outlined above in Question 27, that the "catch and kill" arrangement was typical politics that he left to his campaign team; that Trump and his associates had been involved in similar arrangements prior to running for office; that he had limited knowledge of the arrangements with Daniels, McDougal, and Sajudin; that he trusted Cohen to handle legal issues for him without Trump's oversight or involvement; that he trusted Weisselberg and others at the Trump Organization to run the back-office operations of the company; that Trump was not involved in any decision about Cohen's taxes or what expenses were being attributed to the campaign versus him personally; and that Trump's motivation was protecting his family.

It will be important for Trump to acknowledge some limited involvement in higher-level decisions; claiming not to have known anything will likely not be credible. In this way, Trump may be able to offer a plausible narrative of having known and helped make the big decisions but not knowing the details that are the basis for the alleged crimes.

Lastly, expect Trump to use his case-in-chief to bolster his remaining legal arguments, discussed at Question 33.

30. Will Trump Be Present During Trial?

Generally, a "defendant must be personally present during the trial of an indictment." NY CPL § 260.20. Indeed, the defendant has an affirmative right to be present. The court can, however, remove a defendant "who conducts himself in so disorderly and disruptive a manner that his trial cannot be carried on with him in the courtroom," as long as "he has been warned by the court that he will be removed if he continues such conduct, [and] he continues to engage in such conduct." *Id.*; *see also* McKinney, NY CPL § 260.20. New York case law has recognized that when a defendant who for that or other reasons forfeits his right to be present, no adverse inference can be drawn from non-attendance.

31. Will Trump Testify, and Will it Hurt Him if He Doesn't?

In a strictly legal sense, Trump choosing not to testify cannot be used against him. The Fifth Amendment "forbids either comment by the prosecution on the accused's silence or instructions by the court that such silence is evidence of guilt," and, as New York law and courts have recognized, it prohibits the jury from drawing any adverse inferences from a criminal defendant's choosing not to testify.

A defendant's Fifth Amendment right against self-incrimination is not limited at trial to the decision of whether to testify but extends to putting on a case, offering any evidence, or cross-examining any witness. In short, Trump and his attorneys can say and do nothing throughout the entire trial, and the prosecutors cannot comment on their lack of a defense, nor can the jury infer anything from it. The burden is always on DANY to prove the case.

If Trump chooses not to testify, Merchan will be required to direct the jury on no adverse inference being drawn if Trump requests such a charge (as he surely would). However, Trump not testifying would mean he missed an opportunity to directly present his side of the story. It could also possibly humanize Trump before the jury. (Trump might also have needed to testify in order to establish the factual prerequisites for asserting an advice-of-counsel defense, but as we note in Question 36, Trump waived that defense and the court precluded him from trying to shoe-horn in a similar "presence of counsel" defense).

Conversely, Trump taking the stand "will be a most risky proposition" in light of his 30,000 proven false or misleading statements. Additionally, Trump's recent testimony in the civil fraud trial should give him pause. As Judge Engoron found, "Trump rarely responded to the questions asked, and he frequently interjected long, irrelevant speeches on issues far beyond the scope of the trial. His refusal to answer questions directly, or in some cases, at all, severely compromised his credibility."

Given the volume of ammunition on which to cross him and his poor performance at the civil fraud trial, we would expect Trump's able attorneys to likely advise him not to take the stand. But things could certainly change, as Trump's lawyers have noted. In either case, in and around the courthouse, Trump has often been "his own worst enemy." So the critical question is not what advice his lawyers will give, but whether Trump will follow it.

32. How Long Will the Trial Last?

Justice Merchan said he expects the trial to take around six weeks, with DANY estimating its case-in-chief to last 3-4 weeks. Trials often take longer than anticipated, and our assessment based on the evidence and analysis in this essay is that it could take up to eight weeks. That being said, trials are inherently unpredictable and the case could take shorter or longer than all have estimated.

33. How Long Will Jury Deliberations Take?

It is difficult to predict, but if the trial lasts around six to eight weeks, expect jury deliberations to last from a few days to around one week.

34. What Will be Trump's Main Legal Defenses?

a. What Is Left After Motions Practice

In addition to raising factual defenses that challenge the prosecution's narrative of what happened, Trump will raise legal defenses that focus on the legal insufficiency of the charges. In other words, where the factual defenses amount to "I didn't do what you said I did," the legal defenses are essentially, "Even if I did what you said I did, it's not a crime." These are previewed by the analysis in Questions 4 and 16 above, describing Trump's motions to dismiss, both sides' motions *in limine*, and the justice's decisions on them.

The decisions on the motions *in limine* and the briefing that preceded those decisions substantially trimmed back available defenses. For example, as described more fully above in Question 16, DANY filed a motion *in limine* to preclude Trump from arguing selective prosecution and Trump filed a motion *in limine* to preclude DANY from arguing that Trump's personal or trust account constitute business records. Justice Merchan found DANY's motion to preclude Trump's argument of selective prosecution mooted, since Trump represented "that he does 'not intend to ask the jury to acquit'" on that basis. Merchan also ruled that the Trump Organization and Trump's personal accounts are "intertwined to such a degree" that he rejected Trump's motion to preclude arguments about his personal accounts. Those and other legal defenses are now off the table for trial.

As for the motions to dismiss discussed above in Question 4, Trump raised seven different legal defenses in attempting to dismiss the indictment. The court's rejection of these arguments for purposes of throwing out the entire case, however, does not mean that Trump cannot try to persuade the jury that certain of those defenses are valid. For example, Justice Merchan ruled that the indictment adequately alleged Trump's intent to commit other crimes as to three out of the four predicates set forth in the response to the request for a bill of particulars (state and federal election and campaign crimes and state tax ones). But Trump remains free to argue to the jury that he did not have that intent.

Indeed, Trump's central argument to the jury will likely be that he lacked the requisite intent to commit, aid, or conceal another crime (a hybrid legal and factual question). He will argue that candidates regularly seek to prevent adverse publicity during a campaign, and doing so is not inherently wrongful. Ultimately, the jury instruction for falsifying records will govern the legal standard the jury applies when it evaluates this defense and whether DANY has proven the required intent. (For more about this issue and the jury instructions see Chapter 7.)

b. The John Edwards Defense[1]

Some commentators, and Trump's defense attorney, appear to be trying to equate the hush money payments in this case to the contributions at issue in the unsuccessful prosecution of former Senator and presidential candidate John Edwards. But the Edwards case was borderline as to whether it should have been brought, both legally and factually, whereas the Trump case is relatively straightforward.

Edwards was charged in a North Carolina federal court with five counts of campaign finance violations and one count of conspiracy (essentially, to commit the scheme contained within the other five counts). Many of the facts in the case were uncontested. From early 2006 through approximately August 2008, Edwards had an extramarital affair with Rielle Hunter, a former campaign videographer. The National Enquirer published allegations of the affair in October 2007, and a subsequent article in December 2007 alleging Hunter was pregnant. Edwards initially denied the affair, and his campaign aide Andrew Young claimed paternity over the baby. Over months, Edwards used payments from donors, some of which Young had collected, to pay for travel and accommodations for Young and Hunter to escape media attention. In the background of the affair, its coverup, and Edwards' presidential campaign was his wife Elizabeth, who had stage-IV breast cancer. In an April 2007 interview, she acknowledged the cancer was likely terminal. She passed away in December 2007, survived by three children.

To secure a conviction, federal prosecutors had to prove that each of the six offenses were done willfully, which required a jury to find that Edwards knew his conduct was unlawful. That appears to have been one of their major challenges. The Government relied almost entirely on the testimony of Young—who was granted immunity for cooperating in the prosecution—and that of his wife, Cheri. Both had motivation to fabricate testimony. Young had the threat of criminal prosecution hanging over his head if he failed to implicate Edwards. And Young had significant exposure were he convicted: he testified that he kept approximately $1 million in payments for his own personal use. Cheri's motivation to fabricate was not as strong, but a desire to support her husband and perhaps to seek revenge against the man she believed had wronged them likely played a role in the jury's minds. Additionally, the proof as to whether the donors knew where their payments were going or that the campaign solicited the payments for that purpose was less than ironclad, in part because the donors themselves were unavailable as witnesses.

Among Edwards' defense team's many arguments were (1) that the money was personal and not election-related for the purpose of FECA because he used the money solely to hide the affair from his dying wife, and subsequently from their surviving children; and (2) in any event, he did not know that he could be violating federal campaign finance laws. He mounted a robust defense, calling a number of witnesses, including both a former FEC chairman (who testified as to how complicated campaign finance law is) and one of Edwards' former lawyers (who testified in support of Edwards' contention that he did not know the payments were illegal).

Ultimately, the jury deadlocked on five counts and acquitted Edwards of one count (illegal use of campaign funds). Any prosecutor who tries these types of cases (or defense lawyer who defends them) will tell you that without a proverbial smoking gun, proving a willful violation of a complex statute is challenging. Nevertheless, the fact that the Government came close in this case with a deadlocked jury suggests that when the proof is substantially more compelling, conviction is a real possibility. (In that case, the government decided against re-trying the charges on which the jury hung).

c. Contrasting the Edwards and Trump Cases

Trump's defense will lack many of the attributes that helped Edwards avoid conviction. Compare Cohen (an imperfect, yet credible witness who already has served his time) with Young, whose motivation to stay out of prison clearly had an impact on his credibility. Trump also lacks the personal motivation that Edwards was able to argue— whereas Edwards' wife was unaware of the affair, public evidence suggests that Melania already knew about Trump's affair with Clifford. Edwards therefore could credibly argue he had a strong motive to keep the affair secret from his wife and their children. The fact that Edwards even made a payment after he dropped out of the election further buttresses that point. Moreover, whereas both McDougal and Clifford were in negotiations to go public about their affairs, there is no indication that Edwards' mistress had any similar inclination.

What's more, the Trump payment was made only weeks before the election. And there is likely to be testimony from Cohen, Pecker, and perhaps others that the purpose of the payment was related to the election (the non-prosecution agreement with Pecker's AMI is one piece of evidence, and the audio recording of Trump and Cohen referring to the arrangement with Pecker is another). The Justice Department's sentencing memorandum in Cohen's federal criminal case is also replete with references to how the arrangement was designed—starting two months after Trump announced his presidential run—to suppress stories being published before the election. And whereas Edwards' former lawyer testified in his defense as to his good faith, Trump's former lawyer (Cohen) will testify as to his bad faith. The proof as to the facts of a falsified business record and whichever likely predicate crime is alleged against Trump are also much stronger than were the facts of the campaign finance violations alleged against Edwards.

In short, although the two cases share some overlaps

involving presidential campaigns and secret affairs, the outcome of the cases is likely to be very different.

35. Does Presidential Immunity Apply?

Almost certainly not, although Trump waived the issue in the federal proceedings and then missed the deadlines to bring it up in the state ones.

Let's begin with the proceedings in state court. In a March 7 motion, filed less than three weeks before jury selection, Trump asked Merchan to adjourn the trial pending the U.S. Supreme Court's decision on presidential immunity in *Trump v. United States*, the January 6th federal election interference case. The Supreme Court will hear argument in that case on April 25. Additionally, Trump requested that the court preclude evidence that he describes as constituting his "official acts," based on presidential immunity. He contends that DANY must be precluded from introducing public statements he made while president, since such statements were made within the "outer perimeter" of his official responsibilities as president, and thus cannot be offered as evidence in the case.

On March 13, DANY responded in opposition, arguing that Trump's motion should firstly be denied as untimely. Alternatively, the court should defer ruling until a later date, prior to the end of trial. In any case, DANY rightly contends, Trump's arguments are meritless, as has been made clear, including by the editor of this volume.

On April 3, Merchan denied the motion in its entirety.

a. The Motion was Untimely

Merchan found that Trump had "myriad opportunities

to raise the claim of presidential immunity well before March 7, 2024." New York law strongly disfavors last-minute delaying tactics, even those that might be permissible earlier in the proceedings including arguments of this kind or other maneuvers (like changing lawyers). The court's order described how Trump could have raised this argument in his omnibus motion to dismiss in September 2023, in his motions *in limine*, or in his opposition to DANY's motions *in limine*. Rather than raising the issue at one of those times, Trump chose to wait to do so just weeks before trial, after the February 22 deadline for motions *in limine,* and months after the court-imposed September 2023 deadline for omnibus motions.

Merchan's decision explained how Trump has long been aware of DANY's case against him which he, on the eve of trial, claimed has immunity implications (because the case makes explicit reference to a 2018 pressure campaign and conduct and statements made while he was in office). The proper time for Trump to have advanced a presidential immunity argument was in summer 2023, when he sought to remove his case to New York federal court based on a "colorable" federal defense. But he didn't and, as such, "surrendered that claim." In fact, Judge Hellerstein made clear—when rejecting the removal motion, which was primarily premised on, inter alia, Supremacy Clause immunity—that Trump had "expressly waived any argument premised on a theory of absolute presidential immunity." For that reason alone, many have taken the view that Trump "should not be permitted to reopen the issue" and get another "bite at the apple."

Not only did Trump fail to raise presidential immunity in his unsuccessful bid to be tried in federal court, he later chose to abandon his appeal before the United States

Court of Appeals for the Second Circuit of Hellerstein's ruling and has failed to raise the issue in any of his prior pretrial motions in New York state court, which has already prompted stern words from Merchan.

Trump also could have raised the issue before Justice Merchan in October 2023 when he filed a motion to dismiss before Judge Chutkan in DC, or when he appealed that ruling to the DC Court of Appeals or the U.S. Supreme Court. But he didn't. As DANY noted, "the very existence of" Trump's immunity appeal before the Supreme Court, which he "egregious[ly]" "attempt[s] to link" with Bragg's prosecution, "shows that [Trump] could have raised an immunity argument months before the current motion."

b. The Motion Lacks Merit

Because it denied the motion for being untimely, the court did not need to address the merits of the immunity argument. Nevertheless, the motion appeared to fail on the merits because Trump's conduct is personal or political, and is not official. With respect to Trump's evidentiary contention that his public statements and portions of the grand jury testimony must be excluded, the motion cited no applicable authority to support why DANY should be precluded from introducing, *inter alia*, public social media posts by Trump. The same appeared to be the case regarding evidence of alleged Trump statements constituting intimidation of Michael Cohen that just happened to have been made while president, despite having nothing to do with his official duties. Such an argument was "ridiculous... [and] the very tweets that Trump is trying to keep out of evidence also refute his argument" because they show the personal nature of his behavior.

As Judge Hellerstein ruled, Trump's conduct at issue in this case does not constitute official presidential acts. Even if the alleged acts were within the outer perimeter of his official duties, DANY argued that there is no categorical rule in New York that would preclude the admission of evidence of official acts that are *relevant* to, but do not directly underpin, criminal charges for non-immune conduct.

In any case, as DANY argued, Trump's motion raised no presidential immunity argument specific to the "actual charges in the indictment," having already conceded in federal court that his conduct was not protected by any such immunity and having not raised anything to the contrary in subsequent motions.

36. Can Trump Argue an "Advice-of-Counsel" Defense?

Trump has proclaimed on social media that he relied on counsel. For example, in Jan. 2023 he declared, "I placed full Reliance on the JUDGMENT & ADVICE OF COUNCIL, who I had every reason to believe had a license to practice law, was competent, & was able to appropriately provide solid legal services... [T]here was NO reason not to rely on him, and I did."

Asserting an advice-of-counsel defense on social media, however, is not the same as doing so in a court of law, and the judge has found that Trump has not met the requirements for advancing such a defense and will not be permitted to do so.

On February 7, 2024, Justice Merchan ordered Trump to provide "notice and disclosure of his intent to rely on the defense of advice-of-counsel by March 11, 2024, and to produce all [relevant] discoverable statements and commu-

nications within his possession or control by the same date."
The elements of such a defense are that the defendant:

1. made a complete disclosure to counsel
   [concerning the matter at issue],
2. sought advice as to the legality of his conduct,
3. received advice that his conduct was legal, and
4. relied on that advice in good faith.

Electing to assert the formal defense also requires the waiver of the attorney-client privilege and the production of communications normally protected by it.

On March 11, Trump filed a notice stating that he "does not intend to assert a formal advice-of-counsel defense that would require him to prove at trial" the elements of such a defense. Instead, Trump says he intends to negate unlawful intent by eliciting purported "probative" evidence proving his "awareness that various lawyers were involved in the underlying conduct giving rise to the charges," including "the presence, involvement and advice of lawyers." To corroborate, Trump intends to call witnesses, "including former AMI executives and Michael Cohen." Without formal reliance on an advice-of-counsel defense, Trump contends, "there is no privilege waiver requiring production of communications protected by the attorney-client privilege, and there is no basis for the People to demand a preview of our defenses at trial."

It appeared that Trump was trying to eat his cake and have it too, utilizing attorney advice to rebut the prosecution's case without meeting the legal requirements for doing so. The court agreed, rejecting Trump's distinction between "advice-of-counsel" and "presence of counsel" defenses. To allow the latter, the court reasoned, would "effectively permit Defendant to invoke the very defense he has declared he will not rely upon, without the concomitant obligations that come with it. The result would undoubtedly be to confuse and mislead the jury."

A similar tactic was recently spurned by Judge Lewis Kaplan in the prosecution of Sam Bankman-Fried. In that case, around six weeks before trial the government <u>sought</u> to preclude Bankman-Fried from arguing or adducing evidence at trial regarding the "involvement of lawyers in certain events at" his two cryptocurrency firms, unless he first asserted formal notice of an advice-of-counsel defense. Specifically, the government <u>asked</u> Kaplan to preclude Bankman-Fried "'from unduly focusing on the facts of attorney's involvement'... or 'suggesting that attorneys blessed, for instance, the loans, bank documents, or message deletions.'" In his October 2023 <u>opinion</u> the day before trial, Kaplan ruled that the defense was prohibited from referring in opening statements to the presence or involvement of attorneys.

Trump referred to Judge Kaplan's decision in attempting to distinguish between what he called a "formal advice-of-counsel defense" and an (informal) "presence of counsel" defense. Justice Merchan said Trump's argument quoted a select portion of Judge Kaplan's ruling but ignored the rest, including the critical findings that it was not clear how the formal and informal defenses were different and the substantial risk of jury confusion.

SENTENCING AND APPEAL

37. If Convicted, What Will be Trump's Sentence?

Falsifying records in the first degree is a class E felony, punishable by a maximum of four years in prison and a $5,000 fine. class E felonies generally carry indeterminate sentences, meaning that the court is authorized to impose a sentence within a certain range. For indeterminate sentences, the court often imposes a minimum and a maximum, with the minimum representing the amount of time the defendant must serve before being eligible for parole. For class E felonies, the lowest sentencing range is one to three years, and the highest range is 1 ⅓ to four years. However, for defendants with limited or no criminal history such as Trump, there is no minimum sentence. A court can impose an alternative sentence of a fixed term of less than one year of incarceration, based upon the nature of the crime and the defendant's "history and character."

This means the judge will have discretion in imposing a sentence, taking into account the seriousness of the conduct on which Trump is convicted, the evidence at trial, Trump's testimony, and other factors.

In New York, a jail sentence of less than one year is served in a New York City jail and is ordered as a set period of time (e.g. 5 months or one year). A sentence of more than one year is served in a State Correctional Facility.

As detailed in Chapter 8, there is precedent for imposing a sentence of incarceration for a defendant with no criminal history convicted of falsifying records, although the cases typically include other serious charges. In 2015, an executive of a building construction company was sentenced to two days per week in jail for one year for a bribery scheme in which he falsified records to conceal improper payments to secure a client's business. (The ringleader received a sentence of 2 to 6 years plus a $500,000 forfeiture on other charges.) In two cases in 2013, corporate executives received sentences of four and six months for falsifying records to misclassify more than $1 million of their salaries as expenses as part of a larger scheme involving bribery and fraud by their employer. And as discussed above, Weisselberg received a five-month jail sentence and five months' probation for pleading guilty to all 15 counts, including four falsifying records counts, although the other charges included other serious offenses such as grand larceny, offering a false document for filing and scheme to defraud.

That and much more about sentencing is described in more detail in Chapter 8.

38. If Convicted, Does Trump Have a Right to Appeal?

Yes. Trump can appeal his conviction and/or sentence following final judgment or sentence. NY CPL § 450.10.

All appeals, except those including a sentence of death, are made to the NY appellate division. Trump would have 30 days from judgment/sentence to file notice of appeal to the trial court. NY CPL § 460.10.

If Trump loses the first appeal, he can seek reargument before the First Department or apply for leave to appeal to the New York Court of Appeals. The decision of the First Department will not automatically be remitted to the trial court if Trump pursues these options. If he applies for leave to appeal and it is granted, the execution of any judgment can be stayed pending the determination of the appeal by the New York Court of Appeals.

39. Can the State Appeal?

Yes, the state also has a right to appeal in very limited circumstances, including an order dismissing charges or setting aside the verdict. NY CPL § 450.20. The state cannot appeal an acquittal.

40. Will Trump's Conviction and/or Sentence (If Any) Be Stayed Pending Appeal?

Not automatically. Trump can apply for a stay pending appeal, which can be sought from the trial court or the First Department. NY CPL § 460.50.

41. What Happens if Trump is Reelected?

Should Trump assume the presidency during the pendency of an appeal, he will undoubtedly instruct his personal attorneys and the United States Department of Justice to argue that the U.S. Constitution requires all pending proceedings to be stayed because they interfere with his duties as president. Because no sitting president has ever been charged, much less been convicted, sentenced, and appealed, the courts have not addressed this question. The U.S. Supreme Court has, however, permitted civil proceedings against a sitting president (Clinton v. Jones) and the enforcement of criminal subpoenas (United States v. Nixon & Trump v. Vance). It remains to be seen what the Supreme Court would do with respect to a pending appeal of a criminal sentence, which would not appear to be unduly burdensome, or with respect to serving such a sentence, which presents a more profound prospect of interference with presidential duties.

7

JURY INSTRUCTIONS

S tates can formulate model jury instructions for a given crime. At the conclusion of trials, a judge will draw on these models to instruct the jury on how it is to evaluate the elements of the crime. In this chapter, we explain how the court will approach the jury instructions.

This essay originally appeared as part of "A Complete Guide to the Manhattan Trump Election Interference Prosecution," which was published by Norm Eisen, Andrew Warren and Siven Watt in Just Security on March 27, 2024. It has been slightly modified for this publication.

42. What Does DANY Have to Prove to Convict?

All 34 counts allege the same charge of falsifying business records in the first degree. For each count, per New York's standard jury instructions the two elements that must be proven are:

(1) That on or about the date in question, Trump made or caused a false entry in the business records of an enterprise; *or*

Altered, erased, obliterated, deleted, removed, or destroyed a true entry in the business records of an enterprise; *or*

Omitted to make a true entry in the business records of an enterprise in violation of a duty to do so which the defendant knew to be imposed upon him/her by law or by the nature of his/her position; *or*

Prevented the making of a true entry of caused the omission thereof in the business records of an enterprise;

and

(2) Trump did so with intent to defraud that included an intent to commit another crime or to aid or conceal the commission thereof.

In terms of part (1) of the statute, the first prong ("made or caused") is the only theory pleaded in the indictment, so the other three will not go to the jury. In terms of part (2), intent to defraud, "courts in the First Department have interpreted this culpable mental state broadly. Intent to defraud is not constricted to an intent to deprive another of property or money. In fact, 'intent to defraud' can extend beyond economic concern. Nor is there any requirement that a defendant intend to conceal the commission of his own crime; instead, 'a person can commit First Degree Falsifying Business Records by falsifying records with the intent to cover up a crime committed by somebody else.'" People v. Trump, 2024 NY Slip Op 30560(U). Note that the state's pattern jury instructions say that intent "means conscious objective or purpose. Thus, a person acts with intent to defraud when his or her conscious objective or purpose is to do so."

43. What are the Other Crimes that DANY Has to Prove Trump Intended to Commit, Aid, or Conceal?

As part of establishing the second element of each falsifying records charge, DANY must prove that Trump intended to commit, aid, or conceal another crime—in this case, either a violation of the Federal Election Campaign Act, New York Election Law § 17-152, or New York tax law. Importantly, DANY does not have to prove that Trump actually violated any of the three predicate crimes, but rather that by falsifying (or causing the falsification of) business records he had the *intent* to commit, aid, or conceal the commission of such crime(s). Further, the jury need not find that Trump had that intent as to all three predicate crimes—a conviction is proper if jurors are satisfied beyond a reasonable doubt as to an intent to commit at least one predicate crime per count.

a. Federal Election Campaign Act (FECA)

Throughout 2016, FECA placed the following applicable limitations and prohibitions on campaign contributions: (a) individual contributions to any presidential candidate, including expenditures coordinated with a presidential candidate or her political committee, were limited to $2,700 per election, and presidential candidates and their committees were prohibited from accepting contributions from individuals in excess of this limit (52 U.S.C. § 30116(a)(1)(A), (f); 11 C.F.R. §§ 110.1(b), 110.9); and (b) corporations were prohibited from making contributions directly to presidential candidates, including expenditures coordinated with presidential candidates or their committees, and presidential candidates and their committees were prohibited from accepting corporate contributions (52 U.S.C. § 30118(a); 11 C.F.R. § 114.2(b)). (*See also* Cohen federal criminal information, p. 11; FEC McDougal/AMI/Pecker analysis, pp. 13-15; FEC Cohen analysis, p.2, n. 3). A "contribution" includes "any gift, subscription, loan, advance, or deposit of money or anything of value made by any person for the purpose of influencing any election for Federal office." 52 U.S.C. § 30101(8)(A). (*See also* 11 C.F.R. §§ 100.52(a); 113.1(g)(6))

The amount that Cohen and ultimately Trump paid to purchase and suppress information that could harm Trump's campaign far exceeded those limits as of 2016.

b. State Election Law

New York Election Law § 17-152 prohibits a conspiracy to use "unlawful means" to promote or prevent a person's election. The phrase "unlawful means" is interpreted broadly and is not limited to crimes but rather includes any conduct unauthorized by law. In denying Trump's motion to dismiss, Justice Merchan upheld DA Bragg's theory under this statute, namely: "the People allege that Defendant intended to violate N.Y. Election Law § 17-152 by conspiring to 'promote the election of any person to a public office... by entering a scheme specifically for purposes of influencing the 2016 presidential election; and that they did so by 'unlawful means,' including by violating FECA through the unlawful individual and corporate contributions by Cohen, Pecker, and AMI; and... by falsifying the records of other New York enterprises and mischaracterizing the nature of the repayment for tax purposes.' People's Opposition at pg. 25."

c. State Tax Law

For the purposes of tax violations, Bragg relies on two related tax provisions: New York Tax Law §§ 1801(a)(3) & 1802. Section 1801(a) sets out relevant tax fraud acts, with subsection (3) prohibiting "knowingly suppl[ying] or submit[ting] materially false or fraudulent information in connection with any [tax] return, audit, investigation, or proceeding." The tax fraud includes four elements: (1) a tax document filed, submitted or supplied; (2) falsity; (3) materiality; and (4) intent (willfulness). Any person who commits a tax fraud act, including under 1801(a)(3), is guilty, at a minimum, of criminal tax fraud in the fifth degree, a class A misdemeanor crime under Section 1802, where the tax liability is less than $3,000. No additional mens rea is required, such as an intent to evade taxes or defraud the state. In this case, the primary alleged tax violation was Cohen falsely declaring the reimbursement as income, which artificially *increased* his tax liability. As Justice Merchan already found, however, an allegation of tax fraud where the state "was not financially harmed... and instead would wind up collecting more tax revenue" does not preclude the tax violation from being a predicate act for the first degree falsification of business records.

44. What is the Burden of Proof?

In any criminal case, the prosecution must prove each of the elements of a particular count beyond a reasonable doubt. At the beginning and end of the trial, the judge will instruct the jury on the definition of reasonable doubt. New York's model jury instructions describe reasonable doubt, in part, as follows:

[T]here are very few things in this world that we know with absolute certainty. Therefore, the law does not require the people to prove a defendant guilty beyond all possible doubts. On the other hand, it is not sufficient to prove that the defendant is probably guilty. Criminal case, the proof of guilt must be stronger than that. It must be beyond a reasonable doubt.

A reasonable doubt is an honest doubt of the defendant's guilt for which a reason exists based upon the nature and quality of the evidence. It is an actual doubt, not an imaginary doubt. It is a doubt that a reasonable person, acting in a matter of this importance, would be likely to entertain because of the evidence that was presented or because of the lack of convincing evidence.

Proof of guilt beyond a reasonable doubt is proof that leaves you so firmly convinced of the defendant's guilt that you have no reasonable doubt of the existence of any element of the crime or of the defendant's identity as the person who committed the crime.

45. What Will Be in the Jury Instructions?

Typically, the court will instruct the jury on the applicable law following closing arguments. To determine what instructions will be read to the jury, the parties and the judge will have a charging conference (also called a "pre-charge conference") outside the presence of the jury where they discuss and litigate the applicable law and relevant instructions. Like most states and federal practice, New York has model jury instructions that serve as a benchmark for judges. There are model instructions universal to any criminal case as well as statute-specific instructions depending on the charges involved. These instructions are based on basic legal principles and rely on statutory language and prevailing case law. In some instances, there will not be a model instruction for a relevant issue, and the parties and court will have to draft the instruction based on the law. Model instructions exist for the vast majority of issues, however, and courts generally use the model instruction where possible to avoid a mistaken or confusing instruction that could create an appellate issue.

New York's model final jury instructions include approximately 25 general instructions, covering basic issues including the role of the jury; evidence; presumption of innocence; burden of proof; reasonable doubt; witness credibility; expert witnesses; juror note taking; deliberations; electing a foreperson; and the verdict sheet.

The critical instruction will address the law on the falsification of business records. The wrinkle in this case will be adding instructions to explain the object crimes, so that the jury understands the elements of FECA, New York Election Law § 17-152, and the two tax statutes that Trump is alleged to have intended to violate by falsifying records.

Starting with FECA, DANY alleges that Trump intended to violate 52 U.S.C. § 30116, which limits individual campaign contributions to $2,700, and 52 U.S.C. § 30118, which prohibits corporations from making direct contributions to a federal campaign at all. It is a crime to knowingly and willfully violate these prohibitions.

Regarding the second object crime, DANY's theory is that Trump intended to violate New York Election Law by "entering into this scheme specifically for purposes of influencing the 2016 presidential election; and that they did so by 'unlawful means'—including by violating FECA through the unlawful individual and corporate contributions... by falsifying the records of other New York enterprises and mischaracterizing the nature of the repayment for tax purposes." That is, DANY contends that the "unlawful means" employed by Trump in violation of § 17-152 was the commission of other crimes, namely FECA, tax fraud, and falsification of other business records.

Regarding the third object crime, there is a model jury instruction for tax fraud. Expect that instruction to be given to explain the elements of the tax laws that Trump is alleged to have intended to violate.

Complicating matters is the court's ruling on the motion to dismiss, in which it precluded DANY from using falsification of Cohen's or AMI's business records as a fourth object crime. However, the court wrote that DANY will be "permitted to present evidence at trial that stems from the fourth theory, to the extent that the evidence advances any one or more of the first three theories." It is unclear from the court's opinion whether DANY could satisfy its second object crime theory—violation of state election law—by arguing that Cohen's or AMI's falsification of records constitutes "unlawful means" prohibited by § 17-152.

46. What is in the Relevant Model Jury Instructions?

We reprint the model jury instructions for Penal Law § 175.10 in full as a reference:

FALSIFYING BUSINESS RECORDS IN THE FIRST DEGREE

Penal Law § 175.10

(Committed on or after November 1, 1986)

The (*specify*) count is Falsifying Business Records in the First Degree. Under our law, a person is guilty of falsifying business records in the first degree when, with intent to defraud that includes an intent to commit another crime or to aid or conceal the commission thereof, that person:

Select appropriate alternative:

makes or causes a false entry in the business records of an enterprise;

or

alters, erases, obliterates, deletes, removes or destroys a true entry in the business records of an enterprise;

or

omits to make a true entry in the business records of an enterprise in violation of a duty to do so which he or she knows to be imposed upon him or her by law or by the nature of his or her position;

or

prevents the making of a true entry or causes the omission thereof in the business records of an enterprise.

The following terms used in that definition have a special meaning:

ENTERPRISE means any entity of one or more persons, corporate or otherwise, public or private, engaged in business, commercial, professional, industrial, eleemosynary, social, political or governmental activity.

BUSINESS RECORD means any writing or article, including computer data or a computer program, kept or maintained by an enterprise for the purpose of evidencing or reflecting its condition or activity.

INTENT means conscious objective or purpose. Thus, a person acts with intent to defraud when his or her conscious objective or purpose is to do so.

In order for you to find the defendant guilty of this crime, the People are required to prove, from all of the evidence in the case, beyond a reasonable doubt, each of the following two elements:

1. That on or about (<u>date</u>), in the county of (<u>county</u>), the defendant, (<u>defendant's name</u>),

Select appropriate alternative:

made or caused a false entry in the business records of an enterprise;

or

altered, erased, obliterated, deleted, removed or destroyed a true entry in the business records of an enterprise;

or

omitted to make a true entry in the business records of an enterprise in violation of a duty to do so which the defendant knew to be imposed upon him/her by law or by the nature of his/her position;

or

prevented the making of a true entry or caused the omission thereof in the business records of an enterprise;

and,

2. That the defendant did so with intent to defraud that included an intent to commit another crime or to aid or conceal the commission thereof.

[*Note: If the affirmative defense does not apply, conclude as follows*:

If you find the People have proven beyond a reasonable doubt both of those elements, you must find the defendant guilty of this crime.

If you find the People have not proven beyond a reasonable doubt either one or both of those elements, you must find the defendant not guilty of this crime.

[NOTE: *If the affirmative defense does apply, continue as follows*:

If you find that the People have not proven beyond a reasonable doubt either one or both of those elements, you must find the defendant not guilty of Falsifying Business Records in the First Degree.

If you find that the People have proven beyond a reasonable doubt both of the elements, you must consider an affirmative defense the defendant has raised. Remember, if you have already found the defendant not guilty of Falsifying Business Records in the First Degree, you will not consider the affirmative defense.

Under our law, it is an affirmative defense to this charge of Falsifying Business Records in the First Degree that the defendant, at the time he/she engaged in the conduct constituting the offense, was a clerk, bookkeeper or other employee who, without personal benefit, merely executed the orders of his/her employer or of a superior officer or employee generally authorized to direct his/her activities.

Under our law, the defendant has the burden of proving an affirmative defense by a preponderance of the evidence.

In determining whether the defendant has proven the affirmative defense by a preponderance of the evidence, you may consider evidence introduced by the People or by the defendant.

A preponderance of the evidence means the greater part of the believable and reliable evidence, not in terms of the number of witnesses or the length of time taken to present the evidence, but in terms of its quality and the weight and convincing effect it has. For the affirmative defense to be proved by a preponderance of the evidence, the evidence that supports the affirmative defense must be of such convincing quality as to outweigh any evidence to the contrary.

If you find that the defendant has not proven the affirmative defense by a preponderance of the evidence, then, based upon your initial determination that the People had proven beyond a reasonable doubt both of the elements of Falsifying Business Records in the First Degree, you must find the defendant guilty of that crime.

If you find that the defendant has proven the affirmative defense by a preponderance of the evidence, then you must find the defendant not guilty of Falsifying Business Records in the First Degree.

A GUIDE TO SENTENCING

C*hapter 8 addresses sentencing, specifically the likelihood of incarceration if Trump is convicted. We start by explaining New York's sentencing law before exploring the state's precedent for imposing incarcerative sentences for falsifying business records, using case-specific examples. We conclude by evaluating how Trump's history and character factor into the sentencing analysis.*

Introduction

TRUMP FACES 34 felony counts of falsifying business records to cover up hush money paid to keep a damaging scandal from voters in the 2016 election. Each felony charge of first-degree business record falsification carries a statutory maximum sentence of four years of imprisonment.[1] Normally as a first time offender we would not expect Trump to receive a sentence of incarceration—but he and this case are anything but normal. As we detail below, Trump's case presents legally cognizable aggravating factors that make a sentence of incarceration not only possible but likely, and there are multiple examples of first-time offenders charged with this offense getting jail time. Whether Trump is among them will depend of course on what is proven at trial and also on whether he continues to comport himself as he has so far in this case, in his other criminal cases, and in his recent civil trials in state and federal court. No one knows the answer to that question, perhaps not even Trump himself. But we see little reason to think he will change.

Because falsifying business records in the first degree is a Class E felony, non-incarceral sentences such as probation or conditional discharge are available sentencing option for the court. But District Attorney Bragg can and may well make a strong argument that the court should sentence Trump to prison if he is convicted at trial. Under New York law, its state courts regularly consider "'the nature and circumstances of the crime and . . . history and character of the defendant'" in determining whether to impose a sentence of imprisonment.[2] At sentencing the DA may argue and the judge consider the full context—that is, Trump's misconduct, both here and elsewhere, as well as his character.

That picture will be profoundly adverse to Trump should it be presented at sentencing. His alleged conduct giving rise to the charges here is serious: the payment of hush money to avoid another damaging sex scandal in the last days of the 2016 presidential contest, which could have cost him the election in the wake of the Access Hollywood revelations. He is charged with covering up that hush money scheme with 34 instances of document falsification. This is no minor peccadillo but (if proven at trial) an offense amounting to election interference–a precursor to his alleged 2020 election interference at issue in the federal and Fulton County prosecutions. Facts relevant to all of that may be considered at sentencing under New York law.

As we outline below, many other issues regarding Trump's character may also be relevant: his lack of remorse (assuming that does not change), his attacks on witnesses and court personnel in this case and elsewhere, his penchant for lying, and on and on. There is also precedent for sentencing first-time offenders to incarceration where the charges include felony document falsification. Even defendants who have accepted responsibility and pleaded guilty to felony records falsification have been incarcerated, as have defendants who have pleaded guilty to that felony in the context of campaign finance violations. That includes the outcome of a recent case involving a different falsifica-tion of the Trump Organization's business records, although there and in other cases additional serious misconduct was charged.

The net effect of all of these factors is to make a sentence of incarceration likely should Trump continue his long-established approach to similar allegations and be convicted. That is appropriate given the impact of his misconduct upon our democracy both in 2016 and in paving the way for what happened in 2020.

The Nature of the Charged Crimes

The formal charges in this case for false business records must be understood in the context in which Trump allegedly committed those crimes. In the closing days of the 2016 election, he concealed a potentially devastating political story from the voting public through an alleged scheme to make hush money payments to a porn star. Because he did not want this scheme to be revealed through campaign finance disclosures, he allegedly channeled those payments through his personal lawyer and then allegedly concealed the nature of those payments through the falsification of business records. Those facts, if proven, constitute an attempt to corruptly influence the 2016 presidential election and then conceal it. District Attorney Bragg has in effect charged Trump with committing crimes that harmed voters and democracy itself[3] by covering up[4] the most consequential alleged campaign finance violations[5] in American history.[6] According to the Statement of Facts filed with the indictment,

> The defendant DONALD J. TRUMP repeatedly and fraudulently falsified New York business records to conceal criminal conduct that hid damaging information from the voting public during the 2016 presidential election . . . . From August 2015 to December 2017, the Defendant orchestrated a scheme with others to influence the 2016 presidential election by identifying and purchasing negative information about him to suppress its publication and benefit the Defendant's electoral prospects. In order to execute the unlawful scheme, the participants violated election laws and made and caused false entries in the business records of various entities in New York. The participants also took steps that mischaracterized, for tax purposes, the true nature of the payments made in furtherance of the scheme.[7]

The 34 felony falsifying business records charges against Trump are the result. The consequences of the alleged conduct appear significant. The election was extremely close and decided by fewer than 80,000 votes across three states that Trump won by 0.2, 0.7, and 0.8 percentage points.[8] The story that his hush money payments suppressed was poised to break in the wake of the release of the "Access Hollywood" tape, wherein Trump proclaimed that he was free to sexually assault women, so he could not risk another revelation that could have altered the outcome of that contest.

Thus, the former president allegedly tampered with the 2016 election and got away with it, facing no immediate consequences. That appears to have emboldened him to try again in 2020. Seen in this light, District Attorney Bragg's prosecution is a precursor to the federal 2020 election-over-turn cases and also an important case for our democracy.

New York Sentencing Law Basics

For sentencing purposes, New York classifies crimes into five categories of felonies—A through E—and three categories of misdemeanors—class A, class B, and unclassified. On the most severe end of the spectrum are class A felonies, including murder, terrorism, kidnapping, major drug traf-ficking, and predatory sexual assault. On the other end of the spectrum are unclassified misdemeanors, which include vehicle and traffic offenses. New York also classifies certain low-level offenses as "violations," including trespass and disorderly conduct.

New York's sentencing laws vary based on the type of offender. For example, different provisions apply for repeat offenders, repeat violent offenders, and juveniles. As noted above, falsifying records in the first degree is the lowest severity of felony, class E. Trump has no criminal history, so his sentence if convicted is governed by Chapter 40, Article 70, Section 70.00.

Section 70.00 provides that most felony sentences are "indeterminate," meaning the court imposes a sentencing range consisting of a minimum and maximum term of years. PEN § 70.00(1). The section then defines the maximum term of an indeterminate sentence as "at least three years" and provides that for a class E felony, it "shall not exceed four years." PEN § 70.00(2). This means that, for a class E felony, a court imposes a sentence with the high end of the range being between three and four years. The statute then says for any felony other than class A, "the minimum period shall be fixed by the court and specific in the sentence and shall be not less than one year nor more than one-third of the maximum term imposed." PEN § 70.00(3)(b). This means that for a class E felony with a four-year maximum, the low-end of the sentencing range must be between one and 1 ⅓ years. Therefore, for a class E felony, the lowest range of incarceration a judge may impose as an indeterminate sentence is one to three years, and the highest range is 1 ⅓ to four years.

However, a judge is not required to impose an indeterminate sentence for class E felonies. Section 70.00(4) allows for an "alternative definite sentence" for class D and E felonies. For first time offenders, it provides that if:

> the court, having regard to the nature and circumstances of the crime and to the history and character of the defendant, is of the opinion that a sentence of imprisonment is necessary but that it would be unduly harsh to impose an indeterminate or determinate sentence, the court may

impose a definite sentence of imprisonment and fix a term of one year or less.

This provision gives judges flexibility to sentence a class E offender outside of the minimum and maximum (indeterminate) ranges and instead to a fixed term of one year or less. As expressly provided, such a sentence is warranted where the court determines that imprisonment is "necessary." Pursuant to Section 65.00, a court may impose a sentence of probation rather than incarceration.

Section 65.00 provides several factors for the court to consider in imposing a probationary sentence. First, it requires the court to consider the "nature and circumstances of the crime" and the "history, character and condition" of the defendant. PEN § 65.00(1)(b). It then gives additional criteria: whether (i) confinement is necessary for the protection of the public; (ii) the defendant is in need of guidance, training or other assistance which can be effectively administered through probation; and (iii) probation is "not inconsistent with the ends of justice." Probation is set at a fixed term of three, four or five years. PEN § 65.00(3)(a)(i).

New York sentencing law also provides for a sentence that does not involve incarceration or supervised probation. Called "conditional discharge," a court may impose conditions of restitution and rehabilitation, such as substance abuse treatment, community service, and maintaining gainful employment. Section 65.05 sets similar criteria to that of probation: the nature and circumstances of the offense; the defendant's history, character and condition; the public interest; and the ends of justice. PEN § 65.05(1). The period of conditional discharge is fixed at three years for felonies. PEN § 65.00(3)(a).

In sum, if Trump is convicted, the judge will have a

range of sentencing options at his disposal. Nevertheless, based on these authorities, DA Bragg will be able to make a compelling argument that Trump's crimes warrant incarceration. We now turn to the why: the precedents and how they apply to Trump's circumstances.

New York State Court Precedent

a. Statistical Data

There is precedent in New York state courts for imposing sentences of incarceration upon defendants convicted of felony falsifying business record charges. As set forth above, the statutory sentencing structure contemplates a carceral sentence of up to four years even for a first-time offender convicted of a single charge.[9] New York State aggregate case data suggest that approximately one in ten cases in which the most serious charge at arraignment is falsifying business records in the first degree (and in which the court ultimately imposes a sentence) results in a sentence of imprisonment.[10] Our analysis of the raw data available from New York State shows that between November 2020 and March 20, 2024, there were 457 cases with a final disposition in which the most serious charge at arraignment was falsifying business records in the first degree. Fifty-five of these cases–or approximately 12 percent of the total–resulted in a prison sentence.[11]

In order to perform our analysis, we downloaded the two .csv files available at OCA-STAT Act Report[12] and consolidated them. We refined the data to include only disposed cases in which felony falsification of business records, N.Y.P.L. § 175.10, was the top charge. We further refined that data to remove cases that were likely duplicates (i.e., those that were marked as being "disposed" due to having been sent to the grand jury or transferred to another court, each of which is almost certain to be reflected again in the court to which it was transferred). That yielded 457 cases with the following dispositions:

Count of Disposition Type Most Severe Sentence	Disposition Type						
	Dism-ACD	Dismissed	Other	Plea	Unknown	Verdict-ACQ	Grand Total
	48	35	36	22	4	1	146
Conditional Discharge				95			95
Fee				1			1
Fine		1		120			121
Imprisonment			2	53			55
Probation			2	32			34
Restitution				1			1
Surcharge				1			1
Unconditional Discharge				3			3
Grand Total	48	36	40	328	4	1	457

Table caption: Disposed Cases in Which NYPL 175.10 Was the Top Charge

Some of these sentences of incarceration may of course have resulted from plea agreements where the prosecutor agreed not to file further uncharged offenses, as was the case in the recent guilty plea filed by Allen Weisselberg to the charge of perjury.[13] Nonetheless, a sentence like Weisselberg's was ultimately imposed for the charge for which he was convicted. These numbers thus demonstrate that the defendant was sentenced to incarceration in a meaningful number of cases where felony falsifying business records is the most serious charge in the indictment. Moreover, data show that defendants pleaded guilty in at least 53 of the 55 cases we mentioned above that had falsifying business records in the first degree as the top charge at arraignment and that resulted in sentences of imprisonment; a defendant who is convicted at trial is frequently more worthy of receiving a carceral sentence than one who accepts responsibility and pleads guilty.

Other defendants convicted of this offense when it was not the top charge in the indictment may also have been sentenced to prison as a result of that conviction. The New York State aggregate case data does not, for example, account for cases in which the top charge at arraignment could potentially result in a longer sentence than falsifying business records but the defendant either accepts a plea offer to, or is convicted at trial of, the lower falsifying charge.[14] Such a scenario would not be uncommon where the defendant is charged with one or more crimes more serious than falsifying business records in the first degree, such as the underlying crime(s) that the falsification is intended to hide (which in past cases has included violent crimes, schemes to defraud, campaign finance violations, tax fraud, and grand larceny, to name only a few). Convictions such as these that also result in sentences of imprisonment are not captured by the New York State Unified Court System data presented above but certainly do occur and may even represent a large fraction of all sentences for falsifying business records.

In sum, New York law authorizes a sentence of incarceration for a conviction of felony falsification of a business record. New York courts have not hesitated to impose such sentences in appropriate cases. Whether the court is likely to sentence Donald Trump to prison upon a conviction therefore depends on whether his case is comparable to prior cases in which the defendant was so sentenced.

b. Specific Case Examples

1. Convictions for Falsifying Business Records in the First Degree —General

Past New York state sentences for falsifying business records in the first degree support a sentence of imprisonment for Trump if he is convicted at trial. Consider the case of David Adelhardt.[15] Adelhardt, like Trump, was a corporate chief executive officer conducting business related to constructing buildings. While leading Adelhardt Construction Corporation, he falsified purchase orders to conceal both (1) his firm's construction work at the home of a Citibank real estate executive whom he bribed to hire his firm to do work for Citibank as well as (2) payments for the executive's hunting trips. This was part of a larger scheme involving commercial bribe receiving and money laundering offenses. Mr. Adelhardt accepted responsibility by pleading guilty to just one count of falsifying business records in the first degree and received a one-year intermittent prison sentence (two days per week) totaling 104 days of imprisonment.

Trump's case bears similarities to Adelhardt's. The latter was convicted for falsifying business records as part of a scheme to cover up the commission of serious crimes. He was convicted of no other offense, including the underlying bribery that his business record falsification concealed. While Adelhardt's overall scheme was a serious matter, so is Trump's. He is alleged to have falsified documents with the intent to conceal or commit state and federal campaign finance or election law violations and state tax ones.[16] If that is proven, he will have been shown to have harmed voters by depriving them of important information and may well have affected the outcome of the 2016 presidential election.

Moreover, Trump's case will likely also present aggravating factors that were not present in Adelhardt's. In contrast to Adelhardt, Trump has not yet, and seems unlikely in the future to accept responsibility for his crimes.[17] Trump likely will not conserve judicial resources

264　　　　　　　　　NORMAN EISEN

or spare witnesses from having to testify against him by pleading guilty.

In addition to the Adelhardt case, New York courts have similarly sentenced other defendants to periods of incarceration who pleaded guilty only to falsifying business record felonies where the cases, like Trump's, typically involve allegations of other offenses. For example, a case involving electrical supply corporation executives resulted in jail sentences: Ira Friedman (sentenced to approximately six months of incarceration) and Todd Ehren (sentenced to approximately four months) pleaded guilty in 2013 to falsifying business records by misclassifying their salaries as expenses. The case involved a larger scheme including commercial bribery, theft and fraud by the corporation where they worked.[18] And in 2015, Kerriann Bryan pleaded guilty to one count of falsifying business records in the first degree and was sentenced to one year of incarceration.[19] Like this case, a false invoice was involved; the defendant allegedly created a false invoice to steal a sum in excess of $50,000. She was originally charged with grand larceny before pleading to record falsification.

If Trump is convicted at trial of the 34 counts of falsifying business records counts with which he is charged, then given both the nature of the underlying criminal conduct and the character of the defendant, the court could likewise sentence Trump to a period of incarceration consistent with prior cases.

2. Convictions for Falsifying Business Records in the First Degree —Campaign and Election Violations

Defendant Trump would not be the first person in New York to receive a carceral sentence following conviction for falsifying business records in the first degree related to campaign finance violations. For example, transportation executive Richard Brega was convicted of falsifying business records in just such circumstances.[20] Brega did so by misrepresenting to the New York State Board of Elections the source of funds that he funneled into a county executive campaign. In 2018, Brega pleaded guilty to one count of falsifying business records in the first degree and was sentenced to one year of imprisonment to run concurrently with his federal sentence of 50 months in prison for a separate bribery conviction.

Another political campaign case in which the defendant was convicted of falsifying business records in the first degree and sentenced to incarceration is that of Richard Luthmann. Luthmann was accused of impersonating New York political figures[21] on social media in an attempt to influence campaigns. In 2020, Luthmann pleaded guilty to three counts of falsifying business records in the first degree as well as to two misdemeanor violations of New York Election Law and received a carceral sentence on the felony falsification counts of time served. That amounted to approximately 40 months of incarceration, although the sentence was not solely attributable to the plea.[22]

Similarly, former New York State Assemblyman Clarence Norman was convicted in 2005 in connection with campaign finance violations following two separate trials. At his first trial, Norman was convicted of two felony campaign finance violations for soliciting contributions in excess of the contribution limit in his primary campaigns in 2000 (approximately $4,000 over the limit) and 2002 (approximately $2,000 over the limit) and one felony and one misdemeanor count of falsifying business records related to these contributions.[23] At his second trial[24] a few months later, he was convicted of grand larceny in the third degree, falsifying business records in the first degree, and offering a false instrument for filing in the first degree as a result of his depositing a $5,000 contribution to his campaign into his personal bank account and then falsifying related campaign records.[25] The court ultimately sentenced Norman to a period of incarceration of a minimum of two and a maximum of six years and noted that he had "'willfully and repeatedly'" violated the law and that his attempt to blame associates was "'unconvincing and shameful.'"[26] Although Norman's sentence was not solely attributable to his conviction for falsification of business records,[27] the fact that Norman was charged with the offense of falsifying business records related to campaign finance violations—and later sentenced to incarceration—makes his case yet another reference point.

3. Convictions for Falsifying the Trump Organization's Business Records in the First Degree by Other Trump Employees

Finally, Trump would not be the first person sentenced to a period of incarceration following a conviction for first-degree falsification of the business records of the Trump Organization. Trump Organization Chief Financial Officer Allen Weisselberg was sentenced in 2022 for his role in a Trump Organization tax fraud scheme to five months of incarceration after pleading guilty to all 15 charges he faced, including four counts of falsifying business records in the first degree, grand larceny, four counts of tax fraud, a scheme to defraud, conspiracy, and four counts of offering a false instrument.

Moreover, Trump's former attorney Michael Cohen was sentenced to three years in prison by a federal judge in part for committing, allegedly at the behest of Trump, the underlying criminal campaign finance violations in the instant case that are the basis for Trump's charges. Cohen was arguably a lesser participant in Trump's scheme to defraud voters and suppress information and he pleaded guilty and cooperated with prosecutors. While federal sentences might often be longer than state ones, the fact that Cohen was sentenced to three years in prison is also a relevant data point. Moreover, the fact the Cohen was sentenced to imprisonment for acting as a coconspirator to Trump in these very matters is a substantial reason why a sentencing judge might also sentence Trump to a carceral sentence.

The History and Character of the Defendant

Should Trump be convicted, District Attorney Bragg could develop a presentation on his history and character that would support incarceration. Below is a brief preliminary sketch supporting our conclusion that a sentence of incarceration is appropriate based on Trump's history and character.

There is relevant New York Court of Appeals precedent that supports lengthening the sentence of a defendant based upon evidence of wrongdoing that has not yet been finally adjudicated elsewhere in a court.[28] The misconduct must however be established at sentencing (or have been established elsewhere) by at least a preponderance of the evidence.[29] The judge will have discretion whether to consider merely pending cases and might elect not to do so. Matters which have been adjudicated of course present a more persuasive case for consideration at sentencing.

Trump's legal history is checkered, to say the least. His other pending indictments include two separate federal prosecutions: the Florida stolen classified documents and obstruction of justice case and the Washington, D.C., 2020 election interference case. In Georgia state court, Trump is a defendant in a sweeping multi-defendant RICO indictment for his conduct related to attempting to steal the 2020 election. His family business, the Trump Organization (of which he is the founder and which employs much of his family), has been convicted of numerous felonies including falsifying business records and engaging in a 13-year tax fraud scheme.[30] A federal judge also concluded in a civil case involving one of Trump's attorneys that "[b]ased on the evidence, the Court finds it more likely than not that President Trump corruptly attempted to obstruct the Joint Session of Congress on January 6, 2021," likely committing federal crimes in attempting a "coup."[31]

Moreover, there have been multiple civil cases where Trump has already been found to have committed serious legal violations by a preponderance of evidence; they also inform his history and character and the judge can consider them.[32] A jury found him to have sexually abused and defamed E. Jean Carroll, who has made additional defamation allegations in another pending lawsuit; a New York State judge found him to have engaged in repeated and persistent civil fraud, including falsifying business records in the first degree;[33] and he has been held in contempt repeatedly, warned, fined, sanctioned, and gagged by state and federal judges for statements exposing witnesses, those involved in the judicial system or their families to danger.[34]

Trump's character can also be gleaned from his own words. He taunts, mocks and threatens those who deign to hold him accountable. He openly brags about sexual violence, utilizes racist terminology, and evokes Nazi tropes. He has no respect for the rule of law as evidenced by his calling for "the termination of all rules, regulations, and articles, even those found in the Constitution"[35] and repeated threatening of judges, court staff, prosecutors, and witnesses. For example, in this case alone, his Truth Social account featured a picture of him holding a baseball bat next to District Attorney Bragg's head[36] and a post appearing to warn that "death & destruction" could result from District Attorney Bragg charging him with a crime; this prompted the court to issue a stern warning against making comments that were "'likely to incite violence or civil unrest.'"[37] Moreover, he has repeatedly threatened judges, court staff, prosecutors, and witnesses in his other cases,[38] and Justice Merchan[39] as well as other judges including federal District Court Judge Tanya Chutkan[40] and New York Supreme Court Judge Arthur Engoron[41] have imposed gag orders to prevent him from potentially inciting violence.

Trump is notoriously not truthful[42]—whether it is lying about winning an election or the size of his crowds, apartment, and wealth. His lies know no bounds - he lies about all things big and small, whether they are inconsequential or involve our nation's most closely-held secrets.

These are just a few examples of evidence upon which District Attorney Bragg can draw to argue that defendant Trump's character and conduct deserves a sentence of imprisonment. Much more could be said—and likely will be should Trump face sentencing.

Conclusion

Given the nature and circumstances of Trump's alleged crimes here, his history and character, and New York state court sentencing precedent, District Attorney Bragg can make a strong argument that Trump should receive a sentence of incarceration if convicted. Trump is of course innocent until proven guilty, denies all wrongdoing and has not yet been tried, much less convicted. But it is also true that in order to evaluate the prosecution and its seriousness, we must have an understanding of the range of possible outcomes. Should Trump be convicted, they are serious.

CONCLUSION: THE CASE AGAINST TRUMP IS STRONGER THAN YOU THINK

T his essay was originally published by Norm Eisen, Joshua Kolb, and Barbara McQuade as "There Is Much More at Stake in Trump's Manhattan Case Than Just Hush Money" in The New York Times on February 20, 2024. It has been updated to reflect subsequent events.

WITH JUSTICE JUAN MERCHAN'S proclamation that jury selection in the Manhattan prosecution of Donald Trump will begin on April 15th, 2024, it is time for a reappraisal of the case. The charges brought by Alvin Bragg, the Manhattan district attorney, have been overshadowed by the three other criminal prosecutions of Mr. Trump, but the 34 felony counts constitute a strong case of election interference and fraud in the place where Mr. Trump lived and conducted business for decades.

Mr. Bragg will face tough challenges ahead, fueled by lingering skepticism that critics have harbored about the strength of the evidence and whether Mr. Trump has been unfairly targeted.

But we think he can overcome those hurdles and, by seeking to secure a conviction, reinforce the principle that in Manhattan—as across the country—playing by the rules is critical to the integrity of both our businesses and our democracy.

To understand why this case matters, think about a precedent, an earlier episode of an election-related felony and its cover-up. That was the Watergate scandal, which hung over Richard Nixon's re-election campaign in 1972. Voters did not have the information then to make an informed decision about Mr. Nixon, partly because the criminal investigation and trials of "the plumbers" had not concluded before the election and the majority of the evidence remained concealed. Because the investigation was unresolved, Mr. Nixon's nefarious conduct worked; he was in the White House when the full revelations came out later, to devastating effect.

The salaciousness of the details in Mr. Trump's case obscures what it is actually about: making covert payments to avoid losing an election and then further concealing it. Indeed, that is how Mr. Bragg has described the case, that it is "about conspiring to corrupt a presidential election and then lying in New York business records to cover it up."

It is entirely possible that the alleged election interference might have altered the outcome of the 2016 contest, which was decided by just under 80,000 votes in three states. Coming, as it might have, on the heels of the "Access Hollywood" disgrace, the effort to keep the scandal from voters may have saved Mr. Trump's political prospects.

The charges against Mr. Trump are also a deterrence against business fraud and a support of legitimate business in Manhattan. They target the essence of Mr. Trump's identity and reputation, as a businessman, before his entrance into the political arena.

For decades, Mr. Trump lived and ran his businesses in New York City. We now know as a result of multiple New York court proceedings that fraud appeared to have been a regular part of his dealings. The Trump Organization and Allen Weisselberg, its chief financial officer, were both criminally convicted of fraud (before Justice Merchan) in 2022. In the New York attorney general's civil fraud suit, Justice Arthur Engoron ruled that the former president is liable as a result of fraudulently manipulating his net worth and ordered him to pay a staggering $355 million penalty—over $400 million with interest.

Mr. Bragg's prosecution is the next step in probing—and, however much possible, deterring—this pattern of conduct by Mr. Trump and his display of contempt for the rule of law that every other New York business and Manhattan executive has to follow.

To succeed, Mr. Bragg will need to overcome the first impressions of the case from its critics. In this view, it is nothing more than a years-old, stale case about hush money payments to a porn star on shaky legal ground. But since the indictment in April 2023, the legal foundations of the case have been revealed to be much stronger than the naysayers suggested. A particularly strong endorsement, for example, came from federal Judge Alvin Hellerstein, who rebuffed efforts from Mr. Trump's lawyers to move the case to federal court.

In his opinion sending the case back to state court, Judge Hellerstein seemed to endorse Mr. Bragg's theory of the case. He noted that the evidence against Mr. Trump appeared to support Mr. Bragg's "allegations that the money paid to [Michael] Cohen was reimbursement for a hush money payment."

For the trial itself, Mr. Bragg has that strong evidence and a favorable jury pool in Manhattan, but he will have to overcome two major challenges in order to prevail: one each for the jury and the judge.

First will be the challenge of how Mr. Bragg and his team present Michael Cohen, Mr. Trump's former fixer, to the jury. Mr. Trump's trial team will try to hammer Mr. Cohen as an admitted liar and convicted criminal who pleaded guilty to multiple federal crimes for the alleged election interference in New York. But Mr. Bragg and his own team have deep experience with putting on cooperating witnesses with complex pasts.

Mr. Cohen has not wavered in his account of the hush money payments, their election interference purpose and their cover-up. And perhaps most important, everything Mr. Cohen has said is corroborated by documentary evidence and other witnesses. Even after a tough cross-examination in the New York civil fraud case, Justice Engoron found that "Michael Cohen told the truth." Prosecutors also have the benefit of learning from Mr. Cohen's civil testimony and can focus on his consistency, corroboration and acceptance of responsibility.

Second, Mr. Bragg and his team will be confronted with the challenge of working with Justice Merchan to prevent Mr. Trump from acting out in front of the jury and thereby disrupting the case or introducing irrelevant information to try to prejudice the outcome. We all saw the spectacle that Mr. Trump created in the New York State civil fraud trial. But we also saw Mr. Trump reined in by federal Judge Lewis Kaplan in the E. Jean Carroll case, which, unlike the civil fraud one, featured a jury watching every move.

Justice Merchan is cut more from the cloth of Judge Kaplan. He is a widely respected and experienced jurist. Moreover, criminal trial rules and practice give him even more latitude than Judge Kaplan had in the E. Jean Carroll civil matter. With a jury in the box, Justice Merchan is unlikely to tolerate repeated outbursts. We got a taste of that at the hearing on February 15th, 2024, when he repeatedly and summarily shut down frivolous objections from Mr. Trump's counsel.

The seriousness of the prosecution can also be conveyed at sentencing. If Mr. Trump is convicted, Mr. Bragg should seek jail time. Each count of document falsification carries a term of up to four years in prison. Many individuals, including first-time offenders, are sentenced to imprisonment for this crime in New York.

Whether it comes to American business or constitutional democracy, individuals who flamboyantly and persistently flout the rules of a system must be deterred for that system to endure. That principle underlines the gravity of the forthcoming case in Manhattan and the cases elsewhere against Mr. Trump.

ACKNOWLEDGMENTS

I would like to thank the original coauthors of all the material adapted or anthologized in this book for their work and also for teaching me so much: Fred Wertheimer, Paula Junghans, Gretchen Knaut, Joshua Kolb, Barbara McQuade, E. Danya Perry, Joshua Stanton, Andrew Warren, and Siven Watt. Much of the work in this book was meticulously edited in its original form by the co-editor-in-chief of Just Security and my co-editor of that website's "Trump Trials Clearinghouse and Calendar," Ryan Goodman. I thank him for that and for helping me understand the case more broadly. I would also like to thank his Just Security co-editor-in-chief Tess Bridgeman, Managing Editor Megan Corrarino, Legal Editor Paras Shah, Director of Partnerships and Marketing Pooja Shah, Journalism Fellow Adam Klasfeld, and Just Security itself for permission to reprint my writing there.

I am deeply grateful to the team who worked hard in helping me put together this guide to one of the most historically significant trials in our nation's history. First among them: Tom Joscelyn, my colleague, co-author, and friend who was my main deputy on the effort; Jacob Kovacs-Goodman, who assisted us; Susan Corke, who was instrumental throughout the writing and publishing process; my research team, for their collective effort in making this book a reality– Allison Rice, Francois Barrilleaux, Sasha Matsuki, Maya

Cook, and Michael Nevett; to the communications team for their help on shaping the book and comms about it–Ginny Terzano, David Byron Wagner, Maura McDonough, Zoe Calambokidis, Allyson Rupp, Matthew Kim, Max Flugrath, Jaden Jennings, and Jonathan Carvalho; Miriam Dwinell, for her book cover design; our editor Elizabeth Feifer, whose assistance has been invaluable; Barbara McQuade for her thoughtful foreword; to my wonderful editor at *The New York Times*, John Guida and to the *Times* for permission to reprint my writing there; Domenica Alioto, Michael Podhorzer, and Leslie Dach for their kind assistance; Karen Agnifilo, Adam Kaufmann, Jerry Goldfeder, and other experts for their insights into New York law; Samara Angel, McKenzie Carrier, Colby Galliher, Madison Gee, Vicka Heidt, Greg Phea, Taylor Redd, and other colleagues; and above all, my family, for their love and support–my wife, Lindsay Kaplan, my daughter, Tamar Eisen, and Pete the Cat.

All proceeds of this book benefit State Democracy Defenders Fund, a nonpartisan, nonprofit organization which I chair, which was instrumental to the publication of this book, and which is dedicated to keeping our democracy vibrant.

APPENDIX I: KEY COURT OPINIONS

State Court: Intent and the Predicate Crimes

Trump filed motions to dismiss the case on several grounds. On February 15, 2024, Justice Juan Merchan issued a decision and order addressing Trump's motions to dismiss, denying them all. We include Justice Merchan's reasoning here on intent to defraud, including his rulings that pertain to committing, aiding, or concealing each of the predicate crimes, and several other key issues.

Justice Merchan's Denial of the Motion to Dismiss the Indictment

a. Nexus to Another Crime

As Justice Merchan's opinion noted, DANY had advanced four potential theories for what "other crime" Trump intended to commit: violating FECA restrictions on individual and corporate contributions; unlawful means in promoting the election of a person in violation of NY elec-

tion law; violating NY tax law by offsetting Cohen's potential
tax losses; and the intent to violate Penal Law §§ 175.05 and
175.10. Justice Merchan limited inquiry at trial to the first
three of these four theories.

1. FECA

Merchan noted Trump's argument "that the 'crime'
element in PL § 175.10 must have occurred in New York.
Therefore, an out of state crime or federal crime such as a
violation of FECA cannot satisfy this element of the charge,"
citing *People v. Witherspoon,* 211 AD3d 108 (2nd Dep. 2022).[1]
Merchan noted that the People, by contrast, "stress that
Witherspoon expressly limited its holding to the construction
of the phrase 'any crime' within the context of CPL Section
160.59." Merchan concurred with Bragg: "This Court agrees
and further finds that CPL section 160.59(3)(f) has no application to the issue presently before this Court. The People
submit that courts in New York have considered out of state
offenses as 'other crimes' when necessary to satisfy an
element of an offense. As examples, the People cite *People v.
Kulakov,* 278 AD2d 519 [3d Dept 2000] and *People v. Cornish*
104 Misc2d 72 [Sup. Ct. Kings County 1980]."[2]

Turning to the applicable federal crime itself, Merchan
found that:

> The evidence before the Grand Jury was legally sufficient
> to show that the Defendant, along with Cohen and
> Pecker, among others, planned to promote Defendant's
> presidential campaign by purchasing and suppressing
> information that could negatively impact Defendant's
> campaign. The amount Pecker and Cohen paid exceeded
> allowable federal limits as established by FECA. Indeed,

Cohen pled guilty to violating FECA and served a prison term as a result of his involvement in this scheme. Likewise, the Federal Election Commission ('FEC') found that AMI and Pecker also violated FECA as a result of these payments. Evidence presented to the Grand Jury that the Defendant discussed the above plan with Cohen and then reimbursed him for his payment to Daniels is legally sufficient to establish the requisite *intent* to commit another crime, i.e. FECA. [Emphasis in the original].[3]

2. State Election Crimes

Merchan noted Trump's argument that N.Y. Election Law § 17-152 is not an object offense "because the allegation is that he tampered with the 2016 *presidential* election... [but] its application is limited to elections for 'public office,' a term which Defendant claims does not include federal elections."[4] However, Merchan found:

New York Election Law § 1-102, titled "Applicability of Chapter," explicitly states "This chapter shall govern the conduct of *all* elections at which voters of the state of New York may cast a ballot or the purpose of electing an individual to any party position or nominating or electing an individual to any federal, state, country, city, town or village office..." (emphasis added [by Justice Merchan]). It is clear from the text of § 1-102 that the New York Election Law applies to ballots cast for any election, including federal... This Court is hard pressed to find and indeed cannot, that federal elections are not included in the statute's principal objective.[5]

Next, Merchan turned to the question of whether or not preemption doctrine applied here:

> Defendant's next argument, that N.Y. Election Law § 17-152 is pre-empted by federal law, is also unsuccessful. As Judge Hellerstein reasoned in *People v. Trump*, 2023 WL 4614689 [S.D.N.Y 2023] when he was presented with the same argument by this Defendant, N.Y. Election Law § 17-152 "does not fit into any of the three categories of state law that FECA preempts." *People v. Trump*, 2023 WL 4614689 at 11. This Court agrees and follows Judge Hellerstein's decision. Since FECA does not affect the states' rights to pass laws concerning voter fraud and ballot theft, there is no preemption by FECA in this matter.[6]

3. State Tax Crimes

In his moving papers, Trump argued that he lacked intent to violate tax laws since Cohen's tax returns were not presented to the Grand Jury, since Trump was not aware of the purported "grossing up scheme," and since the State was not financially harmed but rather collected more tax revenue.[7] DANY countered that the evidence presented to the Grand Jury was sufficient to establish intent. Merchan held that:

> The evidence before the Grand Jury was legally sufficient to establish that Defendant knew the amount being paid to Cohen was not for legal services but rather, as reimbursement for the Daniels payoff. Weisselberg's handwritten notes demonstrated the intent and purpose behind the 'grossing up' strategy. Together with the witness testimony, the Grand Jury could infer that Defen-

dant knew about the grossing up scheme and its purpose.... Similarly, this Court disagrees that the alleged New York State tax violation is of no consequence because the State of New York did not suffer any financial harm.[8]

4. Falsification of Business Records as an Object Crime

Justice Merchan struck the last of DANY's four theories for the predicate offense: that Trump intended to commit, aid, or conceal the falsification of Cohen's or AMI's business records. Merchan precluded the DA from arguing that theory to the jury but allowed evidence of the falsification of Cohen's or AMI's business records to establish one of the other three predicates:

> [T]he Court is not convinced that this particular theory fits into the "other crime" element of PL § 175.10, but it does seem that it is intertwined and advances the other three theories discussed *supra*. For example, in support of this fourth theory, the People argue that "the participants in defendant's election fraud scheme also caused the falsification of other New York business records to help defendant execute and conceal the scheme." People's Opposition at pg. 42. It appears that such an argument goes to the People's N.Y. Election Law § 17-152 and FECA theories, which both directly involve the Defendant's intent to violate those particular statutes.[9]

b. Intent to Defraud

With respect to the element of intent to defraud in PL § 175.10, Trump had argued that "he did not intend 'to cheat anyone out of money or property through the allegedly false entries.' Defendant's Memo at pg. 23. and that because the alleged falsification of business records occurred in 2017, any evidence pointing towards an alleged intent to defraud in 2016 is not relevant." Merchan held the opposite:

> Intent to defraud is not constricted to an intent to deprive another of property or money. In fact, "intent to defraud" can extend beyond economic concern. *People v. Headley* 37 Misc3d 815, 829 [Sup Ct, Kings County 2012]; *People v. Schrag*, 147 Misc 2d 517 [Rockland County Ct. 1990]. 'Nor is there any requirement that a defendant intend to conceal the commission of *his own* crime; instead, 'a person can commit First Degree Falsifying Business Records by falsifying records with the intent to cover up a crime committed by somebody else." People's Opposition at pg. 22, *citing to People v. Dove*, 15 Misc3d 1134(A), *judgment aff'd*, 85 AD3d 547 [1st Dept 2011]; *People v. Fuschino*, 278 AD2d 657 [3rd Dept 2000]....The term "intent to defraud" carries a broad meaning and is not limited to the causing of financial harm or the deprivation of money or property. *People v. Sosa-Campana*, 167 AD3d at 464. To reiterate, controlling authority holds that the People need not demonstrate intent to cause financial harm to prove that defendant had the requisite intent to defraud under the Falsifying Business Records statutes. *See Kase*, 53 NY2d at 989 [1981]; *Khalil*, 73 AD3d 509 at 510. The Defendant's argument to the contrary is unavailing and contrary to settled law. *Headley*, 37 Misc3d at 829; *Schrag* 147 Mis.2d at 517. A long line of cases not only within the First Department but in other departments as well, have so held... The Grand Jury, when viewing this evidence, could find reasonable cause that an offense was committed and that the defendant committed it, namely that Defendant possessed the requi-

site intent to defraud either the voting public, the government or both.[10]

c. Business Records

Justice Merchan went into the elements of NYPL § 175.10 to evaluate the legal sufficiency of the charges. The test for legal sufficiency of the indictment is "'whether there was 'competent evidence which, if accepted as true, would establish every element of an offense charged and the defendant's commission thereof.'" *People v. Swamp*, 84 NY2d 725 [1995]."[11]

With respect to the element of "business records," Merchan "agree[d] with the People's contention that the invoices, checks, and general ledger entries are in fact 'business records' for purposes of the charge of Falsifying Business Records in the First Degree."[12] He explained as follows:

The cases cited by the Defendant in support of his theory that because Defendant paid Cohen from his own funds, then the business records at issue were not "kept or maintained to reflect the Trump Organization's condition or activity" are not persuasive. *People v. Golb*, *People v. Papatonis*, and *People v. Banks*, are all inapplicable to the instant matter.... "Indeed, the payments here exemplify the intermingling of the Trump Organization's business records and Defendant's purportedly personal expenses." People's Opposition at pg. 13. Defendant and the Trump Organization are intertwined to such a degree, that it is of no legal relevance that some of the moneys paid to Cohen came from Defendant's personal funds.[13]

Federal Removal: Removal, Immunity, and Preemption

On May 4, 2023, Trump filed to remove the case to the United States District Court for the Southern District of New York, on the basis of the federal officer removal statute. On July 19, 2023, Judge Alvin Hellerstein rejected Trump's attempt to have the case heard in federal court, and remanded it back to the state court. The section below contains key sections of the Hellerstein decision, in particular emphasizing the Judge's analysis of what role federal law and preemption and immunity issues should play in New York state court.

Judge Hellerstein's Denial of Trump's Removal Petition

a. The indictment was not "for or relating to any act under color of such office"

The judge first evaluated a split among the federal circuit courts in how they determine whether an act is "under color" of federal office. The Supreme Court articulated a test that looks for a causal connection between what an officer did, under his or her official authority, and the acts being prosecuted. However, this test dates to 1926 and Congress, in 2011, altered the statute: replacing the language "for any act under color of office" with "for or relating to any act under color of office." Some circuit courts have recently interpreted this addition of "or relating to" as loosening the causal connection requirement. Others, including the circuit that has appellate jurisdiction over New York, have retained the more stringent causal connection test.

Judge Hellerstein found that, "Whatever the standard, and whether it is high or low, Trump fails to satisfy it." He explained that:

Trump contends that Cohen was hired "as a direct result of President Trump's role as President of the United States and his obligations under the Constitution, and in order to separate his business affairs from his public duties," but offers no evidence to support that contention. Trump chose not to testify and chose not to call Cohen or any other witness having knowledge of Trump's purpose in hiring Cohen. Cohen's invoices are the only indication of a retainer, but no one testified to the existence of any retainer agreement or what legal services, if any, Cohen did other than to advance hush money to Clifford. The evidence overwhelmingly suggests that the matter was a purely a [sic] personal item of the President—a cover-up of an embarrassing event. Hush money paid to an adult film star is not related to a President's official acts. It does not reflect in any way the color of the President's official duties.[14]

Judge Hellerstein then offered some analysis of presidential immunity before concluding definitively that all of the acts in the case were solely of a personal nature:

Trump conceded in his Notice that he hired Cohen to attend to his private matters. [Citation omitted]. Cohen's invoices and their associated records were maintained by the Trump Organization, a private enterprise, in New York City, not in Washington, D.C. as official records of the President. Trump paid Cohen from private funds, and the payments did not depend on any Presidential power for their authorization. Trump offered no evidence regarding what Cohen did as Trump's personal attorney. Neither the Constitutional prohibition barring the President from taking compensation beyond that fixed by Congress, nor the Constitutional obligation to take care to execute the laws, converts the President's private acts into acts under the color of his office.[15]

b. Trump did not raise a colorable federal defense

An officer seeking federal removal does not need to clear a high bar for a plausible defense to state prosecution, just one "colorable" in law and fact. Trump needed to demonstrate the "underpinnings" of a valid federal defense. Trump proposed two defenses: immunity and preemption. Judge Hellerstein ruled that neither was colorable, because (i) no presidential duty was in play to warrant immunity and (ii) New York's laws are generally applicable, and so not preempted by FECA. Hellerstein first rejected Trump's immunity claim:

Trump has expressly waived any argument premised on a theory of absolute presidential immunity. (Def.'s Br. 21.) Instead, he argues that he is immune from prosecution under the Supremacy Clause because his conduct "w[as] taken solely because he was President of the United States" and, "[a]s such, [his] decision to retain Michael Cohen to act as his personal lawyer arose out of his duties as President." Trump has not raised a colorable immunity defense.

"[I]mmunity does not attach merely because state criminal prosecutions are based upon acts that happen during the scope of a federal officer's employment," and not everything a President does is "in the context of the discharge of his federal duties." *De Vecchio*, 468 F. Supp. 2d at 460, 462; *see also North Carolina v. Ivory*, 906 F.2d 999, 1003 (4th Cir. 1990) (holding that immunity does not provide federal officers "carte blanche... to proceed as they please" in carrying out every act within the scope of their employment). Rather, Supremacy Clause immunity requires the defendant to show both that he was performing "an act which he was authorized to do by the law of the United States" and that, in performing that authorized act, "he did no more than what was necessary and proper for him to do." *In re Neagle*, 135 U.S. 1, 75 (1890); *see also New York v. Tanella*, 374 F.3d 141, 147 (2d Cir. 2004). The standard is more stringent than the color of office test: "the acts themselves must of necessity be required in the discharge of the officer's duties." *De Vecchio*, 468 F. Supp. 2d at 460....

Trump has not explained how hiring and making payments to a personal attorney to handle personal affairs carries out a constitutional duty. Reimbursing Cohen for advancing hush money to Stephanie Clifford cannot be considered the performance of a constitutional duty. Falsifying business records to hide such reimbursement, and to transform the reimbursement into a business expense for Trump and income to Cohen, likewise does not relate to a presidential duty. Trump is not immune from the People's prosecution in New York Supreme Court.[16]

With respect to preemption, Trump argued that the Federal Election Campaign Act (FECA), a federal statute, preempts certain provisions of New York election law at issue in the case. Judge Hellerstein held that this defense, too, was not colorable due to the distinction between generally applicable state laws (not preempted) from state laws that regulate FECA-covered conduct (preempted). The judge explained that,

FECA does not preempt state laws concerning the "[m]anner of qualifying as a candidate or political party organization"; "[d]ates and places of elections"; "[v]oter registration"; "[p]rohibition of false registration, voting fraud, theft of ballots, and similar offenses"; "[c]andidate's personal financial disclosure"; and "[a]pplication of State law to the funds used for the purchase or construction of a State or local party office building to the extent described in 11 CFR 300.35." 11 C.F.R. § 108.7(c).

There is a "strong presumption against pre-emption" that applies with equal force to FECA. *Weber v. Heaney*, 995 F.2d 872, 875 (8th Cir. 1993). Thus, "even with respect to election-related activities, courts have given [FECA] a narrow preemptive effect...." [Citations omitted].[17]

Judge Hellerstein then engaged in an in-depth analysis of several decisions, including *WinRed, Inc. v. Ellison*, 59 F.4th 934, 942 (8th Cir. 2023), which held that the "FEC regulation defines the statute's scope." In *WinRed*, a political action committee used fine print to set up unexpected recurring donations to its efforts on federal races:

The court of appeals held that FECA is to be narrowly construed, and that the states' investigation in furtherance of consumer protection is not preempted even if solicitations for a federal election are involved. Furthermore, the court of appeals ruled that Minnesota's consumer-protection law, which became the focus of the case, was covered by FECA's regulations providing that state "prohibition[s] on fraudulent voting, registration, and 'similar offenses'" are not preempted. The court of appeals added that WinRed's argument, if upheld, would result in an improper "immuniz[ation]... from many generally applicable state laws" [Citations omitted].[18]

Whereas in *WinRed* and similar cases courts found that FECA does not preempt generally applicable state laws, Judge Hellerstein next noted that FECA does preempt state laws that regulate specifically FECA-covered conduct. For instance, FECA preempted a state law that regulated contributions to state legislators, which included contributions in connection with federal elections. By contrast, FECA does not preempt generally applicable state laws, and both the New York statute for falsifying business records and the New York Election Law at issue in Trump's case fall squarely into this category of a state law of general applicability:

NYPL § 175.10 is a law of general applicability, prohibiting the falsification of business records for a fraudulent purpose. Cf *People v. Bloomfield*, 844 N.E.2d 296,300 (N.Y. 2006). A violation is a misdemeanor. NYPL § 175.05. A violation with intent to commit, aid, or conceal another crime is a felony. *Id.* § 175.10. Any fraudulent falsification, along with an intention to commit, conceal, or aid the commission of any other crime, proves the felony. The law does not target, or make an exception for, election-related activities. There is no mention of disclosures of campaign contributions or spending, elections, or election laws, state or federal.

Trump concedes that FECA does not preempt § 175.10 on its face. He argues that the provision of NYPL § 175.10 that raises falsification of business records to a felony if there is an intent to commit, aid, or conceal another crime is preempted if the crime involves federal elections. But violations of FECA and NYEL § 17-152 are not elements of the crime charged. The only elements are the falsification of business records, an intent to defraud, and an intent to commit or conceal another crime. The People need not establish that Trump or any other person actually violated NYEL § 17-152 or FECA... Trump can be convicted of a felony even if he did not commit any crime beyond the falsification, so long as he intended to do so or to conceal such a crime.[19]

Having dispatched with the idea that the People's use of FECA itself as a predicate is preempted, Judge Hellerstein similarly disposed of Trump's defense arguing that the New York state election statute is preempted by FECA as one of the predicate crimes for felony falsification of business records. He explained that:

NYEL § 17-152 does not fit into any of the three categories of state law that FECA preempts: "law[s] concerning the... [o]rganization and registration of political committees supporting federal candidates;" "law[s] concerning the... [d]isclosure of receipts and expenditures by Federal candidates and political committees;" and "law[s] concerning the... [l]imitation on contributions and expenditures regarding Federal candidates and political committees."[20]

APPENDIX II: TRUMP'S INTENT

As we have noted, the pivotal issue in the case is whether District Attorney Bragg can establish Trump's intent to defraud, including his intent to commit, aid, or conceal other state or federal crimes. This appendix includes a compendium of past pieces coauthored by the editor tackling the question of whether Trump had the "mens rea" —the criminal intent—that Bragg will need to prove beyond a reasonable doubt. The first essay addresses the question of intent to defraud in general and the next essay addresses the issue of whether Trump's intent to defraud included an intent to commit, aid, or conceal another crime. It addresses all three predicates that will be at issue at trial. The third and final essay in this appendix is a deep dive into perhaps the most overlooked of those three predicates: alleged tax fraud. Our analysis includes both state tax offenses, on which Bragg relies, as well as federal ones, since federal case law and scholarly analysis is more well developed and applicable by analogy.

What Does "Intent to Defraud" Mean?

This essay was originally published by Ryan Goodman, Norm Eisen, Siven Watt, Joshua Kolb and Joshua Stanton as "The Broad Scope of 'Intent to Defraud' in the New York Crime of Falsifying Business Records," in Just Security *on April 3, 2023. It has been updated to reflect subsequent events. Emphasis is retained from the original, which made liberal use of bolding to highlight key text.*

AN IMPORTANT QUESTION is whether maintaining false business records to conceal hush money payments in a political campaign meets the "intent to defraud" element of the Falsifying Business Records statute, New York Penal Law (NY PL) § 175.10.

As we explain in this essay, the law is firmly on the side of the DA. Indeed, the jurisdiction in which this case will be brought—the First Department of New York—has settled law on the issue that defines "intent to defraud" in broad terms that cover the allegations in the Trump case. The most important expression of a contrary view was issued by a lower court in a different jurisdiction and on a basis that is demonstrably flawed.

We should note at the outset that some legal experts might assume "intent to defraud" has a narrow construction —limited to deprivation of money or property, or other pecuniary loss—given U.S. Supreme Court decisions to that effect in recent years. But that is a category mistake. The U.S. Supreme Court was interpreting federal fraud statutes, and this case is about New York courts interpreting New York state statutes.

What's more, the U.S. Supreme Court has not only expressly noted the distinction between the federal and state level, but also recognized states' prerogative to fill in the gap. In a 2020 opinion, the Justices explained that due to their narrow construction of the federal criminal statutes, "federal fraud law leaves much public corruption to the States (or their electorates) to rectify." *Kelly v. United States*, 140 S. Ct. 1565, 1571-73 (2020).

So, how does New York State law define the "intent to defraud" for the criminal offense of falsifying business records? A long line of New York state court cases supports an expansive conception with respect to NY PL § 175.00 crimes—namely, that intent can be established when a defendant acts "for the purpose of frustrating the State's power" to "faithfully carry out its own law." *People v. Kase*, 76 A.D.2d 532, 537–538, 431 N.Y.S.2d 531, 534 (N.Y. App. Div., 1st Dept. 1980), *aff'd,* 53 N.Y.2d 989, 441 N.Y.S.2d 671, 424 N.E.2d 558 (1981).

On this standard, the law does not require prosecutors to show "pecuniary or potential pecuniary loss" to the government or otherwise. *Id.* Indeed, New York Jurisprudence (Second Edition 2023) in a section titled, "Indictment or information charging falsification of business records," states: "In an indictment for first degree falsification of business records, the grand jury presentation is not required to establish commercial or property loss."

Applying this broad concept of "intent to defraud" in false business records cases, New York state courts have found such intent in a wide range of cases including when a defendant: made covert contributions to a political campaign, covered up an alleged rape, misled the relatives of a patient about the individual's treatment, operated a motor vehicle without a license, obtained credit cards through false documents but with no proof of intention to miss payments, frustrated the regulatory authorities of the New York City Transit Authority, and much more. We detail all these judicial opinions below.

The DA charging former President Donald Trump with falsifying business records to conceal hush money payments as campaign finance or election law violations fits the test, with government authorities being frustrated in their ability to regulate elections. Nor is the harm limited to them.

Falsifying hush money payments as legal services frustrated New York State authorities more broadly. New York firms are required to "keep correct and complete books and records of account" for the purposes of state regulators and tax authorities, N.Y. Bus. Corp. Law § 624 (McKinney). Indeed, New York Tax Law allows for tax commissioners "to examine or to cause to have examined... any books, papers, records or memoranda" of a corporation "bearing upon the matters to be required in the return." N.Y. Tax Law § 1096(b)(1) (McKinney). Thus any book or record kept by a private corporation is subject to public exposure, and New York law requires these books to be accurate.

In short, the Manhattan DA's case rests on firm legal footing.

a. "Intent to Defraud"

"Intent to defraud" is an element of both the misdemeanor (second degree) and felony (first degree) violations of Falsifying Business Records in New York. Under NY PL § 175.05 (the misdemeanor offense), "A person is guilty of falsifying business records in the second degree when, **with intent to defraud**, he:

1. Makes or causes a false entry in the business records of an enterprise; or
2. Alters, erases, obliterates, deletes, removes or destroys a true entry in the business records of an enterprise; or
3. Omits to make a true entry in the business records of an enterprise in violation of a duty to do so which he knows to be imposed upon him by law or by the nature of his position; or
4. Prevents the making of a true entry or causes the omission thereof in the business records of an enterprise."

NY PL § 175.10 (the felony offense), adds to the language of an "intent to defraud" the following requirement:

> A person is guilty of falsifying business records in the first degree when he commits the crime of falsifying business records in the second degree, **and when his intent to defraud includes an intent to commit another crime or to aid or conceal the commission thereof.**

As noted in McKinney's on New York Penal Law (McKinney's NY PL) §175.05, "there is no Penal Law definition of 'intent to defraud.'" Instead, McKinney's refers to McKinney's NY PL § 15.00 for further practice commentary on "intent to defraud," which, in so far is relevant, states:

> Although a significant number of penal statutes require an "intent to defraud," there is no Penal Law definition of that culpable mental state. It has been suggested that an intent to defraud should be "for the purpose of leading another into error or to disadvantage." *People v. Briggins*, 50 N.Y.2d

302, 309, 428 N.Y.S.2d 909, 406 N.E.2d 766 (1980) (concurring opinion) (Jones, J.). *See also* Black's Law Dictionary (6th ed. 1990) ("*Intent to defraud* means an intention to deceive another person, and to induce such other person, in reliance upon such deception, to assume, create, transfer, alter or terminate a right, obligation or power..."); *Carpenter v. United States*, 484 U.S. 19, 27, 108 S.Ct. 316, 321, 98 L.Ed.2d 275 (1987) (finding that the words "to defraud" meant "wronging one in his property rights by dishonest methods or schemes, and usually signifying the deprivation of something of value by trick, deceit, chicane or overreaching").

While an "intent to defraud" is often directed at gaining property or a pecuniary benefit, it need not be so limited. See *People v. Kase*, 53 N.Y.2d 989, 441 N.Y.S.2d 671, 424 N.E.2d 558 (1981), affirming for reasons stated at 76 A.D.2d 532. In *Kase*, a prosecution for the filing of a false instrument, an intent to defraud was found where a person intentionally filed a false statement with a public office for the purpose of frustrating the State's power to fulfill its responsibility to faithfully carry out its own law. (Emphasis added; unless otherwise indicated, bolded text throughout this essay signifies the same).

Absent a definition of "intent to defraud" in the New York penal code, case law has developed to define its parameters.

b. The Case Law

The First Department decision in *Kase* established the broad conception of "intent to defraud"—that it does not require an intent to deprive another person of money, property rights or a pecuniary interest—in a matter concerning the crime of Offering a False Instrument for Filing in the First Degree (NY PL § 175.35). The defendant was charged with filing a false statement in an application for a liquor license. According to the court, an intent to "frustrat[e] the State's power to fulfill [its obligation to carry out the law] violates the statute." 76 A.D.2d at 537–538, 431 N.Y.S.2d at 534. The decision was affirmed by the highest New York court, the New York Court of Appeals.

There is no need to guess how Justice Merchan would rule as to whether that standard applies in the falsification of business records statutes. The First Department has long said the *Kase* test applies to §§ 175.05 and 175.10, most recently in 2018 in *People v. Sosa-Campana*, 167 A.D.3d 464, 89 N.Y.S.3d 75, (N.Y. App. Div., 1st Dept. 2018), *leave to appeal denied*, 2019 N.Y. Slip Op. 97967, 33 N.Y.3d 981, 101 N.Y.S.3d 257, 124 N.E.3d 746 (N.Y. 2019); *see also Morgenthau v. Khalil*, 73 A.D.3d 509, 902 N.Y.S.2d 501 (N.Y. App. Div., 1st Dept. 2010).

In *Sosa-Campana*, the First Department reaffirmed that "intent to defraud" under §175.05-10 is much broader than deprivation of money or property—or indeed causing any financial harm. The defendant in the case had provided a fraudulent driver's license, in the name of another real person, when stopped for a traffic violation. His intent was to deceive the state authorities to escape government sanctions. He was charged with falsifying business records in the first and second degree, identity theft in the second degree, and aggravated unlicensed operation of a motor vehicle in the third degree. The court found:

> The evidence was legally sufficient to establish the element of intent to defraud, as required for the convic-

tions of identity theft and falsifying business records. When defendant was stopped for a traffic violation and presented a fraudulent driver's license in the name of another actual person, defendant acted with at least two forms of fraudulent intent, each falling within the plain meaning of "defraud." Defendant intended to escape responsibility for the violation by causing the officer to issue a summons to the wrong person, and also intended to conceal his additional offense of unlicensed driving. In order to prove intent to defraud, the People **did not need to make a showing of an intent to cause financial harm** (see *People v. Kase*, 76 A.D.2d 532, 537–38, 431 N.Y.S.2d 531 [1st Dept. 1980] (construing intent-to-defraud element of analogous statute), *affd* 53 N.Y.2d 989, 991, 441 N.Y.S.2d 671, 424 N.E.2d 558[1981]; *see also Morgenthau v. Khalil*, 73 A.D.3d 509, 510, 902 N.Y.S.2d 501 [1st Dept. 2010]).

The First Department in another decision, *People v. Reyes*, demonstrated that an intent to conceal a crime could be a sufficient basis to establish the requisite "generalized 'intent to defraud.'" *Reyes* involved a corrections officer charged with first- and second-degree falsifying business records, both based on the same conduct. The court held that, given the "exclusive theory" of prosecutors that the defendant had "falsely indicated in the logbook that he was off-post during the inmates' mealtime, in order to hide the fact that he had raped the complainant during that time frame,"

[T]here would be no way for the jury to acquit defendant of first-degree falsifying business records—entailing a rejection of an intent to conceal a rape—but still convict him of the second-degree count. **The People simply did not afford the jury any basis, other than intent to conceal the alleged rape, to support any finding of the generalized "intent to defraud."**

Under the facts, **either defendant's intent was to conceal the alleged rape, or he had no fraudulent intent at all.** As such, only the higher count of first-degree falsifying business records should have been submitted to the jury.

69 A.D.3d 537, 538–539, 894 N.Y.S.2d 43, 44–45 (N.Y. App. Div., 1st Dept. 2010).

In a similar case also decided by the First Department, a nurse was charged with falsifying business records by omitting information in her nursing notes recording mistreatment which preceded the death of her patient. *People v. Coe*, 131 Misc.2d 807, 812, 501 N.Y.S.2d 997 (N.Y. Sup. Ct. 1986). The court explained that the target of the intent to defraud need not be the geriatric center, but "might just as well have been [the patient's] relatives, defendant's supervisors or others. Intent to defraud anyone is sufficient." The opinion was affirmed on appeal, with the Court of Appeals simply stating that the "remaining contention pertaining to her conviction for falsifying business records (see, Penal Law § 175.05) is without merit." 126 A.D.2d 436, 510 N.Y.S.2d 470 (N.Y. App. Div., 1st Dept. 1987), *aff'd*, 71 N.Y.2d 852, 522 N.E.2d 1039 (1988).

The 2010 First Department decision in *Morgenthau v. Khalil*, 73 A.D.3d at 510, 902 N.Y.S.2d at 502, is also consistent with this line of cases. In that instance, the defendant challenged a civil forfeiture action in an underlying criminal action arising out of an illegal check scheme, arguing that the prosecutors could not prove there was a substantial likelihood of securing a conviction for falsifying business records in the first degree because the indictment did not allege the intent to defraud a particular person or business entity out of money, property, or pecuniary value. The First Department rejected the defendant's claim. Citing *Ramirez* (from the Fourth Department) and *Elliassen* (a lower court in the Second Department), the court in *Morgenthau v. Khalil* ruled:

> Defendant argues that because the underlying indictment does not allege, and the People cannot prove, that he acted with intent to defraud a particular person or business entity—as opposed to the government or the public at large—out of money, property, or something of pecuniary value, plaintiff fails to demonstrate the requisite substantial likelihood of securing a conviction for falsifying business records in the first degree (see *Morgenthau v. Citisource, Inc.*, 68 N.Y.2d 211, 222, 508 N.Y.S.2d 152, 500 N.E.2d 850 [1986]). **We do not view the meaning of "intent to defraud" in Penal Law § 175.10 to be so limited** (see *People v. Ramirez*, 168 A.D.2d 908, 909, 565 N.Y.S.2d 659 [1990], *lv. denied* 77 N.Y.2d 965, 570 N.Y.S.2d 499, 573 N.E.2d 587 [1991]; *People v. Elliassen*, 20 Misc.3d 1143[A], 2008 N.Y. Slip Op. 51841[U], *2–3, 2008 WL 4193166 [2008]) (emphasis added).

Morgenthau v. Khalil dismissed the argument that intent under §175.10 required either (1) a person or business as the intended victim, or (2) that the intent must be to defraud someone or something out of money or something else of pecuniary value.

This understanding of the law—from Kase through to false business records jurisprudence—has also been adopted elsewhere throughout the state in cases arising under §§ 175.05 and 175.10. *People v. Ramirez*,168 A.D.2d 908, 909, 565 N.Y.S.2d 659, 660 (N.Y. Sup. Ct., 4th Dept. 1990), leave to appeal denied, 77 N.Y.2d 965, 573 N.E.2d 587 (N.Y. Ct. App. 1991); *People v. Schrag*, 147 Misc.2d 517, 558 N.Y.S.2d 451 (Rockland County Ct. 1990); *People v. Elliassen*, 20 Misc.3d 1143(A), 873 N.Y.S.2d 236 (N.Y. Sup. Ct., Richmond County 2008); *People v. Headley*, 37 Misc. 3d 815, 951 N.Y.S.2d 317 (N.Y. Sup. Ct., Kings County 2012), opinion adhered to on reargument, 36 Misc. 3d 1240(A), 960 N.Y.S.2d 51 (N.Y. Sup. Ct., Kings County 2012). *See also* McKinney's NY PL §175.05; McKinney's NY PL § 15.00.

The 1990 Fourth Department case of *People v. Ramirez*, for example, also approved the trial court's jury direction on this definition of "intent to defraud." The defendant allegedly used false information to apply for credit cards to purchase store merchandise. The court held that the defendant could not be prosecuted for petit larceny because there was no proof that she did not intend to pay. Despite there being no proof that the defendant caused or intended to cause any financial loss, the court upheld her conviction for falsifying business records. The Fourth Department held:

> We reject defendant's argument that the evidence was insufficient to convict her of the crimes of falsifying business records and issuing a false financial statement. Citing *People v. Saporita* (132 A.D.2d 713, 715, lv. denied 70 N.Y.2d 937), defendant contends that an element of those crimes, "intent to defraud", requires that a person "be deprived of property or a thing of value or a right" and no person was deprived of property or a thing of value or right. **In *People***

> *v. Saporita* (supra), the court charged a definition of
> "intent to defraud" which was not met by the evidence
> offered by the People. Here, however, the court, in its
> charge, gave a different definition of intent to defraud,
> which was met by the evidence produced. The evidence
> shows that defendant intended to defraud various store
> owners by applying for and obtaining credit cards in the
> name of another person when she could not get credit in
> her own name and that she intended to deceive those
> stores and induce them to extend credit to her, which,
> but for her misrepresentation, they would not have
> done. That evidence proved defendant's "intent to
> defraud" as defined by the court's charge.

168 A.D.2d at 909, 565 N.Y.S.2d at 660 (N.Y. App. Div., 4th
Dept. 1990) (emphasis added).

The defendant tried to appeal the Fourth Department
decision, but leave to appeal was denied by the Court of
Appeals.

In the 2008 decision in *People v Elliassen*, the Richmond
County Supreme Court (within the Second Department)
held that the intent to defraud required no pecuniary loss,
and that interference with the legitimate public administration of the NYPD sufficed. The court stated:

> Counts Two through Thirteen, Falsifying Business
> Records in the First and Second Degrees, charge the
> defendants with not preparing and filing the juvenile log
> report or the UF 250 stop and frisk report relating to their
> interaction with Rayshawn Moreno. These statutes require
> defendants to have an "intent to defraud". It is not neces-

sary to show a property or pecuniary loss from the
fraud, and, in this case, it is sufficient to show that the
NYPD's legitimate official actions and purposes were
impeded. See, *People v Schrag*, 147 Misc 2d 517 (County
Court, Rockland County, 1990); *People v Coe*, 131 Misc 2d
807, 812 (Supreme Court, New York County, 1986) (".... the
target of the intent to defraud could have been defendant's
supervisors, defendant's employer or the victim....")....

Defendants contend that Counts Fourteen through
Twenty-Five, Falsifying Business Records in the First and
Second Degrees (involving defendants' failure to properly
follow NYPD Communications Division radio procedures), likewise are legally insufficient because there is no
evidence of defendants' "intent to defraud"....

The inaccuracy of the records has ramifications
beyond general business practices. Likewise, the failure of
police personnel to promptly notify the Communications
Division dispatcher of their whereabouts and current
status vis a vis handcuffed prisoners, adversely affects the
agency's ability to carry out its mission. It meets the standard of "intent to defraud", since defendants' actions
"intentionally defrauded" or deprived the Police
Department of valuable information and knowledge
that were critical to its public safety mission.

20 Misc. 3d 1143(A), 873 N.Y.S.2d 236 (N.Y. Sup. Ct., Richmond
County 2008) (emphasis added).

The Kings County Supreme Court's 2012 decision in
People v. Headley provides a useful account of the broad
intent to defraud standard under the falsifying business
records statute. 37 Misc. 3d 815, 951 N.Y.S.2d 317, 2012 N.Y. Slip

Op. 22257 (N.Y. Sup. Ct. 2012). *Headley* was a case about ambulance chasing. The defendant, who served as outside counsel for the New York City Transit Authority [NYCTA] in pursuit of personal injury lawsuits, used a fictitious name for his company in order to fraudulently obtain paid assignments from NYCTA to procure independent medical examinations of personal injury claimants who had sued NYCTA. He was charged with first-degree falsifying business records and first-degree offering a false instrument for filing, among other crimes.

The court reviewed relevant precedent—including *Kase*, *Schrag*, and *Elliassen*—and held that "**the term 'intent to defraud' does not require an intent to deprive the state of money or property, but rather intent to frustrate legitimate state interests and processes.** Maintaining a fair vendor selection process free of any potential conflicts of interest is a legitimate function of the NYCTA." *Id.*, at 832-33. (internal citations omitted) (emphasis added).

The court in *Headley*, at 829–830, usefully outlined the law in New York regarding the intent to defraud:

> The lesser included charge of Falsifying Business Records in the Second Degree requires simply "intent to defraud." **The term "intent to defraud" in article 175.00 crimes has been held to be broader than an intent to deprive another of property or money.** See Donnino, Practice Commentary, McKinney's Cons. Laws of N.Y., Book 39, PL § 175.05, pp.408-409. In *People v. Schrag*, 147 Misc.2d 517, 558 N.Y.S.2d 451 (Rockland Co.1990), defendant was a police officer charged with Falsifying Business Records in the First Degree for filing a false police report. He argued that no intent to defraud was proved before the grand jury. **The court found that Penal Law article 175 did not limit the**

term "intent to defraud" to property or pecuniary loss, **and noted that the interests of an entity in keeping accurate business records goes beyond economic concerns and extends to rights of others which may be infringed by false records.** The court in *Schrag* cited *People v. Kase*, 76 A.D.2d 532, 431 N.Y.S.2d 531 (1st Dept. 1980), in which the defendant was charged with Offering a False Instrument in the First Degree, in support of its conclusion that it was **sufficient to show that the Government's legitimate official action and purpose were impeded**.

In *Kase*, the defendant argued that there was no intent to defraud because the instrument in question, an application to transfer a liquor license in connection with the sale of a tavern, did not have the potential to cause pecuniary loss to the State or political subdivisions thereof. The Appellate Division disagreed. "Whoever intentionally files a false statement with a public offense or public servant for the purpose of frustrating the State's power to fulfill [its obligation to carry out the law] violates the statute." *Kase* at 537-538, 431 N.Y.S.2d 531.

In *People v. Elliassen*, 20 Misc.3d 1143(A), 2008 WL 4193166 (Sup. Ct. Richmond Co. 2008), the defendants, police officers, were charged with falsifying business records in the first and second degrees for failing to prepare and fill required reports and for failing to follow NYPD procedures. The defendants argued that the evidence was insufficient to establish an "intent to defraud." The court held that, "[I]t is not necessary to show a property or pecuniary loss from the fraud, and, in this case, it is sufficient to show that the NYPD's legitimate official actions and purposes were impeded." The defendants' conduct inhibited the Police Department's ability to perform its duties and carry out its mission. The court noted that the inaccuracy of the records had ramifications beyond general business practices.

Given this precedent, this court does not agree with the view that defendant was not proved to have an "intent to defraud" sufficient to justify trial on the lesser second degree offense under Counts 13 and 14.

The 1990 Rockland County Court decision in *Schrag* also noted, "When the Legislature intended to limit the scope of a fraud statute it has done so (i.e., Penal Law §§ 195.20, 190.60). While several Penal Law fraud statutes are directed specifically to preventing property or pecuniary loss, the fraud crimes in article 175 of the Penal Law are not so delimited and therefore the 'intent to defraud' terminology must be interpreted so as to effectuate their object, spirit and intent." 147 Misc. 2d 517, 518, 558 N.Y.S.2d 451 (Rockland County Ct. 1990).

A case of election law violations and false business records is also instructive here. In *People v. Norman*, 6 Misc. 3d 1035(A), 800 N.Y.S.2d 353 (N.Y. Sup. Ct., Kings County 2004), the Supreme Court of Kings County held that a defendant causing false information to be entered by a campaign committee and the Board of elections was sufficient to satisfy intent for falsifying business records. The court explained:

> Since it is a crime indeed a felony for a person 'acting on behalf of a candidate or political committee [to] knowingly and willfully... solicit any person to make [expenditures in connection with the nomination for election or election of any candidate] for the purpose of evading the contribution limitations of [article 14 of the Election Law],' Election Law § 14-126(4), this evidence is also sufficient to

establish that the defendant concealed these solicitations and contributions from the treasurer and thus prevented the making of a true entry, and caused the omission of a true entry in the records of both the [campaign] Committee and the Board of elections with 'intent to defraud includ[ing] an intent to commit another crime or to aid or conceal the commission thereof.' Penal Law § 175.10.

Our discussion here focuses on the jurisprudence interpreting the scope of the falsification of business records statute. We should note the practice of district attorneys prosecuting cases under these statutes may also be instructive. See, for example, the 2017 indictment of Richard Brega for falsification of business records in creating a scheme of covert payments to benefit a political campaign.

Of course, the intent to defraud must involve an intent to deceive that is material to another's interest. In *People v. Keller*, the trial court held that the creation of false documentation did not amount to deception because it was immaterial. Defendants who ran an escort service did not intend to defraud a credit card company by falsely billing clients for "limousine service" instead of escort services on charge slips. 176 Misc. 2d 466, 673 N.Y.S.2d 563 (N.Y. Sup. Ct. 1998). The judge explained: "The defendants did not intend for American Express to be deceived by the writing. They knew and expected that the particular falsity of this writing would be of no moment to American Express." *Id.* at 469; see also *id.* at 469 ("Their intention was for American Express to obtain their usual remuneration for a credit card transaction, and there is no evidence that they did not."). While the recipient of the false document suffered no financial loss, that fact was incidental.

c. Contrary cases

Two cases have been cited for the proposition that the intent to defraud is limited to depriving a person of money or property, but there are significant flaws in relying on these cases. The two cases are: a Second Department decision in *People v. Saporita* (1987) and a Kings County Criminal Court one in *People v. Hankin* (1997). In *Saporita*, the court explained that the prosecutors had not objected to a jury instruction on this element of the crime and—whether that instruction was flawed or not—the government was stuck with it on appeal. 132 A.D.2d 713, 715, 518 N.Y.S.2d 625, 627 (N.Y. App. Div., 2nd Dept. 1987) ("No objection was taken by the People to this part of the court's charge and they became bound by it."). Notably, *Saporita* was focused on the element of depriving "another person," not necessarily on the issue of deprivation of money or property. Indeed, the jury instruction read: "The term defraud means to cheat or deprive another person of property **or a thing of value or a right**." 132 A.D.2d at 715 (emphasis added); *id*. ("in the instant record, there is no evidence that 'another person' was deprived of any property or right as a result of the defendants' conduct regarding the public records").

The *Hankin* trial court misconstrued *Saporita*, citing it for the proposition of law described in the jury instruction, thus failing to recognize the highly limited reason for the Second Department's decision.

Other courts in the Second Department have not misconstrued *Saporita*. For example, in the 1990 decision of *People v. Schrag*, the Rockland County Court emphasized the peculiarity of the *Saporita* decision having been predicated on the government's failure to oppose the jury instructions and explained that those jury instructions were, in fact,

erroneous. The *Schrag* court emphasized the broad definition of "intent to defraud" set forth by *Kase* and others. It is
worth quoting the Schrag court's analysis at length:

> The court found that conduct [in *Saporita*] to be insuffi-
> cient to establish an "intent to defraud" as charged since
> there was no evidence that "another person" was deprived
> of any property or right as a result of the defendant's
> actions. A review of the Article 175 crimes illustrates that
> the use of the term "intent to defraud" **is not qualified by
> any language which limits their applicability to prop-
> erty or pecuniary loss....**
>
> Although CJI [Criminal Jury Instructions] refers to the
> object of the intent to defraud as being "another person,"
> there seems to be no basis in law to require the defrauded
> entity to be a person. In fact, because the crime involves
> the false entry or omission of information from business
> records, the defrauded party is most likely to be a business
> entity rather than a person. (See, Penal Law § 175.00 [1].)
> The decision in *People v Saporita* (supra) appears to rely
> heavily upon the fact that the trial court gave the CJI
> instruction without objective by the People, so that the
> People were then limited to showing that another person
> was intended to be defrauded. **Since the instant matter
> has not yet proceeded to trial, and this court does not
> believe the CJI instruction at issue correctly defines the
> statutory language, a dismissal of count 1 on this ground
> is not warranted.**
>
> **Similarly, the language in the CJI instruction which
> refers to depriving another of "property or a thing of
> value or a right" is language which should be given
> more than just a commercial meaning.** The enterprises
> which can be the victims of the falsification of business

records include "any entity of one or more persons, corporate or otherwise, public or private, engaged in business, commercial, professional, industrial, eleemosynary, social, political or governmental activity." Penal Law § 175.00(1). **The interest of these various entities in keeping accurate business records goes far beyond their economic concerns and certainly extends to the rights of the entities and others which may be infringed by false records.** In *People v. Kase*, 76 A.D.2d532, 537, 431 N.Y.S.2d 531 (1st Dept., 198); *aff'd* 53 N.Y.2d 989, 441 N.Y.S.2d 671, 424 N.E.2d 558, the Court favorably cited the federal rule that, in a prosecution for filing a false instrument, it is not necessary to show that the government suffered a property or pecuniary loss from the fraud citing *Hammerschmidt v. United States*, 265 U.S. 182, 188, 44 S.Ct. 511, 512, 68 L.Ed. 968. It was sufficient to show that the government's legitimate official action and purpose were impeded. **Accordingly, this Court will impose no requirement that the Grand Jury presentation establish a commercial or property loss.**

147 Misc. 2d at 518–519, 558 N.Y.S.2d at 452–453 (Rockland County Ct. 1990) (emphasis added).

Subsequent case law in the Second Department has adopted the broad definition of intent to defraud in line with the *Kase* test and *Schrag*. See *People v. Elliassen* (Richmond County Sup. Ct. 2008), which we discussed at length above. *See also People v. D. H. Blair & Co., Inc.* (New York County Sup. Ct. 2002) (rejecting *Hankin* and stating that "prior cases which have defined the statutory scope of a falsifying business records charge have not limited the statute to encompass only the intention to defraud the entity, whose business records were falsified. Rather, the reach of the statute includes the falsification of records, which are designed to thwart possible regulatory scrutiny").

Conclusion

In sum, the New York case law offers clear guidance on the broad scope of the "intent to defraud" for the offense of falsifying business records. While there are other legal hurdles for the Manhattan DA to cross in the indictment of the former president, this element of the relevant offenses poses no obstacle based on the known facts in the case.

Nexus to "Another Crime"

This essay was excerpted from a piece published by Joshua Stanton, Norm Eisen, E. Danya Perry, and Fred Wertheimer and appeared as part of "The Manhattan DA's Charges and Trump's Defenses: A Detailed Preview," in Just Security *on March 20, 2023. It has been updated to reflect subsequent events.*

FALSIFYING business records under New York law can be charged either as a misdemeanor or a felony. The misdemeanor requires proof of one of several potential acts. Relevant to Trump is the statute's prohibition of making "a false entry in the business records of an enterprise." The evidence indicates he personally signed checks to Michael Cohen as reimbursement for the hush money payment. If DA Bragg can prove that Trump signed those checks—and it appears he can—and that Trump knew the payment for hush money was being falsely recorded as "legal expenses," then Trump committed a misdemeanor (or likely a number of misdemeanors, if each false entry is charged separately).

To establish a felony (i.e. falsifying business records in the first degree), prosecutors would need to prove, in addition to the elements of the misdemeanor, that Trump's "intent to defraud include[d] an intent to commit another crime." There are a number of candidate crimes—and we offer below an assessment of just some of the more likely options.

a. Federal Campaign Finance Crimes

There is strong evidence that Trump's conduct in the hush money payments involved federal campaign finance violations. —After all, Cohen was convicted for just such offenses, and the Justice Department's sentencing memorandum stated that he "acted in coordination with and at the direction of Individual-1," who was easily identified as Trump. There are two potential problems with federal campaign finance violations serving as the basis for a felony charge in New York. As we noted in our last article on the subject, there are nuances in the definition of the word "crime" under New York state law. The New York Penal Law defines "crime" as "a misdemeanor or a felony." Both "misdemeanor" and "felony" are separately defined as an "offense" for which a term of imprisonment can be imposed (the distinction between the two being the length of incarceration allowed).

Finally, "offense" is further defined as:

> conduct for which a sentence to a term of imprisonment or to a fine is provided [1] by any law of this state or [2] by any law, local law or ordinance of a political subdivision of this state, or [3] by any order, rule or regulation of any

governmental instrumentality authorized by law to adopt the same.

Clearly, a *federal* law is not a "law of this state" or "any law, local law or ordinance of political subdivision of this state"—the first and second option. The third option in the statute, "any order, rule or regulation of any governmental instrumentality authorized by law to adopt the same," could include federal law. In contrast to the other two clauses, the third does not explicitly limit "governmental instrumentality" to be "of this state." And of course Congress is "authorized by law" to adopt laws imposing sentences of incarceration. Further, the "same" in this context could mean "any order, rule or regulation," which could potentially include federal law. The text of the statute therefore could include federal crimes. Moreover, if the New York state legislature wished to limit the third option to New York state law, they certainly could have said so clearly. There also appear to have been cases in New York brought with a federal crime as a predicate offense.

The Federal Election Campaign Act of 1971 (FECA) regulates campaign spending. It does contain an express preemption statute—meaning its federal provisions are authoritative and preempt any state laws that appear to regulate the same subject matter—and the FEC has interpreted the statute expansively. Yet both Judge Hellerstein and Justice Merchan, as have other judges across the country, found that FECA's preemptive effect is narrow.

FECA imposes contribution limits on both individuals and corporations. When Cohen, through his shell corporation, paid $130,000, this amount exceeded those allowable limits and conferred on Trump a campaign benefit by preventing the release of information that could harm his campaign. DANY does not have to prove that Trump violated FECA, or even intended to violate it, but rather that by falsifying business records he had the intent to commit, aid, or conceal the commission of any FECA violation. Which in this case, could include Michael Cohen's violation.

That the hush money payments were campaign expenditures seems relatively clear (as demonstrated, in good part, by Cohen's conviction of those offenses at the federal level). They transgressed applicable state (and federal) limits and/or reporting rules. Moreover, the evidence supports the proposition that Trump was aware of that. For example, one of Cohen's audio recordings of Trump indicates that Trump knew about the payments that would violate campaign finance laws. The audio recording also supports the contention that Trump knew the hush money payments were being made through a shell company that Cohen would be setting up.

In the recording, Cohen says, "I need to open up a company for the transfer of all of that info regarding our friend David." (David apparently refers to David Pecker, who was involved in the hush money scheme and appears to have testified in front of the Manhattan grand jury investigating Trump.) In proceedings with the federal government, Pecker's company admitted that the scheme was set up "to ensure that a woman did not publicize damaging allegations about that candidate before the 2016 presidential election and thereby influence that election" (AMI non-prosecution agreement).

b. State Election Crimes

Under N.Y. Elec. Law § 17-152: Conspiracy to promote or prevent election, "Any two or more persons who conspire to promote or prevent the election of any person to a public office by unlawful means and which conspiracy is acted upon by one or more of the parties thereto, shall be guilty of a misdemeanor." Trump appears to have conspired with Cohen (and others) to promote his own election by making the hush money payments. The key questions are whether "unlawful means" were used and whether this statute is preempted by federal law.

Under New York law, "unlawful means" appears to be construed broadly—and is not limited to crimes (which would therefore require yet another predicate crime). In a 100-year-old opinion, the state appellate court with authority over Manhattan ruled that "unlawful means" as written in another statute does not necessitate "the commission of a crime." Instead, the court held that "unlawful means" simply refers to conduct "unauthorized by law."

That case, although vintage, is consistent with what we would expect to find when construing the meaning of section 17-152. New York's highest court has noted that when language in a statute is not defined, words are generally to be given their "usual and commonly understood meaning" and that dictionaries are "useful guideposts" in ascertaining that meaning. Merriam Webster defines "unlawful" as "not lawful : ILLEGAL." "Illegal" is further defined as "not according to or authorized by law : UNLAWFUL, ILLICIT." Unlike with the definitions of "a crime" in the books and records statute, there appears to be no issue about the definition precluding the application of federal law. Indeed, these definitions appear to include any conduct that is inconsistent with the law, rather than just criminal conduct. And we would expect a judge ruling on the meaning of the statute to find as much.

Thus the potential "unlawful means" here are legion.

There are the violations of federal campaign finance laws to which Cohen pleaded, as well as violations of state campaign finance laws, and potentially even the bank fraud for which Cohen was convicted in connection to the scheme.

c. State Tax Crimes

This essay was originally published by Paula Junghans, Norm Eisen, Siven Watt, Joshua Stanton and Fred Wertheimer as "The Untold Strength of Tax Crimes in Manhattan DA's Case" in Just Security *on May 24, 2023. It has been slightly updated to reflect subsequent events.*

CHARACTERIZING the payments to Michael Cohen as "legal fees," rather than a series of simple reimbursements for a hush money payment caused the payments to be treated as income to Cohen, which in turn precipitated a tax gross-up so that Cohen would be relieved of any tax burden associated with the mischaracterization. Note that the DA would not have to prove that the tax crimes were actually committed, just that the parties intended them and falsified the business records with that initial intention. We explain these theories of the case below. We describe the law governing offenses involving false statements to tax authorities regardless of whether a defendant's conduct includes an underpayment or other form of evasion of taxes.

We offer this preliminary assessment based on both Bragg's response to Trump's request for a bill of particulars and previously available public information. We note below where further information would be helpful before reaching any firm conclusion on a matter.

Factual and Procedural Background

Some reimbursement payments to Cohen were made from the Donald J. Trump Revocable Trust and others from Trump's personal bank account. While the Trump Organization likely did not label the payments as "income" in its records, the inevitable corollary of characterizing them as legal fees was to cause the payments to be treated as "income" on Cohen's tax returns. According to Bragg, the $130,000 payment was added "to a $50,000 payment for another expense for which" Cohen "also claimed reimbursement, for a total of $180,000." That amount was to $360,000 so that Cohen "could characterize the payment as income on his tax returns, instead of a reimbursement," and so that Cohen "would be left with $180,000 after paying approximately 50% in income taxes." "An additional $60,000" was added "as a supplemental year-end bonus." Together, these amounts totaled $420,000. These allegations are consistent with the Department of Justice's court filings in Cohen's federal criminal case.

In response to Trump's Request for a Bill of Particulars, Bragg responded that "the crimes defendant intended to commit or to aid or conceal may include violations of... New York Tax Law §§ 1801(a)(3) and 1802," in addition to various state and federal election crimes as well as other violations of the falsifying books and records statute. Notably, Bragg declined to state that the list of crimes included in his response as exclusive—suggesting that other crimes, including other state and federal tax crimes as described below, could also later be added to bolster the prosecution's case.

DA Office Statements About the Tax Scheme

The district attorney's office has made the following statements in relation to tax violations.

- "The participants also **took steps that mischaracterized, for tax purposes, the true nature of the payments** made in furtherance of the scheme." Statement of facts, § 2 (emphasis added)
- Bragg: "Participants in the scheme took steps that mischaracterized, for tax purposes, the true nature of the reimbursements." Press release.
- Bragg: "In order to get Michael Cohen his money back, **they planned one last false statement. In order to complete the scheme, they planned to mischaracterize the payments to Mr. Cohen as income to the New York State tax authorities.**" Press conference (emphasis added).
- Bragg: "We have charged falsifying business records for those who were seeking to cover up sex crimes and we have brought this charge for those who committed tax violations." Press conference.
- Assistant District Attorney Christopher Conroy: "After the election, defendant reimbursed the lawyer through a series of disguised monthly payments that hid the true nature of the payoff by causing a series of false business records in the records of the Trump Organization here in Manhattan, **and even mischaracterized for tax purposes the true nature of the payment.**

Defendant falsified these New York business records with the intent to defraud, including the intent to commit[sic] another crime, and to aid and conceal the commission of another crime." Arraignment hearing (emphasis added).

- DA office: "[T]he People further refer defendant to certain facts, among others, set forth in the Statement of Facts relating to... disguising reimbursement payments by doubling them and falsely characterizing them as income for tax reasons Court filing in response to defendant's request for bill of particulars.

The SDNY's Criminal Information and Sentencing Memorandum in Cohen's case also discussed the reimbursement being "'grossed up' for tax purposes."

It is worth noting that in his press conference Bragg also cited false statements to tax authorities as one of the "unlawful means" needed to prove a violation of New York Election Law, § 17-152: conspiracy to promote or prevent election. "I further indicated a number of unlawful means, including more additional false statements, including statements that were planned to be made to tax authorities."

Applicable Law

While New York State tax law is distinct from federal tax law, the two bodies of law, especially in respect of false filing statutes, share similar principles and concepts. As a result, New York State courts often look to federal law for guidance in interpreting and applying state provisions. *See, e.g.*, People v. Essner, 124 Misc. 2d 830, 835-36 (N.Y. Sup. Ct. 1984) (court

looked to federal securities laws for the applicable definition of materiality under § 175.45, issuing a false financial
statement); State v. Rachmani 71 N.Y.2d 718, 725-26 (1988) (for
New York's Martin Act, the court adopted the standard for
materiality used by federal courts). Accordingly, we analyze
the elements of potential charges under New York Tax Law
§§ 1801(a)(3) and 1802 with reference mainly to federal law as
well as state law (where available).

Two statutes appear most relevant: Declaration under
Penalties of Perjury (26 U.S.C. 7206(1)), and Willful
Assistance in Preparation of False or Fraudulent Tax Documents (26 U.S.C. 7206(2)). The two federal statutes are in
many ways similar. Section 7206(1) focuses on those who
cause false statements in their own tax documents—thus
inclusion by Bragg of this statute would focus on Cohen's
criminal conduct of including false statements in his tax
returns, which Trump sought to aid or conceal. Conversely,
§ 7206(2) criminalizes those who cause, assist or aid false
statements in others' tax documents—thus Bragg's focus
here would be on Trump's intent to assist Cohen in making
false statements in his tax returns.

Given their similarities, we discuss all four statutes
together (the two state and the two federal tax offenses).
First, we set out the elements of each offense, which are very
similar. We then address the elements as follows: falsity,
materiality, and intent.

Additionally, a variety of other statutes may be applicable depending on how the facts develop, and, by way of
example, we also include a brief treatment of Conspiracy to
Defraud the United States (18 U.S.C. 371) on the federal side,
and on the state side, Offering a False instrument for Filing
in the First Degree (N.Y. Penal Law, § 175.35) or Second
Degree (N.Y. Penal Law, § 175.30).

Elements of the Offenses

1. New York Criminal Tax Fraud (New York Tax Law, Chapter 60, Article 37, Part 2)

New York Tax Law § 1801(a) defines a "tax fraud act" and is the basis of all New York criminal tax fraud offenses. For Bragg's case, under § 1801, if a person willfully acts (or causes another to act) in any of the following ways, that person has perpetrated a tax fraud act:

1. knowing that **a return, report, statement or other document** under this chapter contains any **materially false or fraudulent information**, or omits any material information, **files or submits** that return, report, statement or document with the state or any political subdivision of the state, or with any public office or public officer of the state or any political subdivision of the state (§ 1801(a)(2))

2. knowingly **supplies or submits materially false or fraudulent information** in connection with any return, audit, investigation, or proceeding or fails to supply information within the time required by or under the provisions of this chapter or any regulation promulgated under this chapter (§ 1801(a)(3))

3. engages in any **scheme to defraud the state** or a political subdivision of the state or a government instrumentality within the state **by false or fraudulent pretenses, representations or promises as to any material matter**, in connection with any tax imposed under this chapter or any matter under this chapter (§ 1801(a)(4)) (emphasis added).

All three of the above tax fraud acts include three elements: (1) falsity; (2) materiality; and (3) intent (willfulness). The first two provisions also require the tax document to be filed, submitted or supplied. The last provision, by its clear wording, also requires an intent to defraud the state.

Any person who commits any tax fraud act listed above is guilty, at minimum, of criminal tax fraud in the fifth degree, a Class A misdemeanor crime under § 1802. No additional mens rea is required. A misdemeanor is sufficient to serve as the predicate to make falsifying business records a felony. For felony criminal tax fraud in the *first to fourth degrees* under §§1803-1806, there are additional elements:

> 1. an intent to evade tax or defraud New York state (such intent to defraud is, as noted above, also required for 1801(a)(4) in the fifth degree); in
>
> 2. a payment to the state (whether **by means of underpayment or receipt of refund** or both) in a tax year; and
>
> 3. of a stated amount (the amount determining the degree of the offense).

2. Declaration under Penalties of Perjury (26 U.S.C. 7206(1))

It is a felony under § 7206(1) for any person who "[w]illfully makes and subscribes any return, statement, or other document, which contains or is verified by a written declaration that it is made under the penalties of perjury, and which he does not believe to be true and correct as to every material matter."

The elements of a Section 7206(1) conviction have been addressed at length by the case law. *See e.g.*, United States v. Bishop, 412 U.S. 346, 350 (1973); United States v. Pirro, 212 F.3d

86, 89 (2d Cir. 2000); United States v. Clayton, 506 F.3d 405, 410, 413 (5th Cir. 2007) (per curiam). Those elements are:

1. The defendant made and subscribed a return, statement, or other document which was **false as to a material matter**;

2. The return, statement, or other document contained a written declaration that it was **made under the penalties of perjury**;

3. The defendant **did not believe the return**, statement, or other document **to be true and correct** as to every material matter; and

4. The defendant falsely subscribed to the return, statement, or other document **willfully, with the specific intent to violate the law.**

3. Willful Assistance in Preparation of False or Fraudulent Tax Documents (26 U.S.C. 7206(2))

Under § 7206(2), it is a felony for any person who "[w]illfully aids or assists in, or procures, counsels, or advises the preparation or presentation under, or in connection with any matter arising under, the internal revenue laws, of a return, affidavit, claim, or other document, which is fraudulent or is false as to any material matter, whether or not such falsity or fraud is with the knowledge or consent of the person authorized or required to present such return, affidavit, claim, or document."

Although § 7206(2) appears calculated to apply primarily to official tax preparers, the statute has been used to prosecute criminal behavior far beyond that group of professionals (*see e.g.*, 43 A.L.R. Fed. 128 (Originally published in

1979), §§ 10-13). It has been used to prosecute participants in any scheme which causes false statements to be made in others' tax documents, whether or not the accused actually prepared the return. See e.g., United States v. Clark, 577 F.3d 273, 285 (5th Cir. 2009) (The statute "reaches all knowing participants in the fraud."); United States v. Crum, 529 F.2d 1380, 1382 (9th Cir. 1976) ("The nub of the matter is that they aided and abetted if they consciously were parties to the concealment of [a taxable business] interest."); United States v. Siegel, 472 F.Supp. 440, 444 (N.D.Ill.1979) (citing *Crum*, 529 F.2d 1380) ("[T]he scope of the statute extends to all participants of a scheme which results in the filing of a false return, whether or not those parties actually prepare it."); United States v. Graham, 758 F.2d 879, 885 (3d Cir.1985) (1985) (quoting United States v. Buttorff, 572 F.2d 619, 623 (8th Cir.) ("[T]here must exist some affirmative participation which at least encourages the perpetrator."); United States v. Hooks, 848 F.2d 785, 791, n.3 (7th Cir. 1988) (citing cases that found liability because of the defendant's concealing actions); United States v. Hastings, 949 F.2d 400 (9th Cir. 1991) (preparing false corporate financial statements that served as the basis for preparing the corporation's tax return); United States v. Aracri, 968 F.2d 1512 (2d Cir. 1992) (creating false invoices and shell companies used to prepare false excise tax returns); United States v. Foley, 73 F.3d 484, 493 (2d Cir. 1996) (a state legislator, accepted financial bribes from political contributors in exchange for agreeing to influence legislation and provided those contributors with fraudulent receipts to help disguise their payments as genuine business expenses). See also, IRS Tax Crimes Handbook (2009), pp.72-3; Justice Department, Criminal Tax Manual, Chapter 13, pp.5-8; Federal Tax Coordinator (2nd Ed.), ¶ V-3115.

The elements of a prosecution under Section 7206(2) are also clear and settled. See e.g., United States v. Perez, 565 F.2d 1227, 1233–34 (2d Cir. 1977); United States v. Klausner, 80 F.3d 55, 59 (2d Cir. 1996); United States v. Salerno, 902 F.2d 1429, 1432 (9th Cir. 1990); IRS Tax Crimes Handbook (2009), pp.71-2. Those elements are:

1. The defendant **aided or assisted in, or procured, counseled, or advised the preparation or presentation of a return**, affidavit, claim, or other document which involved a matter arising under the Internal Revenue laws;

2. The return, affidavit, claim, or other document was fraudulent or **false as to a material matter**; and

3. The defendant **acted willfully**.

Unlike with § 7206(1), under § 7206(2) there is no requirement that the document be signed under penalty of perjury. *Id.*

Although a plain reading of both § 7206(1) and § 7206(2) does not include a filing requirement, some courts have held that the return or statement must be filed. *See e.g.*, United States v. Dahlstrom, 713 F.2d 1423, 1429 (9th Cir. 1983) (filing of a return is a necessary element of § 7206(2)); United States v. Boitano, 796 F.3d 1160 (9th Cir. 2015) (confirming a filing requirement under § 7206(1)); (United States v. Harvey, 869 F.2d 1439, 1448 (11th Cir. 1989) (en banc) (same). Cf. United States v. Feaster, 843 F.2d 1392 (6th Cir. 1988) (per curiam) (holding *Dahlstrom* as contrary to the plain reading of § 7206(2)). See also, Justice Department, Criminal Tax Manual, Chapter 13, p.2.

First Key Issue: Falsity

Bragg may argue that the representations made in Cohen's tax returns were false statements and were false in at least two ways:(1) the mischaracterization of the funds as payment for legal services, and (2) the resulting treatment of the payments "income."

<u>i. False statement as to the mischaracterization of the funds as payment for legal services</u>

According to Bragg, each of the eleven checks made out to Cohen was "issued for a phony purpose." The checks, which were in fact simple repayments, were "illegally disguised" as payment for legal services rendered in 2017 pursuant to a "non-existent retainer agreement." Cohen's plea agreement said the same: "there was no such retainer agreement, and the monthly invoices COHEN submitted were not in connection with any legal services he had provided in 2017." See also Department of Justice Sentencing Memorandum for Michael Cohen ("In fact, no such retainer agreement existed and these payments were not 'legal expenses'—Cohen in fact provided negligible legal services to Individual-1 or the Company in 2017—but were reimbursement payments.").

Trump "could not simply say that the payments were a reimbursement for Mr. Cohen's payments to Stormy Daniels," Bragg said during the press conference. "To do so, to make that true statement, would have been to admit a crime. So instead, Mr. Trump said that he was paying Mr. Cohen for fictitious legal services in 2017 to cover up an actual crime committed the prior year."

ii. False statement of "income"

By characterizing the reimbursement payments to Cohen as legal fees, the Trump Organization necessarily caused Cohen to report the amount as income, subject to tax on Cohen's return. But, the repayment to Cohen of the funds paid to Daniels would simply not be regarded for tax purposes as "income." The payment was a straight dollar-for-dollar reimbursement of a purely personal expense (whether related to Trump's marriage or to his campaign).

It was therefore false for Cohen to then tell tax authorities that he received the $130,000 in "income." Similarly, the Trump Organization was therefore not required to report the full $420,000 worth of payments to Cohen on Cohen's Form W-2, as reimbursements are not "income" to be included on such a form.

However, an argument could be made that both the $130,000 reimbursement amount and the equal $130,000 "bump up" paid to cover Cohen's taxes were income to Trump, as they represented payments by the Trump Organization for personal expenses of Trump. Such a payment is frequently referred to as a "constructive dividend," where a business owner causes the business to pay for personal expenses. Here, it is unclear how the Donald J. Trump Revocable Trust and Trump's personal account, the issuers of the checks, are integrated into the Trump Organization's accounting system and tax reporting. Whether or not a payment is a dividend depends on whether the Trump Organization had earnings and profits, a matter we're fairly certain is entirely too complicated to delve into for the purposes of Bragg's criminal case. *See e.g.*, Boulware v. United States, 552 U.S. 421 (2008). Moreover, it would likely also require analysis of Trump's personal income tax returns —another quagmire.

But it's even more likely that none of this really matters from a criminal prosecution perspective, since all of these issues arise from the same false statement: that the payments to Cohen were for legal services. In prosecuting a criminal case, simplicity is usually better; the focus is on the false statement itself, not its technical tax consequences.

Second Key Issue: Materiality

If Cohen erroneously claimed the repayments as part of his income in submitting tax returns, he would have effectively overstated his income, thus triggering an overpayment of tax. How, then, could Cohen's tax returns form the basis of a tax violation? Indeed, some may argue that the statement was not material if it did not cause any financial loss. But the law does not require such a loss. It is a crime to submit intentionally false statements to tax authorities, even if the statement does not involve evasion of tax.

i. Materiality under federal tax law

We have not identified any New York tax case interpreting the meaning of materiality under state law. Accordingly, as noted above, we first look to federal law for guidance. In contrast to the crime of tax evasion, federal false statement tax statutes generally do not require proof of a tax deficiency, i.e. a difference between what was reported and the taxpayer's correct tax liability. See e.g., United States v. Tsanas, 572 F.2d 340, 343 (2d Cir. 1978) (regarding § 7206(1)); Edwards v. United States, 375 F.2d 862 (9th Cir. 1967) (§ 7206(2) is directed not to evasion or defeat of tax but rather to falsification and counseling and procuring of deception as to any material matter); IRS Tax Crimes Handbook (2009), p.72 (regarding § 7206(2)); Justice Department, Criminal Tax Manual, Chapter 13, pp.12-14 (regarding § 7206(2)). Thus, a defendant may be convicted even where a tax refund is due. See e.g., United States vs. Witasick, W.D. Va., No. 4:07-CR-00030-001, 15-16 (Apr. 7, 2014).

What prosecutors must instead prove is whether the statements made were false as to a "material" matter. This is a question for the jury to decide. See e.g., Neder v. United States, 527 U.S. 1, 4 (1999); United States v. Jackson, 196 F.3d 383, 384-85 (2d Cir. 1999) (reaffirming Neder); United States v. Gaudin, 515 U.S. 506, 522-23 (1995) (holding that "materiality" is a question for the jury in prosecutions for false statements under 18 U.S.C. § 1001). It's worth noting, as the Justice Department has in Chapter 12 of Criminal Tax Manual on § 7206(1), that "[w]hile courts still maintain that proof of a tax deficiency is not required in a section 7206(1) prosecution,... some post-*Gaudin* opinions indicate that the presence or lack of a tax deficiency may be relevant to a jury's determination of materiality."

The three questions Bragg will therefore need to consider are: (1) what "material" means; (2) is the nature of a payment considered material; and (3) does overreporting or overstating income negate materiality. One of the leading authorities on all three questions is United States v. DiVarco, 484 F.2d 670 (7th Cir. 1973), aff'g, 343 F. Supp. 101, (N.D. Ill. 1972).

Under the *DiVarco* definition—adopted by most circuits, including the U.S. Court of Appeals for the Second Circuit —a false statement is "material" if it has a natural tendency to influence or impede the IRS in ascertaining the correctness of reported tax or in verifying or auditing the returns of taxpayers. See, United States v. Bok, 156 F.3d 157, 164-65 (2d Cir. 1998) (regarding § 7206(1)); Neder, 527 U.S. at 16 (adopting for § 7206(1) the definition of materiality in Gaudin, 515 U.S. at 522-23 regarding 18 U.S.C. § 1001: "a natural tendency to influence, or [is] capable of influencing, the decision of the decision making body to which it was addressed"); United States v. Klausner, 80 F.3d 55, 60, n.4 (2d Cir. 1996) (regarding § 7206(2)); United States v. Potstada, 206 F. Supp. 792, 794 (N.D. Cal. 1962) (Under § 7206(2) "it is sufficient to allege and prove obstruction, delay or impairment of governmental functions.").

Importantly, the statement needs to have only the "potential" for influencing or impeding the IRS. United States v. Greenberg, 735 F.2d 29, 31 (2d Cir. 1984) ("The question is rather whether the statement had the potential for an obstructive or inhibitive effect. A consideration of this potential requires an analysis of the responsibilities of the public agency—responsibilities that are assigned by law—and analysis of the relevance of the statement to those responsibilities."); United States v. Pirro, 212 F.3d 86, 89 (2d Cir. 2000); United States v. Moon, 532 F.Supp. 1360, 1366-67 (S.D.N.Y. 1982), aff'd, 718 F.2d 1210 (2d Cir. 1983).

Prosecutors in the *DiVarco* case proved that income reported by the defendant on his personal tax returns as commissions from a mortgage and investment business did not come from that business. The defendant had mischaracterized the source of his taxable income. (Note, there was no dispute in *DiVarco* as to whether the claimed income was, in fact, taxable income, just whether the source of the taxable income was mischaracterized). The court confirmed that "source of income" is to be considered a "material matter" for tax purposes, such that willfully and knowingly stating a false source of income on tax documents is prohibited under § 7206(1)—even in the rarer cases involving an over-statement of taxable income.

> It is true... that most, if not all, of the cases involving misstatement of source of income also involved an under-statement of taxable income. However, "[o]ne of the more **basic tenets running through all the cases is that the purpose behind the statute is to prosecute those who intentionally falsify their tax returns regardless of the precise ultimate effect that such falsification may have."** 343 F.Supp. at 103....
>
> The plain language of the statute does not exclude the matter of the source of income from the definition of "material matter." In light of the need for accurate infor-mation concerning the source of income so that the Internal Revenue Service can police and verify the reporting of individuals and corporations, **a misstatement as to the source of income is a material matter**.

DiVarco, 484 F.2d 670, 673 (emphasis added).

The purpose of the statute is, therefore, "not simply to ensure that the taxpayer pay the proper amount of taxes—though that is surely one of its goals." Instead, the statute "is intended to ensure also that the taxpayer not make misstate-ments that could hinder" the IRS "in carrying out such functions as the verification of the accuracy of that return or a related tax return." United States v. Greenberg, 735 F.2d 29, 31 (2d Cir. 1984). New York district courts of the Second Circuit have similarly held that merely mischaracterizing the source of an income or other matter on tax documents will be considered material. United States v. Goldman, 439 F. Supp. 337, 344 (S.D.N.Y. 1977); United States v. Kaczowski, 882

F. Supp. 304 (W.D.N.Y. 1994); Moon, 532 F.Supp. 1360 (mis-stating source of income on personal tax returns); United States v. Cole, 463 F. 2d 163 (2d Cir. 1972) (related to the mischaracterization of personal legal bills as business expenses); see also United States v. Helmsley, 941 F.2d 71, 93 (2d Cir. 1991) (The district court's instruction that Section 7206(2) would be violated even if the deductions were allow-able but mischaracterized was hardly complex. The alleged offense involved a single predicate act: entering a false state-ment on a tax form."). See also, United States v. Mirelez, 496 F.2d 915 (5th Cir. 1974) (through fear of self-incrimination, taxpayer failed to report true source of income as illegal heroin sales); United States v. Diamond, 788 F.2d 1025 (4th Cir. 1986) (falsely listing losses from commodities transac-tions on Schedule C of Form 1040 as being from a trade or business and misstated occupation to conceal the source of losses).

The bottom line is that Bragg can establish materiality if he can show that Trump intended Cohen to report repay-ment of expenses or illicit campaign contributions as income, and so to overstate that line on his tax returns. Although unusual, there have been a number of prosecu-tions involving overstated income.

For instance, in 1975 former New York City Cultural Affairs Commissioner Irving Goldman was indicted by New York federal prosecutors for, among other things, filing false corporation returns on behalf of a shell company he created, Jola Candy Inc., in that the returns falsely stated gross income by including payments received for goods it had charged at unnecessarily "inflated and excessive prices." In an attempt to have the indictment dismissed, Goldman argued that, as Jola's returns included an "overstatement of income" which resulted in an "overpayment of taxes," the materiality element under was not made out. The Court rejected the argument, citing *DiVarco*:

> [T]he cited authorities do suggest that a statement is material if it is capable of influencing actions of the IRS in any matter within its jurisdiction. The question then is whether overstatement of income is a material matter. **The accuracy of items of taxable income reported on the return of one individual or entity may affect the ability of the IRS to assess the tax liability of another taxpayer.** Furthermore, overstated income may shield from scrutiny falsely inflated deductions. Thus, an overstatement of income impairs the ability of the IRS to determine if the correct amount of tax has been paid. *United States v. DiVarco*, 343 F.Supp. at 103. The conclusion that an overstatement of income may result in a prosecution is buttressed by the Congressional determination to make Section 7206(1) a crime separate and apart from income tax evasion, 26 U.S.C. § 7201.

United States v. Goldman, 439 F. Supp. 337, 342 (S.D.N.Y. 1977) (emphasis added).

In *United States v. Barrow*, the defendant underreported income on his personal tax returns and overreported income on an amended corporate return. The Sixth Circuit held that both underreporting and overreporting were material. "Under this section, false statements are material if they make it more difficult for the IRS to verify defendant's tax returns." United States v. Barrow, 118 F.3d 482, 493-94 (6th Cir. 1997).

Another example is *United States v. Lamberti*, in which the defendant, a parolee, was accused of overstating his hours of work and income on tax returns in order to trick his parole officer into believing that he had worked the minimum hours required under his parole conditions. United States v. Lamberti, 847 F.2d 1531 (11th Cir. 1988). The Eleventh Circuit held that the overstatement of income to the Parole Commission was material for the purposes of false statements under § 18 U.S.C. 1001, and, in respect of the federal tax statute, made its position clear: "As to the completely independent § 7206(1) tax charges, his assertion hinges on his untenable theory that an *overstatement* of income *cannot* be a *material* false statement for purposes of 26 U.S.C. § 7206(1), because it can lead *only* to overestimation and *overpayment* of tax liability." Id. at 1536. As the indictment "did not rest solely upon" overstatements, but instead rested "primarily" upon false statements claiming that he had only one source of income, the court held it unnecessary to consider further Lamberti's contention that an overstatement of income cannot violate § 7206(1). *Id.*

In *United States v. Bouzanis*, one of the defendants was accused of "aiding, counseling and causing the preparation and presentation of a false and fraudulent tax return" belonging to a co-defendant, in that the return included false, inflated income, which was submitted in support of a loan application. The Illinois district court, citing *Divarco* and the Second Circuit decision in *Greenberg*, rejected the defendant's argument that overstated income was not "material." United States v. Bouzanis, 00 CR 1065, 2003 WL 920717, at *2 (N.D. Ill. Mar. 7, 2003).

Another case involving inflated income is *United States v. Barshov*, where the defendants, who had formed limited partnerships to purchase motion picture films for distribution and exhibition, inflated the purchase prices and the income generated by the films in order to maximize depreciation costs and investment credits, and caused returns to be filed based on the inflated figures. United States v. Barshov, 733 F.2d 842, 845-46 (11th Cir. 1984).

ii. Materiality under New York non-tax law

As noted above, our research turned up no New York State criminal cases specifically addressing the concept of "materiality" for the purposes of New York Tax Law. Nevertheless, the general principles of materiality under federal law offer helpful guidance. Given the similarities in wording and purpose between N.Y. Tax Law § 1801(a)(2) and federal § 7206(1) and (2), it is likely that the New York state courts would adopt the federal definition of materiality as set forth in *DiVarco*.

The case of *People v. De Leo*, a decision by the Appellate Division of the Supreme Court of New York, Third Department, offers a glimpse into how New York state courts would likely define materiality under false tax filing laws. People v. De Leo, 185 A.D.2d 374, 585 N.Y.S.2d 629 (N.Y. App. Div. 1992). The defendant was convicted of second degree perjury (as well as second degree forgery and attempted grand larceny) for two false statements he made in a real property transfer gains tax affidavit. First, he falsely claimed to be acting in the capacity of attorney-in-fact for the seller of the property. Second, he significantly understated the amount of consideration he received on transfer for his role as purported attorney. The defendant argued on appeal that the false statements were not "material to the action, proceeding or matter involved" within the meaning of the perjury statute (§ 210.10). Rejecting the defendant's contention and affirming the conviction, the Third Department court stated:

The gravamen of his claim in this regard is that the misstatement of one's authority to act and the amount of consideration received in a transfer gains tax affidavit are not "material to the action, proceeding or matter involved" within the meaning of Penal Law § 210.10. We disagree. **The purpose of the affidavit is to assess the amount of tax due, if any, upon the transfer of realty and to identify those responsible therefor (see, Tax Law art. 31–B). Because calculation of taxes owed is dependent upon the consideration recited in the affidavit, any misrepresentation regarding the consideration is indeed material to the proper assessment of tax. The materiality of a misrepresentation of one's authority to act on behalf of a purported principal, inasmuch as it has the effect of potentially casting the principal in liability for taxes assessed, cannot be doubted.** Upon review, we find the prosecution's evidence that defendant was not an attorney-in-fact for the Colony at the time he executed the affidavit, combined with evidence that defendant effected the transfer as a means of payment for services rendered to the Colony and for which he had not been paid, thus indicating that the transfer was for consideration in excess of the $1 recited in the affidavit, satisfies both the legal sufficiency and weight of the evidence challenges.

Id. at 375 (emphasis added).

Courts have often said that false tax filing statutes are similar to perjury statutes. See e.g., United States v. Scholl, 166 F.3d 964, 980 (9th Cir. 1999) (describing §7206(1) as a perjury statute); Gaunt v. United States, 184 F.2d 284, 288 (1st Cir. 1950) ("purpose is to impose the penalties for perjury upon those who wilfully falsify their returns regardless of the tax consequences of the falsehood"); United States v. Taylor, 574 F.2d 232, 236 (5th Cir. 1978) (noting that to require the government to prove additional tax liability would "seriously jeopardize the effectiveness of section 7206(1) as a perjury statute and would imperil the self-assessment nature of our tax system"); United States v. Fawaz, 881 F.2d 259, 263 (6th Cir. 1989) (The court saw no reason to frame a different rule in the § 7206(1) context than the one applied under § 1623(a) false statement made to federal grand juries.)

The New York Criminal Jury Instruction for perjury also states that, "[d]epending on the facts of the case, it may be appropriate to adapt the language of materiality utilized by the Court of Appeals in the context of a Grand Jury proceeding; namely, that a false statement is material if it has 'the natural effect or tendency to impede, influence or dissuade' the public servant in the performance of his or her official functions in an action, proceeding or matter involved. People v. Davis, 53 N.Y.2d 164, 171 (1981)." (hyperlink added). This language reflects the federal position on false statement statutes, including § 7206.

Third Key Issue: Intent (Willfulness)

When it comes to intent, potential criminal liability under New York State tax law is broader than federal tax law.

N.Y. Tax Law defines willfulness as "acting with either intent to defraud, intent to evade the payment of taxes or intent to avoid a requirement of [New York Tax Law], a lawful requirement of the [tax] commissioner or a known legal duty." Section 1801(c).

Under federal law, willfulness refers to a voluntary, intentional violation of a known legal duty, including the duty to report accurate information on a tax return or other tax related documents. This means that an individual or entity must have acted with a specific intent to provide false or misleading information on their tax documents, and knew or should have known that their conduct was generally unlawful. *See e.g.*, Cheek v. United States, 498 U.S. 192 (1991); United States v. Pomponio, 429 U.S. 10 (1976); United States v. Bishop, 412 U.S. at 412 U. S. 360. Knowledge of the specific statute is not required, so long as the individual knows the information submitted was false.

Willfulness is a question of fact. Direct proof of intent is not necessary, and instead can be inferred from a broad range conduct and evidence (including circumstantial) relating to attempts to conceal or misrepresent income, assets and other material tax matters. United States v. Libous, 645 F. App'x 78, 81 (2d Cir. 2016). The government will often seek to prove willful intent with reference to "affirmative acts" and "acts of commission." See e.g., United States v. Smith, 206 F.2d 905 (3d Cir. 1953) (discussing U.S. Supreme Court authorities); Maxfield v. United States, 152 F.2d 593 (9th Cir. 1945); Battjes v. United States, 172 F.2d 1, 5 (6th Cir. 1949) ("Direct proof of willful intent is not necessary. It may be inferred from the acts of the parties, and such inference may arise from a combination of acts, although each act standing by itself may seem unimportant. It is a question of fact to be determined from all the circumstances."); Katz v United States, 321 F.2d 7, 10 (1st Cir. 1993).

Conclusion

We have argued that DANY has strengthened the case against Trump by bumping up the charges to a felony based on Trump's intent to commit (or aid or conceal) crimes involving false statements to tax authorities. The strongest case involves statements to tax authorities falsely characterizing the payments to Michael Cohen as "legal fees," rather than their true nature (reimbursements for a hush money payment). A strong case could also involve other variations on state criminal tax violations, as well as possible federal ones.

APPENDIX III: TRUMP'S DEFENSES

I n this chapter, we excerpt from three of our previous pieces
that cover Trump's defenses in more depth, such as his
claim that he relied on advice of counsel or that too much
time elapsed before he was indicted. We also digest past cases in
New York and in Bragg's office, which underscore that the DA has
not singled Trump out for disfavored treatment.

Statute of Limitations

*This essay was originally published by Norm Eisen, E. Danya
Perry and Fred Wertheimer as "Trump's Hush Money is News
Again. Here's Why We Should Care" in Just Security on February
7, 2023. It has been updated to reflect subsequent events.*

ALTHOUGH TRUMP'S wrongdoing seems straightforward,
Bragg has faced and will face a series of hurdles in charging
and convicting Trump.

The first hurdle is that the core underlying conduct
occurred at the end of 2016. So more than six years passed

since he was indicted, whereas charges in a case of this kind must usually be brought within five years. The New York legislature has determined that this is the cutoff for all but a handful of crimes, generally violent ones such as murder or terrorism not here at issue. Even if we count from the date of the final payment on December 5, 2017, that was more than five years before the indictment.

But there are exceptions that allow Bragg to overcome this hurdle. For example, under New York law, the statute of limitations is "tolled" (that is, stops running) when a defendant is "continuously" outside of the state. That makes sense: when a defendant is out of New York, it is more difficult to bring them into court, and it is only fair that the prosecution has more time. New York's highest court has interpreted that statute to mean that "all periods of a day or more that a nonresident defendant is out-of-State should be totaled" to determine how long the statute of limitations must be tolled. And the appellate court in Manhattan has found that such tolling applies to residents and nonresidents alike.

The residency distinction is potentially important, as Trump officially changed his residence from Manhattan to Florida only in September 2019. Nevertheless, that judicial decision is currently being reviewed by the Court of Appeals. Although we think the logic of the decision concerning tolling is valid and likely to be upheld, there remains a possibility that it will be overturned.

Trump apparently spent only a small portion of his four-year presidency in New York. Even if he spent a majority of his time since leaving the White House in New York (which of course he has not), the Manhattan District Attorney's office would still have many months and possibly years on the clock, whatever the Court of Appeals decides. That is because the clock definitively stopped running once Trump officially became a nonresident living out of state in 2019, and may even have been stopped for the bulk of his presidency. The Manhattan DA therefore has ample time to prosecute—despite a number of prior statements by Trump proclaiming that the statute of limitations has run out.

Other tolling exceptions might also apply to allow for more time to prosecute. For example, former Governor Andrew Cuomo in 2020 issued executive orders to suspend criminal statutes of limitations due to delays caused by COVID-19. Justice Merchan found that Governor Cuomo's Executive Orders during COVID tolled "'any specific time limit for the commencement of any felony through May 6, 2021. Thus, the deadline for the prosecution of the alleged conduct was extended by one year and 47 days," and the conduct described in the indictment fell within 6 years and 47 days prior to the indictment.

Selective Prosecution I: Campaign Corruption Cases

Here we digest other past cases in Bragg's office, which shows that the DA has not singled Trump out for disfavored treatment.

This essay was originally published by Siven Watt and Norm Eisen as "Survey of Past Criminal Prosecutions for Covert Payments to Benefit a Political Campaign" in Just Security on March 30, 2023.

THE INDICTMENT of former President Donald Trump for conduct involving the alleged concealment of hush money payments to benefit a presidential campaign raises the question whether his case is being treated like other cases. That question is fundamental to ensuring the equal application of the law and protecting free and fair elections. In this essay, we analyze 17 analogous campaign finance and related prosecutions in the State of New York and nationally. Our research shows that third-party payments covertly made to benefit a candidate are routinely and successfully prosecuted as campaign finance violations in New York and elsewhere under a variety of state and federal statutes.

In this essay we make the same point about surreptitious third-party payments benefiting a candidate or campaign: there is nothing novel about prosecuting them. Quite the opposite.

New York State itself offers a number of important, closely analogous campaign finance cases that resulted in convictions for conduct similar to Trump's, including falsifying business records. We begin there.

a. Richard Brega

The Richard Brega case involved campaign finance violations which were prosecuted as a felony violation of New York's books and records statute. In that regard, the Brega case is on all fours with DA Bragg's case which reportedly also will seek to elevate the books and records violation to a felony on a campaign finance basis.

Brega ran Rockland County's bus system and transported students on a multi-million dollar contract.

A Rockland County grand jury indictment in July 2017 accused Brega of, between April 2013 and August 2013, using 10 "straw donors," including his family, friends, and employees of his company, Brega Transportation, to secretly funnel over $40,000 in (cash) campaign donations to the 2013 county executive campaign of legislator Ilan Schoenberger.

The indictment charged Brega with ten felony counts of falsifying business records, namely that "with the intent to defraud and commit another crime and to aid and conceal the commission thereof" Brega "caused" false entries regarding the donations to be entered in the business records of the New York State Board of Elections.

"The campaign contribution limit for an individual donating to Legislator Schoenberger in 2013 was $9,221. The straw donations were reported by 'Friends of Ilan Schoenberger' to the New York State Board of Elections as individual contributions of the ten straw donors," the District Attorney's Office stated. Brega was "accused of causing those records to be false, as the money that was funneled into the Schoenberger account was his own."

In May 2018, Brega pleaded guilty to one count of first-degree falsifying business records, and admitted to using his "brother-in-law, Anielo Feola, as a go-between to conceal the origin of a $6,000 donation" to Schoenberger. In December 2018, Judge David Zuckerman sentenced him to a year's imprisonment to run concurrent with his federal sentence of 4 years and 2 months in prison for a separate bribery conviction which was passed the day earlier.

b. Clarence Norman

Another earlier case that resembles the Trump prosecution is that of Clarence Norman. Among other similarities, Norman's election law violations were treated as the predicate acts for a falsifying business records felony charge—a path that DA Bragg has followed. Indeed, the Norman case may offer an even closer parallel than Brega.

1. Background

Clarence Norman was a member of the New York State Assembly from the 43rd Assembly District in Central Brooklyn for 23 years, and since 1990 the leader of the powerful Kings County Democratic Party in Brooklyn.

Norman's criminal activity was extensive and complex, as too were the criminal investigations, prosecutions, and appeals that followed. Brooklyn District Attorney Charles J. Hynes charged six in a judicial bribery scandal in 2003, and accused local party leadership of facilitating a sham judicial selection process. This spurred a sprawling corruption investigation into Norman's role in Brooklyn's party machine politics. Within months, former judicial candidates alleged that Norman threatened to withdraw party support unless they hired consultants friendly with party leadership—reportedly a $100,000 proposition. As part of this investigation, prosecutors pored over Norman's financial records, including his interactions with campaign funds and government reimbursements.

In early October 2003, DA Hynes presented evidence of Norman's campaign spending practices and other matters to two Brooklyn grand juries. Both grand juries returned indictments, and at the time charges were reported as including: (1) failing to report a lobbyist's political contribution, worth thousands of dollars, to the State Board of Elections; (2) grand larceny for depositing a $5,000 check for his campaign into his personal bank account; and (3) 76 counts of filing for reimbursement from taxpayer money for over $5,000 in travel expenses already paid for by the party.

It was alleged by prosecutors that in 2000 and 2002, Norman spoke with Ralph Bombardiere, the executive director of the New York State Association of Service

Stations and Repair Shops ("the Association"), a political action committee, and "knowingly and willfully" solicited him to pay certain campaign expenses. People v. Norman, 2007 NY Slip Op 04667 [40 AD3d 1128] (May 29, 2007). "Pursuant to the agreements each year that the Association would do so, the executive director received invoices for purchases made for various campaign expenses, and he caused the Association to pay all but one of those invoices. Although those payments constituted in-kind contributions to" Norman's campaigns, he did not inform the treasurer of the Committee to Re-Elect Assemblyman Clarence Norman, Jr. ("the Committee"), the political organization formed to receive contributions and make expenditures on behalf of Norman's re-election campaigns, that the Association had made the payment. "Because she was unaware of the payments, the treasurer did not include them in the January 2001 Periodic Report ("the January 2001 Report") or the January 2003 Periodic Report ("the January 2003 Report") she was required to file with the New York State Board of Elections ("the Board of Elections")." People v Norman, 2004 NY Slip Op 51851(U).

Contributions were reported to total $7,423.30 in 2000 and $5,400 in 2002. "There was no accusation that the money had gone into Mr. Norman's pocket. Rather, it was used to pay expenses for the primary elections, like printing and shopping bags." Prosecutors argued that Norman had tried to conceal the contributions, because he knew they exceeded the maximum of $3,100 then permitted by state law.

2. *Charges 1: First Indictment*

A ten-count indictment was returned in respect of

Norman's solicitation of contributions and falsification of business records, for which he stood trial. People v Norman, 2004 NY Slip Op 51851(U) (Dec. 15, 2004).

Counts related to expenses paid by the Association in 2000:

- Count 1 – Offering a False Instrument for Filing in the 1st Degree, alleging that Norman presented the January 2001 Report to the Board of Elections, knowing the report contained "a false statement and false information" and with intent to defraud the Board.
- Counts 3 & 4 – Falsifying Business Records in the 1st Degree, alleging that Norman prevented the making of a true entry and caused the omission of such an entry in the records of the Committee (count 3) and the Board of Elections (count 4).
- Count 9 – A felony election law violation, alleging that Norman "knowingly and willfully" solicited a person to make expenditures in connection with his candidacy, "for the purpose of evading the contribution limitations" of Article 14 of the Election law, in violation of what was then Election Law §14-126(4), now Election Law §14-126(6).

Counts related to expenses paid by the Association in 2002:

- Count 2 – Offering a False Instrument for Filing in the 1st Degree, alleging that Norman presented the January 2003 Report to the Board of Elections, knowing the report contained "a false statement and false information" and with intent to defraud the Board.

- Counts 5 & 6 – Falsifying Business Records in the 1st Degree, alleging that he prevented the making of a true entry and caused the omission of such an entry in the records of the Committee (count 5) and the Board of Elections (count 6).
- Count 7 – "received a contribution and failed to provide the treasurer of the Committee with 'a detailed account' of it within 14 days of its receipt, in violation of Election Law §14-122.
- Count 8 – received a contribution from a single contributor that amounted to more than ninety-nine dollars and failed to file a statement of its receipt, in violation of Election Law §14-102.
- Count 10 – A felony election law violation, alleging that Norman "'knowingly and willfully' solicited a person to make expenditures in connection with his candidacy, 'for the purpose of evading the contribution limitations' of Article 14 of the Election Law, in violation of Election Law §14-126(4)," now Election Law §14-126(6).

Counts 4, 6, 7 and 8 were eventually dismissed, with Norman standing trial for the remaining counts. People v. Norman 2004 NY Slip Op 51851(U). In dismissing some counts, the court helpfully identified election law violations as the predicate crime to the felony count for falsifying business records:

Since it is a crime indeed a felony for a person "acting on behalf of a candidate or political committee [to] knowingly and willfully... solicit any person to make [expenditures in connection with the nomination for election or election of any candidate] for the purpose of evading the contribution limitations of [article 14 of the Election Law]," Election Law § 14-126(4), this evidence is also sufficient to establish that the defendant concealed these solicitations and contributions from the treasurer and thus prevented the making of a true entry, and caused the omission of a true entry in the records of both the Committee and the Board of Elections with "intent to defraud includ[ing] an intent to commit another crime or to aid or conceal the commission thereof." Penal Law § 175.10.

3. Charges 2: Second Indictment

The second indictment returned a seven-count indictment against Norman in respect of, in main, his stealing of the $5,000 check. People v. Norman, 2004 NY Slip Op 51392(U) (Nov. 16, 2004):

During the months of October and November of 2001, the treasurer of the Club wrote a number of checks, including three payable to the Committee. One, dated October 17, 2001, was for three thousand dollars, and included the notation 'Election Expenses.' Another, dated November 20, 2001, was for two thousand five hundred dollars, and had no notation indicating its purpose. The treasurer of the Committee deposited both of these checks in the Committee's account at Carver Federal Savings Bank. The treasurer of the Club also wrote a third check payable to the Committee, dated October 30, 2001, for five thousand dollars, and wrote on the check the notation 'contribution.' On October 31, 2001, the defendant signed his name on the back of this check and deposited it in a personal account he maintained at another bank in Kings County. The defendant told neither the treasurer nor the secretary of the Committee about this check....

In January 2002, the treasurer of the Club filed a report with the Board of Elections, which listed the contributions the Club had received and the disbursements it had made during the period between July 16, 2001, and January 15, 2002. In that report, the treasurer included the five-thousand dollar check, along with the other two checks, as contributions the Club had made to the Committee. On January 23, 2002, the treasurer of the Committee mailed to the Board of Elections the Committee's January Report. In that report, the treasurer listed the contributions the Committee had received during the period between July 2001, and January 2002, including the two checks from the Club that she had deposited in the Committee's account, but not the five-thousand dollar check, of which she was unaware.

The counts on the indictment were as follows:

- Count 1 – Grand Larceny in the 3rd Degree, and alleges that he stole more than three thousand dollars from the Committee.
- Counts 2 and 3 – Falsifying Business Records in 1st Degree, and allege that, with intent to defraud, including the intent to aid and conceal the commission of a crime, the defendant prevented the making of a true entry, and caused the omission of a true entry in the records of the Committee (count 2) and of the Board of Elections (count 3).
- Count 4 – Offering a False Instrument for Filing in the 1st Degree, and alleges that he presented the January Report to the Board of Elections,

knowing the report contained "a false statement and false information" and with intent to defraud the Board.

- Counts 5, 6 and 7 – criminal violations of the Election Law, see Election Law § 126(2), and allege, respectively, that he received a contribution and failed to provide the treasurer of the Committee with 'a detailed account' of it within 14 days of its receipt, in violation of Election Law §14-122 [count 5]; that he received a contribution from a single contributor that amounted to more than ninety-nine dollars and failed to file a statement of its receipt, in violation of Election Law §14-102 [count 6]; and that he received a contribution to a political committee and converted it to his personal use, in violation of Election Law §14-130 [count 7].

Counts 3, 5, 6, and 7 were eventually dismissed, and Norman stood trial on the remaining counts. People v. Norman, 2004 NY Slip Op 51392(U) (Nov. 16, 2004).

4. Convictions

In respect of the first trial and indictment, in September 2005, Norman was convicted of two felony New York campaign finance laws for soliciting illegal contributions in his 2000 and 2002 primary campaigns for his seat in the New York State Assembly (counts 9 and 10), as well as one felony and one misdemeanor count of falsifying business records of those contributions and preventing the making of a true entry and causing the omission of an entry in the Committee's records (counts 3 and 5).

The second trial and indictment led to a conviction in December 2005 for Norman's taking of the $5,000 check, on counts of grand larceny in the third degree, falsifying business records in the first degree, and offering a false instrument for filing in the first degree. The conviction was affirmed in People v. Norman, 40 A.D.3d 1130, 837 N.Y.S.2d 277 (App. Div. 2007). In January 2006, he was sentenced to a prison term of 2 to 6 years for the convictions in both trials.

Other Examples

Brega and Norman are just two examples of predicating a books and records felony on campaign finance violations. As we note in the Table, there are other New York prosecutions combining charges of falsifying business records in the first degree with New York Election Law violations, though only in relation to state, not federal, elections.

In the John Dote case, the defendant pleaded guilty to felony falsification of business records and to two violations of New York Election Law—unlawful use of campaign funds and failure to account to the party treasurer. He did so in connection with his stealing over $59,000 from his own campaign funds. The books and records charge accused him of filing false financial reports with the state Board of Elections "with the intent to conceal his ongoing larcenies."

In the Richard Luthmann case, the defendant was accused of impersonating New York political figures on social media in an attempt to influence campaigns. He too pleaded guilty to felony falsifying business records as well as to misdemeanors under New York's election law. The falsifying business records charges against Luthmann related to his creating false records on the social media sites, "with the intent to injure them."

Of course, there are distinctions with the Trump case, including that the foregoing cases concerned state candidates whereas Trump was seeking federal office. But as we explained in the second essay in this series, Bragg has formidable arguments on preemption and other possible Trump defenses that enable the Manhattan DA to prosecute the former presidential candidate as others have been prosecuted in New York.

What's more, there are many other cases—in New York and nationally—that address this type of conduct as a campaign finance violation. These cases, individually and collectively, contradict the assertion that there is anything novel about prosecuting covert benefits to a campaign as alleged in the Trump hush money scheme.

That is not to say that every case of this kind that has been prosecuted in New York or nationally has resulted in conviction. The vast majority have. But where they did not result in conviction, the charges generally still made it to the jury. We discussed one of those cases, that of John Edwards, at length in the second essay in this series, rebutting common misunderstandings of the matter. Another similar (non-hush money) example covered in the Table is the prosecution by then-Manhattan DA Cyrus Vance against Nora Anderson and Seth Rubenstein.

Finally, of course, there is also the federal case against Michael Cohen. As former U.S. Attorney for the Southern District of New York Preet Bharara succinctly put it on Meet the Press:

> Michael Cohen, who was not only charged with this type
> of crime but this particular crime. And he thought it was a
> crime, pled guilty to it. His lawyer thought it was a crime,
> allowed him to plead guilty to it. The prosecutors in the

Southern District of New York thought it was a crime. The judge accepted the guilty plea, thought it was a crime.

What's more, the "[Federal Election] Commission's Office of the General Counsel (OGC) recommended finding reason to believe that Cohen and the Trump Organization made, and Trump and Donald J. Trump for President, Inc. (the Committee) accepted and failed to report, illegal contributions," according to the Chair and another commissioner of the FEC. (In a split decision that fell along partisan lines, the full FEC voted against investigating charges that Trump and his Committee had violated campaign finance laws.)

The Table

In the Table at Just Security, we looked at a total of 15 additional cases beyond Brega and Norman, all of which concern covert benefit to a campaign, either by a third-party providing cash or in-kind support, or services, or through covertly funneling other contributions. The Table is not a comprehensive survey of all past cases, but provides strong insight into these types of cases. It can be found at https://www.justsecurity.org/85745/survey-of-prosecutions-for-covert-payments-to-benefit-campaigns/.

Selective Prosecution II: Falsifying Business Records Cases

This essay was originally published by Siven Watt, Norm Eisen and Ryan Goodman as "Survey of Past New York Felony Prosecutions for Falsifying Business Records," in Just Security on March 21, 2023.

THE CORE CRIME is "falsifying business records in the first degree," a felony under New York State law (N.Y. Penal Code § 175.10). Prosecutors and indeed all of us are compelled by the rule of law to consider how such a charge compares to past prosecutions. Are like cases being treated alike?

Here it appears they are. Prosecution of falsifying business records in the first degree is commonplace and has been used by New York district attorneys' offices to hold to account a breadth of criminal behavior from the more petty and simple to the more serious and highly organized. We reach this conclusion after surveying the past decade and a half of criminal cases across all the New York district attorneys' offices.

The Table appears in full on Just Security, which provides full details of many examples of cases we identified in the survey. A sample of representative precedents includes:

- *The People of the State of New York v. Josue Aguilar Dubon*, AKA Saady Dubon, AKA Alejandro Ortiz (October 2022)—Bronx business owner indicted for failing to report over $1 million in income, avoiding paying $60,000 in taxes.
- *The People of the State of New York v. Scott Kirtland* (February 2022)—Insurance broker indicted for allegedly creating/filing fraudulent certificates of liability insurance to further scheme to defraud.
- *The People of the State of New York v. James Garner* (November 2021)—Mental health therapy aide indicted for allegedly defrauding over $35,000 in workers' compensation benefits.
- *The People of the State of New York v. Jose Palmer* (November 2016)—Pleaded guilty to petit larceny

for unemployment benefits fraud of over $3,000, having initially been indicted for grand larceny and falsifying business records in the first degree.

- *The People of the State of New York v. Jason Holley* (November 2016)—Convicted by jury of falsifying business records in the first degree but acquitted of the predicate crime, insurance fraud.
- *The People of the State of New York v. Christina Murray* (May 2015) & *People v. Terrel Murray* (May 2014)—Married couple convicted of house fire insurance claim, attempting to recover the cash value of various items of property that were ostensibly lost in the fire.
- *The People of the State of New York v. Barbara A. Freeland* (June 2013)—Convicted for falsely claiming on a food stamps application that a young adult lived with her.
- *The People of the State of New York v. Maria F. Ramirez* (August 2010)—Convicted for returning unpurchased items to a store in exchange for store credit, thus causing a false entry in a business record of an enterprise, and using the store credit to purchase additional items one day.

The Table

In the Table at Just Security, we looked at 24 pages of additional cases, all of which concern felony prosecutions for Falsifying Business Records. The Table is not a comprehensive survey of all past cases, but provides strong insight into these types of cases. It can be found at https://www.just security.org/85605/survey-of-past-new-york-felony-prosecu tions-for-falsifying-business-records/.

NOTES

1. The Essential Court Filings Explained

1. Michael Cohen's lawyer Lanny Davis provided images of this check and others cited in this book to *The New York Times*.

2. Chronology of Events

1. The timeline of events on Oct. 8 is supplied primarily from two sources: *The Fixers* and Cohen's search warrant. Each source provides information about the conversations that occurred between Trump, Cohen, Hicks, Pecker, Howard, Davidson, and Rodriguez. However, where *The Fixers* provides precise details about the contents of the conversations, it fails to include the precise times of those conversations. Cohen's search warrant, conversely, provides precise details about the times of calls, but not their contents. In order not to mangle the timeline, we present the information below as it appears in the original sources. Where we were able to confirm facts in both sources, we have indicated so with an additional in-text citation.

3. Cast of Characters

1. Despite its name, the New York Supreme Court is actually the state's trial court for felonies.

5. From Indictment to Jury Selection

1. Trump's removal petition asserted this immunity defense under the Supremacy Clause, but as Judge Hellerstein noted, he "expressly waived any argument premised on a theory of absolute presidential immunity."
2. Trump's March 8 letter seeking permission to file the motion was a result of the court's order from earlier the same day requiring the parties to first seek permission to file new motions. The court issued that order in response to Trump filing on March 7 a motion for

adjournment based on presidential immunity, two weeks after the Feb. 22 pretrial motion deadline had passed.

3. In November 2023, DANY filed a motion with the court to compel Trump to provide reciprocal discovery, stating that Trump had provided the prosecution with nothing he sought to rely on. There are no public court filings confirming Trump has since complied with his discovery duties, although in its opposition to Trump's motions *in limine*, on the matter of expert witness Bradley Smith, DANY said that Trump "should not be permitted to evade or delay reciprocal discovery by retaining a law professor 'as an expert consultant and witness'... but then claiming that 'he is not being called as an 'expert.'" In any case, the public may not necessarily be privy to what, if any, discovery has been provided by the defense as this is not required to be filed with the court and so it likely will not be in the public record.

4. The Census figures do not add up to exactly 100 percent.

6. The Trial

1. The content under this header originally appeared as part of "The Manhattan DA's Charges and Trump's Defenses: A Detailed Preview," in Just Security on March 20, 2023, and has been updated to reflect subsequent events. Material from our Just Security and other prior publications is interspersed throughout this volume.

8. A Guide to Sentencing

1. Falsifying business records in the first degree is a Class E felony. *Id*. "For a class E felony, the term shall be fixed by the court, and shall not exceed four years." N.Y. Penal Law § 70.00(2)(e). In New York, felonies are classified from Class "A" to Class "E" with Class "E" being the lowest-level felony.

2. *See* N.Y. Penal Law § 70.00(4); *People v. Williams*, 79 N.Y.2d 281, 286, 590 N.E.2d 1199, 1203 (1992).

3. Special Counsel Jack Smith has similarly charged defendant Trump with committing crimes against all American voters and American democracy itself, for his actions four years later as part of an alleged conspiracy to overturn the 2020 presidential election.

4. Such a coverup is somewhat like Special Counsel Smith's obstruction of justice charges in his separate prosecution against defendant Trump over retention of classified national defense information.

5. Defendant Trump's former attorney, Michael Cohen, was convicted of campaign finance violations for his role in this scheme.

6. *See People v. Trump*, Statement of Facts, at 1.

7. *Id.*

8. "Donald Trump will be president thanks to 80,000 people in three states," The Washington Post, December 1, 2016.

9. Falsifying business records in the first degree is a class E felony. N.Y. Penal Law § 175.10. For a class E felony, the term shall be fixed by the court, and shall not exceed four years. N.Y. Penal Law § 70.00(2)(e).

10. *See* OCA-STAT Act Report.

11. Our full dataset and analysis based upon the .csv files at OCA-STAT Act Report is available at https://docs.google.com/spreadsheets/d/1-gme6iJ84bOTGQNmpr9vFYQmFJHoGwDrRg6psgxybsE/edit?usp=sharing.

12. *See* OCA-STAT Act Report.

13. "Former Trump CFO Allen Weisselberg pleads guilty to perjury in deal that doesn't require cooperation," Associated Press, March 4, 2024.

14. Analogously, there may be instances in which defendants have been convicted yet not imprisoned where falsifying business records was not the top charge. In our experience, although such instances are not captured by the available data, they are highly unlikely to be sufficiently large in number to alter our analysis.

15. *See* "Ex-Citigroup Construction Executive Admits Taking $500,000 in Bribes," *New York Times*, December 1, 2015. *And* "Former CitiGroup Exec Gets 2 Years in Prison for Taking Bribes," NBC News, December 1, 2015.

16. *See* Sections 40 and 41 *in* "A Complete Guide to the Manhattan Trump Election Interference Prosecution," Just Security, March 27, 2024.

17. *See People v. Crump*, 197 A.D.2d 414, 415, 602 N.Y.S.2d 394, 394 (1st Dept. 1993).

18. *See Berger ex rel. Nominal v. Friedman*, 2015 N.Y. Slip Op. 32189 (N.Y. Sup. Ct. 2015); *DA Vance Announces 24-Count Indictment in Major Electrical Contracting Kickback Scheme*, New York County District Attorney's Office, Dec. 18, 2013; "Three-Year Investigation Leads to 24-Count Indictment in Electrical Contracting Kickback Scheme," EC&M, December 20, 2013; Brief of Appellant-Respondent, *Meryl R. Berger, Suing Individually and Derivatively on Behalf of Nominal Defendant I.G. Federal Electrical Supply Corporation, Plaintiff-Respondent, v. Ira M. Friedman and Jodi B. Ehren, Defendants-Appellants, I.G. Federal Electrical Supply Corporation, Nominal Defendant-Appellant*, No. 2015-10682, 2015 WL 13809960, at *9 (2d Dept. Dec. 29, 2015).

19. *See People v. Bryan*, No. 990-2015 (Apr. 23, 2015). *and People v. Bryan*, 2015NY037198 (June 12, 2015). Case files were accessed at the New York County Criminal Court Clerk's Office in Manhattan, NY. Scans on file with author.

20. "Richard Brega sentenced in Rockland political case," The Journal News, Dec. 11, 2018.

21. "Lawyer Accused of Using Fake Facebook Pages to Sway Elections in Staten Island," *New York Times*, November 30, 2018.

22. "Already disbarred, former Staten Island lawyer is released from federal prison," Staten Island Advance, August 6, 2021.

23. "Top Brooklyn Democrat Convicted of Campaign Violations," N.Y. Times, Sept. 28, 2005.

24. "NORMAN GUILTY OF stealing. 2nd conviction for ex-pol," New York Daily News, December 16, 2005.

25. *See People v Norman*, 2004 NY Slip Op 51392(U) (Nov. 16, 2004).

26. *See* "Ex-Lawmaker Sentenced to 2 to 6 Years in Corruption Case," The *New York Times*, January 12, 2006. Trump has previously blamed his attorney, Michael Cohen, in connection with the crimes charged in this case. *See* "Trump Admits To Authorizing Stormy Daniels Payoff, Denies Sexual Encounter," NPR, May 2, 2018. ("Trump denied knowledge of the payments, telling reporters on Air Force One, "You'll have to ask Michael Cohen. Michael is my attorney. You'll have to ask Michael.").

27. Appellant's Brief, The People of the State of New York, Plaintiff-Respondent, v. Clarence NORMAN, Jr., Defendant-Appellant., No. 2006-00428, 2006 WL 4844734, at *43–44 & n.14 (2d Dept. July 31. 2006) (noting that Norman was sentenced concurrently to "one to three years for grand larceny in the third degree, one to three years for falsifying business records in the first degree, and one to three years for offering a false instrument for filing in the first degree" and consecutive to his sentence in the other indictment, resulting in a total sentence of two to six years").

28. *People v. Outley*, 610 N.E.2d 356 (N.Y. 1993) (sentencing enhancement based upon evidence of a mere arrest so long as the court finds there is a "legitimate basis for the arrest on that charge"; the defendant had agreed not to be arrested as a condition of probation and later was).

29. *United States v. Watts*, 519 U.S. 148, 157 (1997) (holding that even acquitted criminal conduct can constitutionally be used to enhance a sentence so long as the charges are separately proved by a preponderance of the evidence); *but see People v. Varlack*, 259 A.D.2d 392, 394, 687 N.Y.S.2d 93, 96 (1999) (holding that if the other case resulted in acquittal, a "sentencing court may not base its sentence on crimes of which the accused has been acquitted" under New York law); *see also* 3 Crim-

inal Procedure in New York § 49:2 (2d), Nature and definition of sentence—Consideration of conduct for which defendant was never tried or was acquitted ("the Court of Appeals has ruled that in order to satisfy due process requirements, the sentencing court must have reliable and accurate information, which standard is a lower standard of proof than the beyond a reasonable doubt standard applied in criminal trials, and that an acquittal is not equivalent to a finding that a defendant is innocent.") (citing *People v. Naranjo*, 681 N.E.2d 1272 (N.Y. 1997)).

30. Trump Organization Chief Financial Officer Allen Weisselberg was sentenced in 2022 for his role in a tax fraud scheme to five months of incarceration after pleading guilty to all 15 charges he faced, including four counts of falsifying business records in the first degree, grand larceny, four counts of tax fraud, a scheme to defraud, conspiracy, and four counts of offering a false instrument.

31. "Judge: 'More likely than not' that Trump 'corruptly attempted' to block Congress from counting votes on January 6," CNN, March 28, 2022.

32. *See United States v. Mackbee*, 894 F.2d 1057 (9th Cir.) (holding that a conviction is considered final for criminal history purposes at the time of the trial court's determination of guilt notwithstanding any pending appeals), *cert. denied*, 495 U.S. 962 (1990).

33. *See People by James v. Trump*, Complaint at 2.

34. "Prominent conservatives issue report rebutting Trump election claims," CNN, July 14, 2022.

35. "Trump calls for the termination of the Constitution in Truth Social post," CNN, December 4, 2022.

36. "Trump posts disturbing baseball bat photo with Alvin Bragg, threatens 'death and destruction'," New York Post, March 25, 2023.

37. "Jan. 6 Prosecutors Ask for Protective Order, Citing Threatening Trump Post," The *New York Times*, August 5, 2023.

38. "Jan. 6 Prosecutors Ask for Protective Order, Citing Threatening Trump Post," The *New York Times*, August 5, 2023.

39. "Judge issues gag order barring Donald Trump from commenting on witnesses, others in hush money case," AP News, March 26, 2024; "Read the new gag order muzzling Trump in his hush-money case," Business Insider, May 8, 2023.

40. "Judge reimposes gag order on Trump in federal election interference case," NPR, October 30, 2023.

41. "Judge defends fining Trump $10,000 for breaking gag order," CNN, October 26, 2023.

42. "Trump's false or misleading claims total 30,573 over 4 years," The Washington Post, January 24, 2021.

Appendix I: Key Court Opinions

1. *People v. Trump* NY Slip Op 30560(U) [2024], at 13.
2. *Id.*
3. *Id.* at 14.
4. *Id.* at 15.
5. *Id.* at 16.
6. *Id.*
7. *Id.*
8. *Id.* at 17.
9. *Id.* at 17-18.
10. *Id.* at 7,19.
11. *Id.* at 7.
12. *Id.* at 9.
13. *Id.* at 10-11.
14. *People of The State of New York v. Trump*, No. 1:2023cv03773 (S.D.N.Y. 2023) at 13.
15. *Id.* at 15.
16. *Id.* at 16-17.
17. *Id.* at 18.
18. *Id.* at 19.
19. *Id.* at 21.
20. *Id.* at 22.